Learning RxJava
Second Edition

Build concurrent applications using reactive programming
with the latest features of RxJava 3

Nick Samoylov
Thomas Nield

BIRMINGHAM - MUMBAI

Learning RxJava
Second Edition

Commissioning Editor: Kunal Chaudhari
Acquisition Editor: Denim Pinto
Content Development Editor: Digvijay Bagul
Senior Editor: Rohit Singh
Technical Editor: Ketan Kamble
Copy Editor: Safis Editing
Project Coordinator: Francy Puthiry
Proofreader: Safis Editing
Indexer: Pratik Shirodkar
Production Designer: Aparna Bhagat

First published: June 2017
Second edition: February 2020

Production reference: 1280220

Published by Packt Publishing Ltd.
Livery Place
35 Livery Street
Birmingham
B3 2PB, UK.

ISBN 978-1-78995-015-1

www.packt.com

To my wife, Luda, for her support and helpful advice.

– Nick Samoylov

Packt.com

Subscribe to our online digital library for full access to over 7,000 books and videos, as well as industry leading tools to help you plan your personal development and advance your career. For more information, please visit our website.

Why subscribe?

- Spend less time learning and more time coding with practical eBooks and Videos from over 4,000 industry professionals

- Improve your learning with Skill Plans built especially for you

- Get a free eBook or video every month

- Fully searchable for easy access to vital information

- Copy and paste, print, and bookmark content

Did you know that Packt offers eBook versions of every book published, with PDF and ePub files available? You can upgrade to the eBook version at www.packt.com and as a print book customer, you are entitled to a discount on the eBook copy. Get in touch with us at customercare@packtpub.com for more details.

At www.packt.com, you can also read a collection of free technical articles, sign up for a range of free newsletters, and receive exclusive discounts and offers on Packt books and eBooks.

Contributors

About the authors

Nick Samoylov graduated from the Moscow Institute of Physics and Technology, has worked as a theoretical physicist, and learned to program as a tool for testing his mathematical models. Following the demise of the USSR, Nick created and successfully ran his own software company. In 1999, with his wife Luda and two daughters, he emigrated to the USA and has been living in Colorado ever since, working as a Java programmer. In his spare time, Nick likes to write and hike in the Rocky Mountains.

Thomas Nield is a business consultant for Southwest Airlines in Schedule Initiatives, and a maintainer for RxJavaFX and RxKotlin. Early in his career, he became fascinated with technology and its role in business analytics. After becoming proficient in Java, Kotlin, Python, SQL, and reactive programming, he became an open source contributor and an author/speaker at O'Reilly Media. He is passionate about sharing what he learns and enabling others with new skill sets. He enjoys making technical content relatable and relevant to those unfamiliar with it or who are intimidated by it. He is interested in data science, reactive programming, and the Kotlin language.

He has also authored the book Getting Started with SQL, by O'Reilly Media.

About the reviewer

Aristides Villarreal Bravo is a Java developer, a member of the NetBeans Dream Team, and a Java User Groups leader. He lives in Panama. He has organized and participated in various conferences and seminars related to Java, JavaEE, NetBeans, the NetBeans platform, free software, and mobile devices. He is the author of the jmoordb framework and tutorials, and blogs about Java, NetBeans, and web development. He has participated in several interviews pertaining to topics such as NetBeans, NetBeans DZone, and JavaHispano. He is also a developer of plugins for NetBeans.

Packt is searching for authors like you

If you're interested in becoming an author for Packt, please visit `authors.packtpub.com` and apply today. We have worked with thousands of developers and tech professionals, just like you, to help them share their insight with the global tech community. You can make a general application, apply for a specific hot topic that we are recruiting an author for, or submit your own idea.

Table of Contents

Section 2: Reactive Operators

Preface

This book is the second—substantially enhanced and updated to include the latest software versions–edition of the popular book *Learning RxJava*. The authors know the subject intimately and provide the most effective and simple approach and step-by-step guide to mastering this new modern programming called **reactive programming**.

You will find clear and succinct definitions, insightful discussions, and demo code that cuts into the essence of this new, rapidly emerging field that has already accomplished a lot and promises even more. Anybody who is thinking about Java programming–especially for Android applications–must read this book and use it at every level of the programming experience.

Who this book is for

This book is for those who have some experience of coding in Java and would like to learn about modern reactive programming, especially in the area of Android development, where RxJava has proven to be the most productive so far. The book contains appendices that introduce the principal RxJava concepts, and each chapter has detailed instructions on how to use them.

What this book covers

Chapter 1, *Thinking Reactively,* covers a brief history of Reactive Extensions and RxJava, and describes how to set up your first RxJava project and build your first reactive application. It also touches on the differences between RxJava 1.x, 2.x, and 3.0.

Chapter 2, *Observable and Observer,* provides the foundation for the following presentation of RxJava by introducing the two main terms Observable and Observer. It also presents the Observable specializations of Single, Completable, Maybe, and Disposable.

Chapter 3, *Basic Operators,* presents the basic RxJava operators. This is necessary for understanding the more complex operators described in the chapters that follow.

Chapter 4, *Combining Observables,* starts the transition from making RxJava useful to making it powerful. It covers the operators that allow several source observables to be combined into one resulting Observable.

Chapter 5, *Multicasting, Replaying, and Caching,* explains what multicasting is, and how to replay and cache emissions. It also presents how to use the Subject object and automatic connections.

Chapter 6, *Concurrency and Parallelization,* explores more of the nuances of RxJava and how to effectively leverage concurrency.

Chapter 7, *Switching, Throttling, Windowing, and Buffering,* explains and demonstrates the buffering, windowing, throttling, and switching of emissions.

Chapter 8, *Flowable and Backpressure,* discusses different ways to cope with backpressure while processing reactive streams. Backpressure happens when data/events are produced faster than they can be consumed.

Chapter 9, *Transformers and Custom Operators,* explains how to compose new operators from existing ones, how to create a new one from scratch, and how to use rxjava2-extras and rxjava2-extensions for that purpose.

Chapter 10, *Testing and Debugging,* covers configuring JUnit, blocking subscribers, blocking operators, using TestObserver and TestSubscriber, manipulating time with TestScheduler, and debugging RxJava code.

Chapter 11, *RxJava on Android,* explains step by step how to create an Android project, how to configure Retrolambda, and how to use RxJava and RxAndroid using RxBinding and other RxAndroid binding libraries.

Chapter 12, *Using RxJava with Kotlin,* covers several miscellaneous but essential topics, including custom operators, as well as how to use RxJava with testing frameworks, Android, and the Kotlin language.

Appendix A, *Introducing Lambda Expressions,* provides a short introductory course on Java lambda expressions, which does not require any prior knowledge of the topic.

Appendix B, *Functional Types,* lists functional interfaces that are included in RxJava 1.*, RxJava 2.*, and RxJava 3.0 – listed with their single-method signature and an indication of which RxJava version has it.

Appendix C, *Mixing Object-Oriented and Reactive Programming,* presents a discussion on using object-oriented programming in conjunction with RxJava.

`Appendix D`, *Materializing and Dematerializing*, introduces the concepts of materializing and dematerializing, along with code examples that demonstrate how they can be used.

`Appendix E`, *Understanding Schedulers*, defines the purpose and functionality of schedulers and demonstrates their usage.

To get the most out of this book

Read the chapters systematically and do not rush. The material presented is very condensed and contains a lot of detail. Clone the source code repository (see below) and run all the code samples that demonstrate the topics discussed. To get up to speed in programming, there is nothing better than executing the examples provided, modifying them, and then trying your own ideas.

Download the example code files

You can download the example code files for this book from your account at `www.packt.com`. If you purchased this book elsewhere, you can visit `www.packt.com/support` and register to have the files emailed directly to you.

You can download the code files by following these steps:

1. Log in or register at `www.packt.com`.
2. Select the **Support** tab.
3. Click on **Code Downloads**.
4. Enter the name of the book in the **Search** box and follow the onscreen instructions.

Once the file is downloaded, please make sure that you unzip or extract the folder using the latest version of:

- WinRAR/7-Zip for Windows
- Zipeg/iZip/UnRarX for Mac
- 7-Zip/PeaZip for Linux

The code bundle for the book is also hosted on GitHub at `https://github.com/PacktPublishing/Learning-RxJava-Second-Edition`. In case there's an update to the code, it will be updated on the existing GitHub repository.

We also have other code bundles from our rich catalog of books and videos available at `https://github.com/PacktPublishing/`. Check them out!

Run code examples

If you open the downloaded code as an **IntelliJ** project, make sure to do the following on the **Project Settings** screen in a **Modules** section:

- Remove the **Android** and **Kotlin** modules, if such are present.
- Mark the `Chapter01` through `Chapter09` and `Chapter12` folders as `Source`.
- Mark the `Chapter10/src/test/java` folder as `Tests`.
- Exclude the `Chapter11` folder and **gen** (right-click and select **Exclude**).

All the examples are written for **Java 1.8**. However, some examples can be run only by **JRE 9.** In such cases, the comments in the examples advise on how to proceed.

Download the color images

We also provide a PDF file that has color images of the screenshots/diagrams used in this book. You can download it here: `https://static.packt-cdn.com/downloads/9781789950151_ColorImages.pdf`.

Code in Action

Please visit the following link to check out the CiA videos: `http://bit.ly/32xFDAh`.

Conventions used

There are a number of text conventions used throughout this book.

`CodeInText`: Indicates code words in text, database table names, folder names, filenames, file extensions, pathnames, dummy URLs, user input, and Twitter handles. Here is an example: "In our `main()` method, we have an `Observable<String>` that will push three string objects."

A block of code is set as follows:

```
repositories {
    mavenCentral()
}
```

When we wish to draw your attention to a particular part of a code block, the relevant lines or items are set in bold:

```
public static void sleep(long millis) {
    try {
        Thread.sleep(millis);
    } catch (InterruptedException e) {
```

Any command-line input or output is written as follows:

```
$ mkdir css
$ cd css
```

Bold: Indicates a new term, an important word, or words that you see on screen. For example, words in menus or dialog boxes appear in the text like this. Here is an example: "Click on the **Latest Version** link and copy the dependency description provided."

Warnings or important notes appear like this.

Tips and tricks appear like this.

Get in touch

Feedback from our readers is always welcome.

General feedback: If you have questions about any aspect of this book, mention the book title in the subject of your message and email us at customercare@packtpub.com.

Errata: Although we have taken every care to ensure the accuracy of our content, mistakes do happen. If you have found a mistake in this book, we would be grateful if you would report this to us. Please visit www.packt.com/submit-errata, selecting your book, clicking on the Errata Submission Form link, and entering the details.

Piracy: If you come across any illegal copies of our works in any form on the internet, we would be grateful if you would provide us with the location address or website name. Please contact us at `copyright@packt.com` with a link to the material.

If you are interested in becoming an author: If there is a topic that you have expertise in, and you are interested in either writing or contributing to a book, please visit `authors.packtpub.com`.

Reviews

Please leave a review. Once you have read and used this book, why not leave a review on the site that you purchased it from? Potential readers can then see and use your unbiased opinion to make purchase decisions, we at Packt can understand what you think about our products, and our authors can see your feedback on their book. Thank you!

For more information about Packt, please visit `packt.com`.

Section 1: Foundations of Reactive Programming in Java

This module sets the stage for the book. It introduces reactive programming in general and quickly brings the reader up to speed on all the basic stream processing functionality.

The following chapters are included in this module:

- Chapter 1, *Thinking Reactively*
- Chapter 2, *Observable and Observer*
- Chapter 3, *Basic Operators*

Thinking Reactively 1

We assume that you are fairly comfortable with Java and know how to use classes, interfaces, methods, properties, variables, static/non-static scopes, and collections. If you are not familiar with concurrency or multithreading, that is okay. RxJava makes these advanced topics much more accessible.

Have your favorite Java development environment ready, be it IntelliJ IDEA, Eclipse, NetBeans, or any other environment of your choosing. We will be using IntelliJ IDEA, although it should not matter or have an impact on the examples in this book. We recommend that you have a project building framework such as Gradle or Maven, which we will explain how to use shortly.

In this chapter, before diving deeper into RxJava, we will cover some core topics:

- A brief history of Reactive Extensions and RxJava
- Thinking reactively
- Leveraging RxJava
- Setting up your first RxJava project
- Building your first reactive applications
- The differences between RxJava 1.x, 2.x, and 3.0

A brief history of ReactiveX and RxJava

As developers, we tend to think in counterintuitive ways. Modeling our world with code has never been short of challenges. It was not long ago that object-oriented programming was seen as the silver bullet to solve this problem. Making blueprints of what we interact with in real life was a revolutionary idea, and this core concept of classes and objects still impacts how we code today. However, business and user demands continued to grow in complexity. As 2010 approached, it became clear that object-oriented programming solved only part of the problem.

Classes and objects do a great job of representing an entity with properties and methods, but they become messy when they need to interact with each other in increasingly complex and often unplanned ways. Decoupling patterns and paradigms emerged, but this yielded an unwanted side effect of growing amounts of boilerplate code. In response to these problems, functional programming began to make a comeback, not to replace object-oriented programming, but rather to complement it and address the challenges.

Reactive programming, a functional event-driven programming approach, began to receive special attention. A couple of reactive frameworks emerged, including **Akka** and **Sodium**. But at Microsoft, a computer scientist named Erik Meijer created a reactive programming framework for .NET called **Reactive Extensions**. In a matter of years, Reactive Extensions (also known as **ReactiveX** or **Rx***)* was ported to several languages and platforms, including JavaScript, Python, C++, Swift, and Java, of course. Soon, ReactiveX became a cross-language standard of reactive programming.

RxJava, the ReactiveX port for Java, was created in large part by Ben Christensen from Netflix and David Karnok. RxJava 1.0 was released in November 2014, followed by RxJava 2.0 in November 2016. RxJava is the backbone for other ReactiveX JVM ports, such as **RxScala**, **RxKotlin**, and **RxGroovy**. It has become a core technology for Android development and has also found its way into Java backend development.

Many RxJava-supporting libraries, such as **RxAndroid** (`https://github.com/ReactiveX/RxAndroid`), **RxJava-JDBC** (`https://github.com/davidmoten/rxjava-jdbc`), **RxNetty** (`https://github.com/ReactiveX/RxNetty`), and **RxJavaFX** (`https://github.com/ReactiveX/RxJavaFX`) adapted several Java frameworks to become reactive and work with RxJava out of the box. This all shows that RxJava is more than a library. It is part of a greater ReactiveX ecosystem that represents an entire approach to programming. The fundamental idea behind ReactiveX is that *events are data and data are events*. This is a powerful concept that we will explore later in this chapter, but first, let's step back and look at the world through the reactive lens.

Thinking reactively

Suspend everything you know about Java (and programming in general) for a moment, and let's make some observations about our world. These may sound like obvious statements, but as developers, we can easily overlook them. Try to become aware of the fact that everything is in motion. Traffic, weather, people, conversations, financial transactions, and so on are constantly changing or moving through stages.

Technically, even something as stationary as a rock is in motion, as its spatial location changes constantly due to the earth's rotation and orbiting through space. When you consider the possibility that everything can be modeled as being in motion, you may find it a bit overwhelming as a developer.

Another observation to note is that these different events are happening concurrently. Multiple activities are happening at the same time. Sometimes, they act independently, but at other times, they can converge and interact. For instance, a car can drive with no impact on a person jogging. They are two separate streams of events. However, they may converge at some point and the car will stop when it encounters the jogger.

If this is how our world works, why do we not model our code this way? Why do we not model code as multiple concurrent streams of events or data? It is not uncommon for developers to spend more time managing the states of objects and doing this in an imperative and sequential manner. You may structure your code to execute two independent processes, **Process 1** and **Process 2**, and then **Process 3**, which depends on **Process 1** and **Process 2**. Why not kick off **Process 1** and **Process 2** simultaneously, and then kick off **Process 3** after the completion of these two processes? Of course, you can use callbacks and Java concurrency tools, but RxJava makes this much easier and safer to express.

Let's make one last observation. A book or music CD is static. A book is an unchanging sequence of words and a CD is a collection of tracks. There is nothing dynamic about them. However, when we read a book, we read one word at a time. Those words are effectively put in motion as a stream being consumed by our eyes. It is no different with a music track on a CD, where each track is put in motion as sound waves and your ears consume each track. Static items can, in fact, be put in motion too. This is an abstract but powerful idea because we create from each of these static items a series of events. When we level the playing field between data and events by treating them both the same, we unleash the power of functional programming and unlock abilities we previously might have thought impractical.

The fundamental idea behind reactive programming is that *events are data and data are events*. This may not seem intuitive, but it really does not take long to grasp when you consider our real-world examples. The runner and car both have properties and states, but they are also in motion. The book and CD are put in motion when they are consumed. Merging the event and data allows the code to feel organic and represent the world we are modeling.

Why should I learn RxJava?

ReactiveX and RxJava address many problems that programmers face daily, allowing them to express business logic and spend less time engineering code. Have you ever struggled with concurrency, event handling, obsolete data states, and exception recovery? What about making your code more maintainable, reusable, and evolvable so it can keep up with your business? It might be presumptuous to call reactive programming a silver bullet that eliminates these problems, but it certainly is a progressive leap toward addressing them.

There is also a growing user demand to make applications responsive in real time. Reactive programming allows you to quickly analyze and work with live data sources such as Twitter feeds or stock prices. It can also cancel and redirect work, scale with concurrency, and cope with rapidly emitting data. Composing events and data as streams that can be mixed, merged, filtered, split, and transformed opens up radically effective ways to compose and evolve the code.

In summary, reactive programming makes many hard programming tasks easy, enabling you to add value in ways you might have thought impractical earlier. If you have a process written reactively and you discover that you need to run part of it on a different thread, you can implement this change in a matter of seconds. If you find network connectivity issues crashing your application intermittently, you can gracefully use reactive recovery strategies that wait and try again. If you need to inject another operation in the middle of your process, it is as simple as inserting a new operator.

Reactive programming models data/event processing as a modular chain of links that can be added or removed quickly. Such a chain is also called a **processing chain** or **processing pipeline**. In essence, RxJava allows applications to be tactical and evolvable while maintaining stability in production.

What will you learn in this book?

As stated earlier, RxJava is the ReactiveX port for Java. In this book, we will focus primarily on RxJava 3.0, but we will highlight the significant differences between RxJava 1.x, 2.x, and 3.0 where they exist. We will place a priority on learning to think reactively and leverage the practical features of RxJava. Starting with a high-level understanding, we will gradually move deeper into how RxJava works. Along the way, you will learn about reactive patterns and tricks to solve common problems that programmers encounter.

We will cover core Rx concepts and the three core entities of RxJava: **Observable, Observer,** and **Operator**. You will start writing reactive programs immediately and will acquire a solid foundation to build upon throughout the rest of the book. Then, we will explore more of the nuances of RxJava and how to effectively leverage concurrency. You will also learn the different ways to deal with reactive streams that produce data/events faster than they can be consumed.

Finally, we will touch on several miscellaneous but essential topics, including custom operators, as well as how to use RxJava with testing frameworks, Android, and the Kotlin language.

Setting up

Currently, there are three co-existing versions of RxJava: 1.x, 2.x, and 3.0. We will go through some of the major differences later in the section entitled *RxJava 1.x, 2.x, 3.0 – which one do I use?* and discuss which version you should use.

RxJava 3.0 is a fairly lightweight library and comes in at fewer than 4 **megabytes** (**MBs**) in size. This makes it practical for Android and other projects that require a low dependency overhead. RxJava 3.0 has only one dependency, called **Reactive Streams** (`http://www.reactive-streams.org/`), which is a core library (made by the creators of RxJava) that sets a standard for asynchronous stream implementations, one of which is RxJava 3.0.

RxJava 2x is even smaller—closer to 2 MB—and has only one dependency on Reactive Streams too.

It may be used in other libraries beyond RxJava and is a critical effort in the standardization of reactive programming on the Java platform. Note that RxJava 1.x does not have any dependencies, including Reactive Streams, which was realized after 1.0.

If you are starting a project from scratch, try to use RxJava 3.0. This is the version we will cover in this book, but we will point out significant differences between versions 1.x and 2.x. While RxJava 1.x and 2.x will be supported for a good while due to the countless projects using it, innovation will likely only continue onward in RxJava 3.0. RxJava 1.x reached end-of-life on March 31, 2018, and RxJava 2.x will only be maintained by fixing bugs until February 28, 2021.

All RxJava versions can run on Java 1.6+. In this book, we will use Java 8, and it is recommended that you use a minimum of Java 8 so that you can use lambdas out of the box. For Android, there are ways to leverage lambdas in earlier Java versions that will be addressed later. But due to the fact that Android Nougat uses Java 8 and Java 8 has been out since 2014, we hope that you will not have to do any workarounds to leverage lambdas.

Navigating the central repository

To bring in RxJava as a dependency, you have a number of options. The best place to start is to go to the Maven central repository, called **The Central Repository** (`http://search.maven.org`) and search for `rxjava`. You should see RxJava 3.0, 2.x, and 1.x as separate repositories at the top of the search results, as shown in the following screenshot:

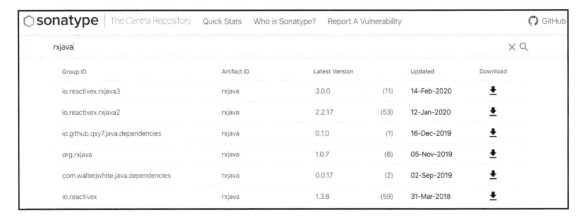

You can also use classic search, if you're already used to its look and feel, and get the same results as shown in the following screenshot:

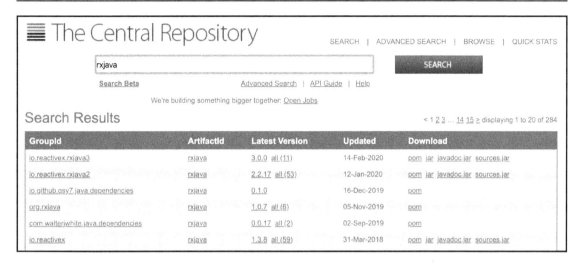

At the time of writing, RxJava 3.0.0 is the latest version of RxJava 3.x, RxJava 2.2.17 is the latest version of RxJava 2.x, and RxJava 1.3.8 is the latest version of RxJava 1.x. You can download the latest JAR file by clicking the link on the far right under the **Download** column and then configuring your project using the downloaded JAR file.

Alternatively, you can use Gradle or Maven to automatically import these libraries into your project. This way, you can easily share and store your project (through Git or other version control systems) without having to download and configure RxJava manually each time. To view the latest configurations for Maven, Gradle, and several other build automation systems, click on the **Latest Version** link and copy the dependency description provided into the `pom.xml` file (for Maven) or `build.gradle` file (for Gradle) of your project.

In the next two subsections, we will walk you through how to do it.

Using Gradle

There are several automated build systems available, but the two most popular ones are Gradle and Maven. Gradle is somewhat of a successor to Maven and used mostly for Android development. If you are not familiar with Gradle and would like to learn how to use it, check out the Gradle **Getting Started** guide (`https://gradle.org/getting-started-gradle-java/`).

There are also several books that cover Gradle in varying degrees of depth that you can find at `https://gradle.org/books/`. The following is the fragment of the above screenshot that contains Maven and Gradle configurations:

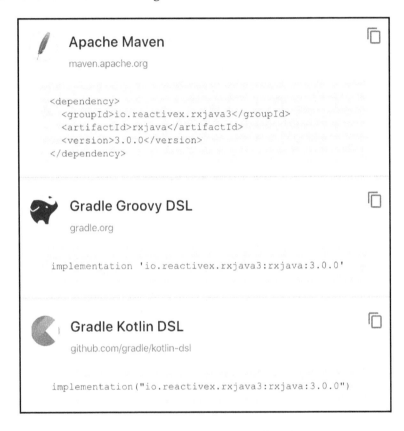

In your `build.gradle` script, ensure that you have declared `mavenCentral()` as one of your repositories. Type in or paste this dependency line, `compile` `'io.reactivex.rxjava2:rxjava:x.y.z'`, where `x.y.z` is the version number you want to use, as shown in the following code snippet:

```
apply plugin: 'java'
sourceCompatibility = 1.8
repositories {
    mavenCentral()
}
dependencies {
    compile 'io.reactivex.rxjava2:rxjava:x.y.z'
}
```

Build your Gradle project and you should be good to go! You will then have RxJava and its types available for use in your project.

Using Maven

You also have the option to use Maven, and you can view the appropriate configuration in **The Central Repository** by selecting the **Apache Maven** configuration information, as shown in the following screenshot:

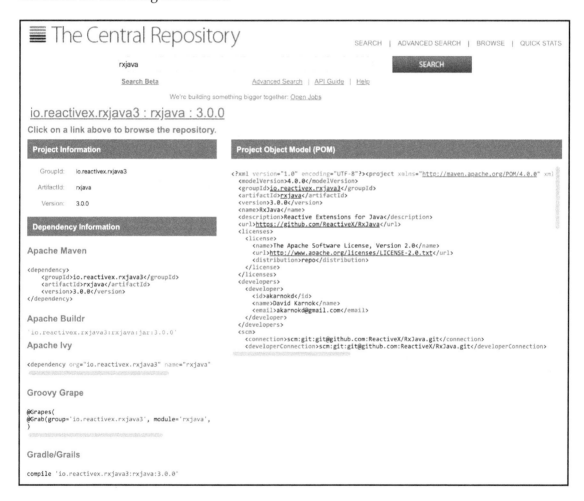

You can then copy and paste the `<dependency>` block containing the RxJava configuration and paste it inside a `<dependencies>` block in your `pom.xml` file. Rebuild your project, and you should now have RxJava set up as a dependency. The `x.y.z` version number corresponds to the desired RxJava version that you want to use:

```
<project>
  <modelVersion>4.0.0</modelVersion>
    <groupId>org.nield</groupId>
    <artifactId>mavenrxtest</artifactId>
    <version>1.0</version>
  <dependencies>
   <dependency>
    <groupId>io.reactivex.rxjava2</groupId>
    <artifactId>rxjava</artifactId>
    <version>x.y.z</version>
   </dependency>
  </dependencies>
</project>
```

A brief exposure to RxJava

Before we dive deep into the reactive world of RxJava, here is a quick immersion to get your feet wet first. In ReactiveX, the core type you will work with is the `Observable` class. We will be learning more about the `Observable` class throughout the rest of this book. But essentially, an `Observable` pushes things. A given `Observable<T>` pushes things of type `T` through a series of operators until it arrives at an `Observer` object that consumes the items.

For instance, create a new `Ch1_1.java` file in your project and put in the following code:

```
import io.reactivex.rxjava3.core.Observable;
public class Ch1_1 {
    public static void main(String[] args) {
      Observable<String> myStrings =
              Observable.just("Alpha", "Beta", "Gamma");
    }
}
```

In our `main()` method, we have an `Observable<String>` that will push three string objects. An `Observable` can push data or events from virtually any source, whether it is a database query or live Twitter feeds. In this case, we are quickly creating an `Observable` using `Observable.just()`, which will emit a fixed set of items.

In RxJava 1.x, the types are contained in the `rx` package. In RxJava 2.x, most types you will use are contained in the `io.reactivex` package. In RxJava 3.0, most types you will use are contained in the `io.reactivex.rxjava3` package.

However, running this `main()` method is not going to do anything other than declare `Observable<String>`. To make this `Observable` actually push (or emit) these three strings, we need an `Observer` object to subscribe to it and receive the items. We can quickly create and connect an `Observer` object by passing a lambda expression that specifies what to do with each value it receives:

```
import io.reactivex.rxjava3.core.Observable;
public class Ch1_1 {
    public static void main(String[] args)  {
        Observable<String> myStrings =
            Observable.just("Alpha", "Beta", "Gamma");
        myStrings.subscribe(s -> System.out.println(s));
    }
}
```

When we run this code, we should get the following output:

```
Alpha
Beta
Gamma
```

What happened here is that our `Observable<String>` pushed each string object one at a time to our `Observer` object, which we shorthanded using the `s ->` `System.out.println(s)` lambda expression. We passed each string through the (arbitrarily named) `s` parameter and instructed it to print each one. Lambda expressions are essentially mini-functions that allow us to quickly pass instructions on what action to take with each incoming item. Everything to the left of the arrow (`->`) are arguments (which, in this case, is a string we named `s`), and everything to the right is the action (which is `System.out.println(s)`).

If you are unfamiliar with lambda expressions, turn to *Appendix A, Introducing Lambda Expressions,* to learn more about how they work. If you want to invest extra time in understanding lambda expressions, I highly recommend that you read at least the first few chapters of *Java 8 Lambdas* (O'Reilly) (`http://shop.oreilly.com/product/0636920030713.do`), by Richard Warburton. Lambda expressions are a critical topic in modern programming and have become especially relevant to Java developers since their adoption in Java 8. We will be using lambdas constantly in this book, so definitely take some time to get comfortable with them.

We can also use several operators in the pipeline between `Observable` and `Observer` to transform each pushed item or manipulate it in some way. Each such operator applies the transformation and returns a new `Observable` that emits the transformed item. For example, we can use `map()` to turn each string emission into its `length()`, and each length integer will then be pushed to `Observer`, as shown in the following code snippet:

```
import io.reactivex.rxjava3.core.Observable;
public class Ch1_2 {
  public static void main(String[] args) {
    Observable<String> myStrings =
        Observable.just("Alpha", "Beta", "Gamma");
    myStrings.map(s -> s.length())
            .subscribe(s -> System.out.println(s));
  }
}
```

When we run this code, we should get the following output:

```
5
4
5
```

If you have used Java 8 streams or Kotlin sequences, you might be wondering how `Observable` is any different. The key difference is that `Observable` pushes the items, while the streams and sequences pull the items. This may seem subtle, but the impact of a push-based iteration is far more powerful than a pull-based one. As we saw earlier, you can push not only data but also events. For instance, `Observable.interval()` will push a consecutive `Long` at each specified time interval, as shown in the following code snippet. This `Long` emission is not only data but also an event! Let's take a look:

```
import io.reactivex.rxjava3.core.Observable;
import java.util.concurrent.TimeUnit;
public class Ch1_3 {
  public static void main(String[] args) {
    Observable<Long> secondIntervals =
            Observable.interval(1, TimeUnit.SECONDS);
    secondIntervals.subscribe(s -> System.out.println(s));
    /* Hold main thread for 5 seconds
       so Observable above has chance to fire */
    sleep(5000);
  }
  public static void sleep(long millis) {
    try {
      Thread.sleep(millis);
    } catch (InterruptedException e) {
      e.printStackTrace();
```

```
                    }
                }
            }
```

When we run this code, we should get the following output:

```
0
1
2
3
4
```

Notice that a consecutive emission fires every second. This application runs for about 5 seconds before it quits, and you likely see emissions 0 to 4 fired, each separated by a just a second-long gap. This simple idea that data is a series of events over time unlocks new possibilities in programming.

As a side note, we will get more into concurrency later, but we had to create a `sleep()` method because this `Observable` fires emissions on a computation thread when the `Observable` is subscribed to. The main thread used to launch our application is not going to wait on this `Observable` since it fires on a computation thread, not the main thread. Therefore, we use `sleep()` to pause the main thread for 5,000 milliseconds and then allow it to reach the end of the `main()` method (which will cause the application to terminate). This gives `Observable.interval()` a chance to fire for the 5-second window before the application quits.

Throughout this book, we will uncover many mysteries about `Observable` and the powerful abstractions it takes care of for us. If you've conceptually understood what's been going on here so far, congrats! You are already becoming familiar with how reactive code works. To emphasize again, emissions are pushed one at a time, all the way to `Observer`. Emissions represent both data and an event, which can be emitted over time. Of course, beyond `map()`, there are hundreds of operators in RxJava, and we will learn about the key ones in this book. Learning which operators to use for a situation and how to combine them is the key to mastering RxJava. In the next chapter, we will cover `Observable` and `Observer` much more comprehensively. We will also demystify how events and data are being represented in `Observable` a bit more.

RxJava 1.x, 2.x, or 3.0 – which one do I use?

As stated earlier, you are encouraged to use RxJava 3.0 if you can. This version will continue to grow and receive new features, while RxJava 1.x has not been developed further since March 21, 2018, and 2.x will be maintained for bug fixes only until February 28, 2021. However, there are other considerations that may lead you to use RxJava 1.x or 2.x.

If you inherit a project that is already using RxJava 1.x or 2.x, you will likely continue using it until it becomes feasible to migrate to RxJava 3.0. You can also check out David Karnok's *RxJava2Interop* project (`https://github.com/akarnokd/RxJava2Interop`), which converts Rx types from RxJava 1.x to RxJava 2.x and vice versa. After you finish this book, you may consider using this library to leverage RxJava 2.x even if you have the RxJava 1.x legacy code.

Migration to RxJava 3.0 requires mostly a change of import statements only. However, a few methods were dropped between RxJava 2.x and 3.0, some methods renamed, and new methods added (refer to the details at `https://github.com/ReactiveX/RxJava/wiki/What's-different-in-3.0`). The compiler will guide you and, for a typical, not overly large application, migration to RxJava 3.0 should be pretty straightforward, unless, of course, your application uses very particular version-specific features. In such a case, a rewrite would be the only way to proceed.

In RxJava, there are multiple libraries that can be used to make several Java APIs reactive and plug into RxJava seamlessly. To name just a few, these libraries include RxJava-JDBC, RxAndroid, RxJava-Extras, RxNetty, and RxJavaFX. At the time of writing, only RxAndroid and RxJavaFX have been fully ported to RxJava 2.x, and many other libraries will follow. By the time you are reading this, all major RxJava extension libraries will hopefully be ported to RxJava 2.x and some to RxJava 3.0, too.

You may prefer RxJava 3.0 because it was built on much of the hindsight and wisdom gained from RxJava 1.x and 2x. It has better performance, simpler APIs, a cleaner approach to backpressure, and is a bit safer when it comes to putting together your own operators.

When to use RxJava

A common question ReactiveX newcomers ask is: What circumstances warrant a reactive approach? Do we always want to use RxJava? As someone who has been living and breathing reactive programming for a while, I have learned that there are two answers to this question.

The first answer, when you first start out, is *yes!* You always want to take a reactive approach. The only way to truly become a master of reactive programming is to build reactive applications from the ground up. Think of everything as `Observable` and always model your program in terms of data and event flows. When you do this, you will leverage everything reactive programming has to offer and see the quality of your applications go up significantly.

The second answer is that as you become experienced in RxJava, you will find cases where RxJava may not be appropriate. There will occasionally be times where a reactive approach may not be optimal, but usually, this exception applies only to a part of your code. Your entire project itself should be reactive. There may be parts that are not reactive for good reason. These exceptions only stand out to a trained Rx veteran who sees that returning `List<String>` is perhaps better than returning `Observable<String>`.

Rx greenhorns should not worry about when something should be reactive versus not reactive. Over time, they will start to see cases where the benefits of Rx are marginalized, and this is something that only comes with experience.

So for now, no compromises. Go reactive all the way!

Summary

In this chapter, you have learned how to look at the world in a reactive way. As a developer, you may have to retrain yourself from a traditional imperative mindset and develop a "reactive" view. If you have done imperative, object-oriented programming for a long time, this may not be easy to accomplish, but the return on investment will be significant as your applications will become more maintainable, scalable, and evolvable. You will also have a faster turnaround and more readable code.

We also have covered how to configure an RxJava project using Gradle or Maven, and what decisions should drive whether you should choose RxJava 3.0, 2.x, or 1.x. We also got a brief introduction to reactive code and how `Observable` works through push-based iteration.

By the time you finish this book, you will hopefully find reactive programming intuitive and easy to work with. We hope you find that RxJava not only makes you more productive, but also helps you take on tasks you hesitated to do earlier. So let's continue!

In the next chapter, you will learn about the `Observable` and how it works together with the `Observer`. We will discuss how to create an `Observable` and how to use its operators. This will create a foundation that allows us to move on to more complex topics later.

2
Observable and Observer

We already got a glimpse into `Observable` and how it works in `Chapter 1`, *Thinking Reactively*. You probably have many questions on how exactly it operates and what practical implications it brings to code.

This chapter will provide a foundation for the understanding of `Observable`, as well as the critical relationship it has with `Observer`. We will also cover several ways to create an `Observable` and how to use its operators. To make the rest of the book flow smoothly, we will also cover all critical nuances head-on to build a solid foundation, so that you do not have surprises later.

Here is what we will cover in this chapter:

- The `Observable` class
- The `Observer` interface
- `Observable` factories
- `Single`, `Completable`, and `Maybe`
- `Disposable`

The Observable

As introduced in `Chapter 1`, *Thinking Reactively*, the `Observable` class is a push-based composable iterator. For a given `Observable<T>`, it pushes items (called emissions) of type `T` through a series of operators until they finally arrive at a final `Observer`, which consumes them. We will present several ways of creating an `Observable`, but first, let's dive into how an `Observable` works through its `onNext()`, `onCompleted()`, and `onError()` calls.

The workings of Observable

Before we do anything else, we need to study how an `Observable` sequentially passes items down the chain to an `Observer`. At the highest level, an `Observable` works by passing three types of events:

- `onNext()`: This passes each item one at a time from the source `Observable` all the way down to the `Observer`.
- `onComplete()`: This communicates a completion event all the way down to the `Observer`, indicating that no more `onNext()` calls will occur.
- `onError()`: This communicates an error down the chain to the `Observer`, which typically defines how to handle it. Unless a `retry()` operator is used to intercept the error, the `Observable` chain typically terminates, and no more emissions occur.

These three events are initiated by the three corresponding abstract methods that compose the `Observer` interface, and we will cover some of their implementations later.

 In RxJava 1.*, the `onComplete()` event is actually called `onCompleted()`.

For now, we will just look pragmatically at how they work in everyday usage. But first, we will discuss how an `Observable` object can be created.

Using Observable.create()

Let's start by creating a source `Observable` using `Observable.create()`. A source `Observable` is an `Observable` from where emissions originate. It is the starting point of our `Observable` chain (pipeline of operators). The `Observable.create()` factory allows us to create an `Observable` by providing a lambda that accepts an `Observable` emitter.

Actually, the `create()` method accepts as a parameter an object of the `ObservableOnSubscribe` type that has only one method, `subscribe(ObservableEmitter emitter)`, which accepts an `ObservableEmitter` type, which, in turn, extends the `Emitter` interface that has three methods: `onNext()`, `onError()`, and `onComplete()`. Since `ObservableOnSubscribe` is a functional interface – it has one abstract method only – we can implement it using a lambda expression.

In RxJava 1.*, ensure that you use `Observable.fromEmitter()` instead of `Observable.create()`. The latter is something entirely different in RxJava 1.* and is intended to be used only by advanced RxJava users.

We can call the `Observable` emitter's `onNext()` method to pass emissions (one at a time) down the chain of operators as well as `onComplete()` to signal completion and communicate that there will be no more items. These `onNext()` calls will push these items down the chain toward the `Observer`, which, for example, will print them, as shown in the following code snippet:

```java
import io.reactivex.rxjava3.core.Observable;

public class Ch2_01 {
  public static void main(String[] args) {
    Observable<String> source = Observable.create(emitter -> {
        emitter.onNext("Alpha");
        emitter.onNext("Beta");
        emitter.onNext("Gamma");
        emitter.onComplete();
    });
    source.subscribe(s -> System.out.println("RECEIVED: " + s));
  }
}
```

When we run this code, the output appears as follows:

```
RECEIVED: Alpha
RECEIVED: Beta
RECEIVED: Gamma
```

The `onNext()` method is a way to hand each item, starting with `Alpha`, to the next step in the chain. In this example, the next step is the `Observer`, which prints the item using the `s -> System.out.println("RECEIVED: " + s)` lambda expression. This lambda is invoked in the `onNext()` call of `Observer`. We will look at `Observer` in more detail in a moment.

Note that the `Observable` contract (`http://reactivex.io/documentation/contract.html`) dictates that emissions must be passed sequentially and one at a time. Emissions cannot be passed by an `Observable` concurrently or in parallel. This may seem like a limitation, but it does, in fact, simplify programs and make Rx easier to reason with. We will learn some powerful tricks to effectively leverage concurrency and parallelization in `Chapter 6`, *Concurrency and Parallelization*, without breaking the `Observable` contract.

The `onComplete()` method is used to communicate down the chain to the `Observer` that no more items are coming. Observables can indeed be infinite, and if this is the case, the `onComplete()` event will never be called. Technically, a source could stop emitting `onNext()` calls and never call `onComplete()`. This would likely be bad design, though, if the source no longer plans to send emissions.

Although this particular example is unlikely to throw an error, we can catch errors that may occur within our `Observable.create()` block and emit them through `onError()`. This way, the error can be pushed down the chain and handled by the `Observer`. Its `subscribe()` method is overloaded multiple times and this particular `subscribe()` version does not handle exceptions. But we can use another version, `subscribe(Consumer<String> onNext, Consumer<Throwable> onError)`, that accepts two functions; the first handles the `onNext` event, while the other handles `onError`, as shown here:

```
import io.reactivex.rxjava3.core.Observable;

public class Ch2_02 {
    public static void main(String[] args) {
        Observable<String> source = Observable.create(emitter -> {
            try {
                emitter.onNext("Alpha");
                emitter.onNext("Beta");
                emitter.onNext("Gamma");
                emitter.onComplete();
            } catch (Throwable e) {
                emitter.onError(e);
            }
        });
        source.subscribe(s -> System.out.println("RECEIVED: " + s),
                Throwable::printStackTrace);
    }
}
```

Note that the `onNext()`, `onComplete()`, and `onError()` methods of the emitter do not necessarily push the data directly to the final `Observer`. There can be another operator between the source `Observable` and its `Observer` that acts as the next step in the chain. In the following code, we have added the `map()` and `filter()` operators that apply their actions on the passed value and return the result as a new `Observable`, as shown in the following code block:

```
import io.reactivex.rxjava3.core.Observable;
public class Ch2_03 {
    public static void main(String[] args) {
        Observable<String> source = Observable.create(emitter -> {
            try {
                emitter.onNext("Alpha");
                emitter.onNext("Beta");
                emitter.onNext("Gamma");
                emitter.onComplete();
            } catch (Throwable e) {
                emitter.onError(e);
            }
        });
        Observable<Integer> lengths = source.map(String::length);
        Observable<Integer> filtered = lengths.filter(i -> i >= 5);
        filtered.subscribe(s -> System.out.println("RECEIVED: " + s));
    }
}
```

This is the output after running the code:

```
RECEIVED: 5
RECEIVED: 5
```

With the `map()` and `filter()` operators between the source `Observable` and `Observer`, `onNext()` hands each item to the `map()` operator. Internally, it acts as an intermediary `Observer` and converts each string to an integer using its `length()` method. Then, it calls `onNext()` on `filter()` to pass that integer, and the lambda condition `i -> i >= 5` skips the emissions that are not at least five characters in length. Finally, the `filter()` operator calls `onNext()` to hand each item to the final `Observer`, where it is printed.

Please note that the `map()` operator yields a new `Observable<Integer>` derived from the original `Observable<String>`. The `filter()` operator also returns an `Observable<Integer>`, but ignores emissions that do not pass the criteria. Since operators such as `map()` and `filter()` yield new observables (which internally use `Observer` implementations to receive emissions), we can chain all our returned observables with the next operator, rather than unnecessarily saving each one to an intermediary variable, as follows:

```
import io.reactivex.rxjava3.core.Observable;

public class Ch2_04 {
    public static void main(String[] args) {
        Observable<String> source = Observable.create(emitter -> {
            try {
                emitter.onNext("Alpha");
                emitter.onNext("Beta");
                emitter.onNext("Gamma");
                emitter.onComplete();
            } catch (Throwable e) {
                emitter.onError(e);
            }
        });
        source.map(String::length)
            .filter(i -> i >= 5)
            .subscribe(s -> System.out.println("RECEIVED: " + s));
    }
}
```

The output of the preceding code appears as follows:

```
RECEIVED: 5
RECEIVED: 5
```

Chaining operators is common (and encouraged) in reactive programming. It has the nice quality of being readable from left to right and from top to bottom, much like a book, which helps with maintainability and readability.

In RxJava 2.*, `Observable` no longer supports the emission of a `null` value. If an `Observable` attempts to emit `null`, `NullPointerException` is generated with the message `onNext called with null`. Null values are generally not allowed in `2.x` operators and sources. If you need to emit `null`, consider wrapping it in a Java 8 or Google Guava `Optional`.

Using Observable.just()

In our previous example with `Observable.create()`, we could have used `Observable.just()` instead and accomplished the same effect. It is likely that you will not need to use the `Observable.create()` factory often. Certain non-reactive sources can be helpful too, and we will see them in a couple of places later in this chapter. But typically, we use streamlined factories to create an `Observable` object:
see `Observable.just()` described in this section and other factories in the following *Other Observable sources* section.

We can pass into the `just()` method up to 10 items that we want to emit. This will invoke `onNext()` for each one and then invoke `onComplete()` when they have all been pushed. Look at the following code block by way of an example:

```
import io.reactivex.rxjava3.core.Observable;

public class Ch2_05 {
    public static void main(String[] args) {
        Observable<String> source =
                        Observable.just("Alpha", "Beta", "Gamma");
        source.map(String::length).filter(i -> i >= 5)
            .subscribe(s -> System.out.println("RECEIVED: " + s));
    }
}
```

We can also use `Observable.fromIterable()` to emit the items from any `Iterable` type, such as a `List`, for example. It will also call `onNext()` for each element and then call `onComplete()` once all the elements are emitted. You will likely use this factory frequently since `Iterable` in Java is used often and can easily be made reactive:

```
import io.reactivex.rxjava3.core.Observabl;
import java.util.List;
public class Ch2_06 {
    public static void main(String[] args) {
        List<String> items = List.of("Alpha", "Beta", "Gamma");
        Observable<String> source = Observable.fromIterable(items);
        source.map(String::length).filter(i -> i >= 5)
            .subscribe(s -> System.out.println("RECEIVED: " + s));
    }
}
```

We will explore other factories that create an `Observable` later in this chapter, but for now, let's put that on hold and learn more about `Observer`.

The Observer interface

The `onNext()`, `onComplete()`, and `onError()` methods actually compose the `Observer` type – an interface implemented throughout RxJava to communicate the corresponding events. The following is the `Observer` interface definition (do not concern yourself with `onSubscribe()` for now, as we will cover it at the end of this chapter):

```
import io.reactivex.rxjava3.disposables.Disposable;

public interface Observer<T> {
    void onSubscribe@NonNull Disposable d);
    void onNext(@NonNull T value);
    void onError(Throwable e);
    void onComplete();
}
```

An `Observer` and source `Observable` are somewhat related. In one context, a source `Observable` is where emissions originate and the processing chain starts. In our previous examples, you could say that the `Observable` was returned by the `Observable.create()` or `Observable.just()` methods. But to the `filter()` operator, the `Observable` looked as if it had been returned from the `map()` operator. It has no idea where the emissions were originating. It just knows that it is receiving emissions from the operator immediately upstream from it, which is `map()` in this case.

Conversely, each `Observable` returned by an operator is internally an `Observer` that receives, transforms, and relays emissions to the next `Observer` downstream. It does not know whether the next `Observer` is another operator or the final `Observer` at the end of the chain. When we talk about the `Observer`, we are often talking about the final `Observer` at the end of the processing chain that consumes the emissions. But each operator, such as `map()` and `filter()`, also implements `Observer` internally.

We will learn in detail about how operators are built in Chapter 9, *Transformers and Custom Operators*. For now, we will focus on using the `subscribe()` method that accepts an `Observer`. In fact, `Observable` implements the functional interface `ObservableSource`, which has only one method, `void subscribe(Observer<T> observer)`. When we call the `subscribe()` method on `Observable` and pass into it an object that implements the `Observer` interface or just a lambda expression that represents the `Observable` implementation, we subscribe this `Observer` to the emissions (data and events) of the `Observable`.

The `Subscriber` of RxJava 1.* essentially became `Observer` in RxJava 2.*. There is an `Observer` type in RxJava 1.*, too, which defines the three event methods, but the `Subscriber` is what you pass to the `subscribe()` method, and it implements `Observer`. In RxJava 2.*, a `Subscriber` only exists for `Flowable`, which we will discuss in `Chapter 8`, *Flowable and Backpressure*.

Implementing and subscribing to an Observer

When you call the `subscribe()` method on an `Observable`, an `Observer` receives three events—onNext, onError, and onComplete—that are processed by the corresponding methods. Instead of specifying lambda expressions as we were doing earlier, we can implement an `Observer` and pass an instance of it to the `subscribe()` method as follows:

```
import io.reactivex.rxjava3.core.Observable;
import io.reactivex.rxjava3.core.Observer;
import io.reactivex.rxjava3.disposables.Disposable;

public class Ch2_07 {
    public static void main(String[] args) {
        Observable<String> source =
                        Observable.just("Alpha", "Beta", "Gamma");
        Observer<Integer> myObserver = new Observer<>() {
            @Override
            public void onSubscribe(Disposable d) {
                //do nothing with Disposable, disregard for now
            }
            @Override
            public void onNext(Integer value) {
                System.out.println("RECEIVED: " + value);
            }
            @Override
            public void onError(Throwable e) { e.printStackTrace(); }

            @Override
            public void onComplete() { System.out.println("Done!"); }
        };
        source.map(String::length)
            .filter(i -> i >= 5)
            .subscribe(myObserver);
    }
}
```

Do not bother about `onSubscribe()` at the moment. Just leave its implementation empty until we discuss it at the end of this chapter. The output of the preceding code looks as follows:

```
RECEIVED: 5
RECEIVED: 5
Done!
```

We have created an `Observer<Integer>` object that receives integer emissions at the end of the processing chain and serves as the endpoint where the emissions are consumed. This means they reach the end of the process where they are written to a database, text file, a server response, displayed in a UI, or (in our example) just printed to the console.

Let's look at the process again in more detail. We start with string emissions at our source. We declare our `Observer` in advance and pass it to the `subscribe()` method at the end of the processing chain. Note that each string is transformed into an integer. The `onNext()` method receives each integer and prints it using `System.out.println("RECEIVED: " + value)`.

We will not get any errors running this simple process, but if an error did occur anywhere in the chain, it would be pushed to our `onError()` implementation on `Observer`, where the stack trace of `Throwable` is printed. Finally, when the source has no more emissions (after pushing Gamma), it calls `onComplete()` and the corresponding event moves along the chain all the way to the final `Observer`, where its `onComplete()` method is called, which prints `Done!` to the console.

Shorthand Observer with lambdas

Implementing `Observer` is a bit verbose and cumbersome. Thankfully, the `subscribe()` method is overloaded to accept lambda arguments for our three events. This is likely what you will want to use in most cases. You can specify three lambda expressions separated by commas: the `onNext` lambda, the `onError` lambda, and the `onComplete` lambda. For our previous example, we can change it to look as follows:

```
Consumer<Integer> onNext = i -> System.out.println("RECEIVED: " + i);
Consumer<Throwable> onError = Throwable::printStackTrace;
Action onComplete = () -> System.out.println("Done!");
```

We can pass these three lambdas as arguments to the `subscribe()` method, and it will use them to implement an `Observer` for us. This is much more concise and requires far less boilerplate code:

```
import io.reactivex.rxjava3.core.Observable;
public class Ch2_08 {
    public static void main(String[] args) {
        Observable<String> source =
                        Observable.just("Alpha", "Beta", "Gamma");
        source.map(String::length)
            .filter(i -> i >= 5)
            .subscribe(i -> System.out.println("RECEIVED: " + i),
                    Throwable::printStackTrace,
                    () -> System.out.println("Done!"));
    }
}
```

The output of this code does not change:

```
RECEIVED: 5
RECEIVED: 5
Done!
```

Note that there are other overloads for `subscribe()`. You can omit `onComplete()` and only implement `onNext()` and `onError()`. This will no longer perform any action for `onComplete()`, but there will likely be cases where you do not need one:

```
import io.reactivex.rxjava3.core.Observable;

public class Ch2_09 {
    public static void main(String[] args) {
        Observable<String> source =
                        Observable.just("Alpha", "Beta", "Gamma");
        source.map(String::length)
            .filter(i -> i >= 5)
            .subscribe(i -> System.out.println("RECEIVED: " + i),
                    Throwable::printStackTrace);
    }
}
```

The output changes and does not have the message **Done!** anymore:

```
RECEIVED: 5
RECEIVED: 5
```

You can even omit `onError` and just specify `onNext`:

```java
import io.reactivex.rxjava3.core.Observable;

public class Ch2_10 {
    public static void main(String[] args) {
        Observable<String> source =
                        Observable.just("Alpha", "Beta", "Gamma");
        source.map(String::length)
                .filter(i -> i >= 5)
                .subscribe(i -> System.out.println("RECEIVED: " + i));
    }
}
```

However, not implementing `onError()` is something you want to avoid doing in real-life code. An error that happens anywhere in the chain will propagate to `onError()` to be handled and then terminate the `Observable` with no more emissions. If you do not specify an action for `onError`, the chain will stop processing anyway, but the error will not be handled by the application and propagate all the way into the JVM, and most likely will force the application's exit.

 You can use `retry()` operators to attempt recovery and resubscribe to an `Observable` if an error occurs. We will cover how to do that in the next chapter.

It is critical to note that most of the `subscribe()` overload variants (including the shorthand lambda we have just covered) return a `Disposable` that we did not do anything with. A `Disposable` allows the `Observable` to be disconnected from its `Observer` so emissions are terminated early, which is critical for an infinite or a long-running `Observable`. We will cover `Disposable` at the end of this chapter.

Cold versus hot observables

There are subtle differences in behavior depending on how `Observable` is implemented. A major characteristic to be aware of is a *cold* versus a *hot* `Observable`, which defines how an `Observable` behaves when it has multiple observers. First, we will cover a cold `Observable`.

A cold Observable

A cold `Observable` is much like a music CD that is provided to each listener, so each person can hear all the tracks any time they start listening to it. In the same manner, a cold `Observable` replays the emissions to each `Observer`, ensuring that it gets all the data. Most data-driven observables are cold, and this includes the observables produced by the `Observable.just()` and `Observable.fromIterable()` factories.

In the following example, we have two observers subscribed to one `Observable`. The `Observable` first pushes all the emissions to the first `Observer` and then calls `onComplete()`. Then, it pushes all the emissions again to the second `Observer` and calls `onComplete()`. Both observers receive the same datasets by getting two separate streams each, which is typical behavior for a cold `Observable`:

```
import io.reactivex.rxjava3.core.Observable;;

public class Ch2_11 {
    public static void main(String[] args) {
        Observable<String> source =
                        Observable.just("Alpha", "Beta", "Gamma");
        //first observer
        source.subscribe(s -> System.out.println("Observer 1: " + s));
        //second observer
        source.subscribe(s -> System.out.println("Observer 2: " + s));
    }
}
```

The output looks as follows:

```
Observer 1: Alpha
Observer 1: Beta
Observer 1: Gamma
Observer 2: Alpha
Observer 2: Beta
Observer 2: Gamma
```

Even if the second `Observer` transforms its emissions with operators, it will still get its own stream of emissions. Using operators such as `map()` and `filter()` against a cold `Observable` preserves the cold nature of the produced observables:

```
import io.reactivex.rxjava3.core.Observable;

public class Ch2_12 {
    public static void main(String[] args) {
        Observable<String> source =
                        Observable.just("Alpha", "Beta", "Gamma");
```

```
        source.subscribe(s -> System.out.println("Observer 1: " + s));

        source.map(String::length)
            .filter(i -> i >= 5)
            .subscribe(s -> System.out.println("Observer 2: " + s));
    }
}
```

The output does not change:

```
Observer 1: Alpha
Observer 1: Beta
Observer 1: Gamma
Observer 2: Alpha
Observer 2: Beta
Observer 2: Gamma
```

As stated earlier, `Observable` sources that emit finite datasets are usually cold.

Here is a more real-world example: Dave Moten's RxJava-JDBC (https://github.com/davidmoten/rxjava2-jdbc) allows the creation of a cold `Observable`, built off of a SQL database query using RxJava 2.0. We will not digress into this library for too long, but if you want to use the built-in Apache Derby test database, for instance, include the following dependency in your project:

```
<dependency>
    <groupId>org.apache.derby</groupId>
    <artifactId>derby</artifactId>
    <version>10.15.1.3</version>
</dependency>
```

You can then create a database, populate it with data, and query the database reactively, as shown in the following code snippet:

```
import org.davidmoten.rx.jdbc.Database;

public class Launcher {
    public static void main(String[] args) {
        Database.test()
                .select("select name from person")
                .getAs(String.class)
                .blockingForEach(System.out::println);
    }
}
```

If there is a `person` table that has a `name` column and three rows with the values `John`, `Bill`, and `Jill`, the output will be as follows:

```
John
Bill
Jill
```

This SQL-driven `Observable` is cold. Many observables emit from finite data sources such as databases, text files, or JSON are cold.

It is still important to note how the source `Observable` is architected. RxJava-JDBC runs the query each time for each `Observer`. This means that if the data changes between the two subscriptions, the second `Observer` gets different emissions to the first one. But the `Observable` is still cold since it is replaying the query even if the resulting data changes.

Again, cold observables repeat the operation to generate these emissions to each `Observer`.

Next, we will cover a *hot* `Observable`, which more closely resembles events than data.

A hot Observable

You just learned about the cold `Observable`, which works much like a music CD. A hot `Observable` is more like a radio station. It broadcasts the same emissions to all observers at the same time. If an `Observer` subscribes to a hot `Observable`, receives some emissions, and then another `Observer` subscribes later, that second `Observer` will have missed those emissions. Just like a radio station, if you tune in too late, you will have missed that song.

Logically, a hot `Observable` often represent events rather than finite datasets. The events can carry data with them, but there is a time-sensitive component, and late subscribers can miss previously emitted data.

For instance, a JavaFX or Android UI event can be represented as a hot `Observable`. In JavaFX, you can create an `Observable<Boolean>` from a `selectedProperty()` operator of a `ToggleButton` using `Observable.create()`. You can then transform the `Boolean` emissions into strings indicating whether the `ToggleButton` is UP or DOWN and then use an `Observer` to display them in `Label`, as shown in the following code snippet:

```
public class Ch2_13 extends Application {
    @Override
    public void start(Stage stage) {
        ToggleButton toggleButton = new ToggleButton("TOGGLE ME");
        Label label = new Label();
        Observable<Boolean> selectedStates =
```

```
                        valuesOf(toggleButton.selectedProperty());
        selectedStates.map(selected -> selected ? "DOWN" : "UP")
                    .subscribe(label::setText);
        VBox vBox = new VBox(toggleButton, label);
        stage.setScene(new Scene(vBox));
        stage.show();
    }
}
```

Note that `ObservableValue` of JavaFX has nothing to do with an RxJava `Observable`. It is proprietary to JavaFX, but we can easily turn it into an RxJava `Observable` using the `valuesOf()` factory implemented earlier to hook `ChangeListener` as an `onNext()` call. The `valuesOf()` method looks as follows:

```
private static <T> Observable<T> valuesOf(final
                                ObservableValue<T> fxObservable) {
    return Observable.create(observableEmitter -> {
        //emit initial state
        observableEmitter.onNext(fxObservable.getValue());
        //emit value changes uses a listener
        final ChangeListener<T> listener = (observableValue, prev,
                    current) -> observableEmitter.onNext(current);
        fxObservable.addListener(listener);
    });
}
```

And the following are `import` statements for your reference:

```
import io.reactivex.rxjava3.core.Observable;
import javafx.application.Application;
import javafx.beans.value.ChangeListener;
import javafx.beans.value.ObservableValue;
import javafx.scene.Scene;
import javafx.scene.control.Label;
import javafx.scene.control.ToggleButton;
import javafx.scene.layout.VBox;
import javafx.stage.Stage;
```

To run the preceding example, you need to add the following dependency to the `pom.xml` file if you are using Maven:

```
<dependency>
  <groupId>org.openjfx</groupId>
  <artifactId>javafx-controls</artifactId>
  <version>x.y.z</version>
</dependency>
```

You also need to download and unzip the JavaFX SDK. Assuming you have unzipped it to a `<javafx>` folder, you also need to add the following VM options to the command line:

```
--module-path <javafx>/lib --add-modules=javafx.controls
```

And, finally, add the following `main()` method to the class:

```
public static void main(String... args) {
    launch(args);
}
```

Now, you can run this example using JRE 9 (the earliest JDK version that allows the module-path option) the same way you run any Java application.

If you are using Gradle, add `compile("org.openjfx:javafx-controls:x.y.z")` to the `build.gradle` file.

The result of running this code looks as follows:

Every time you click **TOGGLE ME**, the `ToggleButton` is invoked and the `Observable<Boolean>` emits a `true` or `false` value that switches the selection state. This is a simple example, showing that this `Observable` is emitting events, but is also emitting data in the form of `true` or `false`. It transforms that `boolean` value into a `String` object and forces an `Observer` object to modify the text of the `Label`.

We only have one `Observer` in this JavaFX example. If we were to add more observers to listen to the `ToggleButton` events after emissions have occurred, those new observers would have missed earlier emissions.

UI events on JavaFX and Android are prime examples of hot observables, but you can also use a hot `Observable` to emit server requests. If you created an `Observable` from a live Twitter stream emitting tweets for a certain topic, that would also be a hot `Observable`. All of these sources are likely infinite, and while many hot observables are indeed infinite, they do not have to be. They just have to share emissions to all observers simultaneously and not replay missed emissions for tardy observers.

Note that RxJavaFX (as well as RxAndroid, covered in Chapter 11, *RxJava on Android*) has factories to turn various UI events into observables and bindings. Using RxJavaFX, you can simplify the previous example using the valuesOf() factory.

Note that we did leave a loose end with this JavaFX example, as we never handled disposal. We will revisit this when we cover Disposable at the end of this chapter.

ConnectableObservable

A helpful form of a hot Observable is the ConnectableObservable class. It takes any Observable, even if it is cold, and makes it hot so that all emissions are played to all observers at once. To do this conversion, you simply need to call publish() on an Observable, and it will yield a ConnectableObservable object.

But note that subscribing does not start the emission. You need to call the connect() method on the ConnectableObservable object to start it. This allows you to set up all your observers first, before the first value is emitted.

Take a look at the following code snippet:

```
import io.reactivex.rxjava3.core.Observable;
import io.reactivex.rxjava3.observables.ConnectableObservable;

public class Ch2_14 {
    public static void main(String[] args) {
        ConnectableObservable<String> source =
                Observable.just("Alpha", "Beta", "Gamma").publish();
        //Set up observer 1
        source.subscribe(s -> System.out.println("Observer 1: " + s));
        //Set up observer 2
        source.map(String::length)
            .subscribe(i -> System.out.println("Observer 2: " + i));
        //Fire!
        source.connect();
    }
}
```

The result is going to be as follows:

```
Observer 1: Alpha
Observer 2: 5
Observer 1: Beta
Observer 2: 4
Observer 1: Gamma
Observer 2: 5
```

Note how one `Observer` is receiving a `String` value, while the other is receiving an integer (the `String` value length) and the two are printing them in an interleaved fashion. Both subscriptions are set up in advance, before the `connect()` method is called to fire the emissions.

Rather than `Observer 1` processing all the emissions before `Observer 2`, each emission goes to all observers simultaneously. Using `ConnectableObservable` to force each emission to go to all observers is known as **multicasting**, which we will cover in detail in `Chapter 5`, *Multicasting, Replaying, and Caching*.

The `ConnectableObservable` is helpful in preventing the replaying of data to each `Observer`. You may want to do this when the replaying is expensive and you decide that emissions should go to all observers at the same time. You may also do it simply to force the operators upstream to use a single stream instance, even if there are multiple observers downstream.

Multiple observers normally result in multiple stream instances upstream. But using `publish()` to return `ConnectableObservable` consolidates all the upstream operations into a single stream. Again, these nuances will be covered more in `Chapter 5`, *Multicasting, Replaying, and Caching*. For now, remember that `ConnectableObservable` is hot, and therefore, if new subscriptions occur after `connect()` is called, they will have missed emissions fired earlier.

Other Observable sources

We have already covered a few factories to create `Observable` sources, including `Observable.create()`, `Observable.just()`, and `Observable.fromIterable()`. After our detour discussing observers, let's pick up where we left off and cover a few more `Observable` factories.

Observable.range()

`Observable.range()` creates an `Observable` that emits a consecutive range of integers. It emits each number from a start value and increments each subsequent value by one until the specified count is reached. These numbers are all passed through the `onNext()` event, followed by the `onComplete()` event:

```
import io.reactivex.rxjava3.core.Observable;

public class Ch2_15 {
    public static void main(String[] args) {
        Observable.range(1, 3)
                .subscribe(s -> System.out.println("RECEIVED: " + s));
    }
}
```

The output looks as follows:

```
RECEIVED: 1
RECEIVED: 2
RECEIVED: 3
```

Note closely that the two arguments for `Observable.range()` are not lower and upper bounds. The first argument is the initial value. The second argument is the total count of emissions, which will include both the initial value and subsequent incremented values. Try emitting `Observable.range(5,10)`, and you will notice that it emits 5 followed by the next 9 consecutive integers upto a grand total of 10 emissions:

```
import io.reactivex.rxjava3.core.Observable;

public class Ch2_16 {
    public static void main(String[] args) {
        Observable.range(5, 3)
                .subscribe(s -> System.out.println("RECEIVED: " + s));
    }
}
```

The output becomes as follows:

```
RECEIVED: 5
RECEIVED: 6
RECEIVED: 7
```

Note that there is also a long equivalent called
`Observable.rangeLong()` if you need to emit larger numbers.

Observable.interval()

As we have seen, `Observable` produces emissions over time. Emissions are handed from the source down to the `Observer` sequentially. The emissions can be spaced out over time depending on when the source provides them. Our JavaFX example with `ToggleButton` demonstrated this, as each click resulted in the emission of `true` or `false`.

But let's look at a simple example of a time-based `Observable` using `Observable.interval()`. It emits consecutive long values (starting at 0) with the specified time interval between emissions. Here, we have an `Observable<Long>` that emits every second:

```
import io.reactivex.rxjava3.core.Observable;
import java.time.LocalDateTime;
import java.util.concurrent.TimeUnit;

public class Ch2_17 {
    public static void main(String[] args) {
        Observable.interval(1, TimeUnit.SECONDS)
            .subscribe(s -> System.out.println(LocalDateTime.now()
                        .getSecond() + " " + s + " Mississippi"));
        sleep(3000);
    }
}
```

The `sleep()` method looks as follows:

```
    private static void sleep(int millis) {
        try {
            Thread.sleep(millis);
        } catch (InterruptedException e) {
            e.printStackTrace();
        }
    }
```

The output consists of three lines:

```
34 0 Mississippi
35 1 Mississippi
36 2 Mississippi
```

In each line, the first is the current second (different at each run), and the second is the emitted value, followed by the same constant, `Mississippi`.

`Observable.interval()` emits infinitely at the specified interval (which is 1 second in our example). However, because it operates on a timer, it needs to run on a separate thread, which is the computation *scheduler* by default. We will cover concurrency in `Chapter 6,` *Concurrency and Parallelization*, and learn about schedulers. For now, just note that our `main()` method kicks off the `Observable`, but does not wait for it to finish. The `Observable` starts emitting on a separate thread.

To keep our `main()` method from finishing and exiting the application before our `Observable` has a chance to finish emitting, we use the `sleep()` method to keep this application alive for 3 seconds (from now on, we are going to use this method throughout the book without presenting its source code anymore). This gives our `Observable` enough time to fire all emissions before the application quits. When you create production applications, you likely will not run into this issue often because non-daemon threads for tasks such as web services, Android apps, or JavaFX will keep the application alive.

Trick question: does `Observable.interval()` return a hot or a cold `Observable`? Because it is event-driven (and infinite), you may be tempted to say it is hot. But put a second `Observer` on it, wait for 3 seconds, and then add another `Observer`. What happens? Let's take a look:

```java
import io.reactivex.rxjava3.core.Observable;
import java.util.concurrent.TimeUnit;

public class Ch2_18 {
    public static void main(String[] args) {
        Observable<Long> seconds =
                            Observable.interval(1, TimeUnit.SECONDS);
        //Observer 1
        seconds.subscribe(l -> System.out.println("Observer 1: " + l));
        //sleep 3 seconds
        sleep(3000);
        //Observer 2
        seconds.subscribe(l -> System.out.println("Observer 2: " + l));
        //sleep 3 seconds
        sleep(3000);
    }
}
```

The output will be as follows:

```
Observer 1: 0
Observer 1: 1
Observer 1: 2
Observer 1: 3
Observer 2: 0
Observer 1: 4
Observer 2: 1
Observer 1: 5
Observer 2: 2
```

As you can see, after 3 seconds have elapsed and Observer 2 has come in, it is executed on its own separate timer and starts at 0! Each of these two observers actually gets its own emissions, each starting at 0, which tells us that the source Observable is cold.

To put all observers on the same timer with the same emission, you can use ConnectableObservable, which forces these emissions to become hot:

```
import io.reactivex.Observable;
import io.reactivex.observables.ConnectableObservable;
import java.util.concurrent.TimeUnit;

public class Ch2_19 {
    public static void main(String[] args) {
        ConnectableObservable<Long> seconds =
                Observable.interval(1, TimeUnit.SECONDS).publish();
        //observer 1
        seconds.subscribe(l -> System.out.println("Observer 1: " + l));
        seconds.connect();
        //sleep 3 seconds
        sleep(3000);
        //observer 2
        seconds.subscribe(l -> System.out.println("Observer 2: " + l));
        //sleep 3 seconds
        sleep(3000);
    }
}
```

The output changes to the following:

```
Observer 1: 0
Observer 1: 1
Observer 1: 2
Observer 1: 3
Observer 2: 3
Observer 1: 4
Observer 2: 4
```

```
Observer 1: 5
Observer 2: 5
```

`Observer 2` subscribes 3 seconds later, misses the previous values, and stays in sync with `Observer 1` for the rest of the emission.

Observable.future()

The RxJava `Observable` is much more robust and expressive than `java.util.concurrent.Future`, but if you have existing libraries that yield `Future`, you can easily turn it into an `Observable` using `Observable.future()`:

```
Future<String> future = ...;
Observable.fromFuture(future)
        .map(String::length)
        .subscribe(System.out::println);
```

Observable.empty()

Although this may not seem useful yet, it is sometimes helpful to create an `Observable` that emits nothing and calls `onComplete()`:

```
import io.reactivex.rxjava3.core.Observable;

public class Ch2_20 {
    public static void main(String[] args) {
        Observable<String> empty = Observable.empty();
        empty.subscribe(System.out::println,
                Throwable::printStackTrace,
                () -> System.out.println("Done!"));
    }
}
```

The output is as follows:

```
Done!
```

Note that no emissions were printed because there were none. It went straight to emitting the `onComplete` event processed by the third parameter of the `subscribe(Consumer<String> onNext, Consumer<Throwable> onError, Action onComplete)` method, which printed the `Done!` message.

Empty observables typically represent empty datasets. They can also result from operators such as `filter()` when none of the emitted values pass the criterion. Sometimes, you need to deliberately create an empty `Observable` using `Observable.empty()`, as in the preceding demonstration. We will see other examples of this in a few places throughout this book.

An empty `Observable` is essentially RxJava's concept of `null`. It represents an absence of value or, technically, values. However, it is more elegant than `null` because operations do not throw `NullPointerExceptions`. The `onComplete` event is emitted, and the processing stops. Then, you have to trace through the chain of operators to find which one caused the flow of emissions to become empty.

Observable.never()

A close cousin of `Observable.empty()` is `Observable.never()`. The only difference between them is that the `never()` method does not generate the `onComplete` event, thus leaving the observer waiting for an emission forever:

```java
import io.reactivex.rxjava3.core.Observable;

public class Ch2_21 {
    public static void main(String[] args) {
        Observable<String> empty = Observable.never();
        empty.subscribe(System.out::println,
                Throwable::printStackTrace,
                () -> System.out.println("Done!"));
        sleep(3000);
    }
}
```

This `Observable` is primarily used for testing and not that often in production. We have to use `sleep()` here just like `Observable.interval()` because the main thread is not going to wait for it after kicking it off. In this case, we just use `sleep()` for 3 seconds to prove that no emissions are coming from it. Then, the application exits.

Observable.error()

This, too, is something you likely will use only with testing. It creates an `Observable` that immediately generates an `onError` event with the specified exception:

```
import io.reactivex.rxjava3.core.Observable;

public class Ch2_22 {
    public static void main(String[] args) {
        Observable.error(new Exception("Crash and burn!"))
                .subscribe(i -> System.out.println("RECEIVED: " + i),
                        e -> System.out.println("Error captured: " + e),
                        () -> System.out.println("Done!"));
    }
}
```

The second parameter of the `subscribe(Consumer<String> onNext,` `Consumer<Throwable> onError)` method prints the following line:

Error captured: java.lang.Exception: Crash and burn!

You can also provide the exception using a lambda expression so that it is created from scratch and a separate exception instance is provided to each `Observer`:

```
import io.reactivex.rxjava3.core.Observable;

public class Ch2_23 {
    public static void main(String[] args) {
        Observable.error(() -> new Exception("Crash and burn!"))
                .subscribe(i -> System.out.println("RECEIVED: " + i),
                        e -> System.out.println("Error captured: " + e),
                        () -> System.out.println("Done!"));
    }
}
```

Observable.defer()

`Observable.defer()` is a powerful factory due to its ability to create a separate state for each `Observer`. When using certain `Observable` factories, you may run into some nuances if your source is stateful and you want to create a separate state for each `Observer`. Your source `Observable` may not capture something that has changed regarding its parameters and send emissions that are obsolete. Here is a simple example: we have an `Observable.range()` built from two static `int` properties, `start` and `count`.

If you subscribe to this Observable, modify the count, and then subscribe again, you will find that the second Observer does not see this change:

```java
import io.reactivex.rxjava3.core.Observable;

public class Ch2_24 {
    private static int start = 1;
    private static int count = 3;

    public static void main(String[] args) {
        Observable<Integer> source = Observable.range(start, count);
        source.subscribe(i -> System.out.println("Observer 1: " + i));
        //modify count
        count = 5;
        source.subscribe(i -> System.out.println("Observer 2: " + i));
    }
}
```

The output is as follows:

```
Observer 1: 1
Observer 1: 2
Observer 1: 3
Observer 2: 1
Observer 2: 2
Observer 2: 3
```

To remedy this problem of Observable sources not capturing state changes, you can create a fresh Observable for each subscription. This can be achieved using Observable.defer(), which accepts a lambda expression. This lambda creates an Observable for every subscription and, thus, reflects any change in its parameters:

```java
import io.reactivex.rxjava3.core.Observable;

class Ch2_25 {
    private static int start = 1;
    private static int count = 3;

    public static void main(String[] args) {
        Observable<Integer> source = Observable.defer(() ->
                Observable.range(start, count));
        source.subscribe(i -> System.out.println("Observer 1: " + i));
        //modify count
        count = 5;
        source.subscribe(i -> System.out.println("Observer 2: " + i));
    }
}
```

The output is as follows:

```
Observer 1: 1
Observer 1: 2
Observer 1: 3
Observer 2: 1
Observer 2: 2
Observer 2: 3
Observer 2: 4
Observer 2: 5
```

That's better! When your `Observable` source is not capturing changes to the things driving it, try putting it in `Observable.defer()`. If your `Observable` source was implemented naively and behaves in a broken manner with more than one `Observer` (for example, it reuses an `Iterator` that only iterates data once), `Observable.defer()` provides a quick workaround for this as well.

Observable.fromCallable()

If you need to perform a calculation or some other action and then emit the result, you can use `Observable.just()` (or `Single.just()` or `Maybe.just()`, which we will present later). But sometimes, we want to do this in a lazy or deferred manner.

A word of caution: if that procedure throws an error, no emission (data or event) happens, and the exception propagates in the traditional Java fashion. For example, let's divide one by zero in it:

```java
import io.reactivex.rxjava3.core.Observable;

public class Ch2_26a {
    public static void main(String[] args) {
        Observable.just(1 / 0)
                .subscribe(i -> System.out.println("RECEIVED: " + i),
                    e -> System.out.println("Error captured: " + e));
    }
}
```

The output is as follows:

```
Exception in thread "main" java.lang.ArithmeticException: / by zero
<the stack trace follows>
```

That is because the `Observable` was not even created, so we do not see the **Error captured:** message. By the way, if the exception is thrown anywhere after the source `Observable` was created, the exception is processed by the `Observer`, and the **Error captured:** message will be displayed. For example, let's generate an exception in the very first operator after the `Observable` is created:

```
import io.reactivex.rxjava3.core.Observable;

public class Ch2_26b {
    public static void main(String[] args) {
        Observable.just(1)
                .map(i -> i / 0)
                .subscribe(i -> System.out.println("RECEIVED: " + i),
                    e -> System.out.println("Error captured: " + e));
    }
}
```

The output is as follows:

```
Error captured: java.lang.ArithmeticException: / by zero
```

As you can see, the exception was captured by the `Observer` and successfully processed by the second lambda expression.

Now, back to the exception in the `just()` method. If you want it to be emitted down the `Observable` chain along with an `onError` event, even if thrown during the emission initialization, use `Observable.fromCallable()` instead. It accepts a functional interface, `Supplier<T>`. For example, we have the following:

```
import io.reactivex.rxjava3.core.Observable;

public class Ch2_27 {
    public static void main(String[] args) {
        Observable.fromCallable(() -> 1 / 0)
  .subscribe(i -> System.out.println("Received: " + i),
  e -> System.out.println("Error captured: " + e));
    }
}
```

The output is as follows:

```
Error captured: java.lang.ArithmeticException: / by zero
```

That is better! The error was emitted to the `Observer` rather than being thrown without being emitted. If initializing your emission has a likelihood of throwing an error, use `Observable.fromCallable()` instead of `Observable.just()`.

Single, Completable, and Maybe

There are a few specialized flavors of Observable that are explicitly set up for one or no emissions: Single, Maybe, and Completable. They all follow Observable closely and should be intuitive to use in your reactive coding workflow.

You can create them in similar ways as the Observable (for example, they each have their own create() factory), but certain Observable operators may return them too.

Single

The Single<T> class is essentially an Observable<T> that emits only one item and, as such, is limited only to operators that make sense for a single emission. Similar to the Observable class (which implements ObservableSource), the Single class implements the SingleSource functional interface, which has only one method, void subscribe(SingleObserver observer).

There is the SingleObserver interface as well:

```
interface SingleObserver<T> {
    void onSubscribe(@NonNull Disposable d);
    void onSuccess(T value);
    void onError(@NonNull Throwable error);
}
```

In contrast with the Observer interface, it does not have the onNext() method and has the onSuccess() method instead of onComplete(). This makes sense because Single can emit one value at the most. onSuccess() essentially consolidates onNext() and onComplete() into a single event. When you call subscribe() on a Single object, you provide one lambda expression for onSuccess() and, optionally, another lambda expression for onError():

```
import io.reactivex.rxjava3.core.Single;

public class Ch2_28 {
    public static void main(String[] args) {
        Single.just("Hello!")
                .map(String::length)
                .subscribe(System.out::println,
                    e -> System.out.println("Error captured: " + e));
    }
}
```

The result of the execution of this example is as follows:

```
6
```

There are operators on `Single` that turn it into an `Observable`, such as `toObservable()`. And, in the opposite direction, certain `Observable` operators return a `Single`, as we will see in the next chapter. For instance, the `first()` operator will return a `Single` because that operator is logically concerned with a single item. However, it accepts a default value as a parameter (which is specified as `Nil` in the following example) if the `Observable` comes out empty:

```
import io.reactivex.rxjava3.core.Observable;

public class Ch2_29 {
    public static void main(String[] args) {
        Observable<String> source = Observable.just("Alpha", "Beta");
        source.first("Nil")   //returns a Single
                .subscribe(System.out::println);
    }
}
```

The output is as follows:

```
Alpha
```

The `Single` must have one emission, so you can use it only if you have only one emission to provide. This means that instead of using `Observable.just("Alpha")`, you can use `Single.just("Alpha")`.

But if there are 0 or 1 emissions, you should use `Maybe` instead.

Maybe

The `Maybe` is just like a `Single`, except that it also allows no emissions to occur at all (hence `Maybe`). The `MaybeObserver` is much like a standard `Observer`, but `onNext()` is called `onSuccess()` instead:

```
public interface MaybeObserver<T> {
    void onSubscribe(@NonNull Disposable d);
    void onSuccess(T value);
    void onError@NonNull Throwable e);
    void onComplete();
}
```

A given `Maybe<T>` emits 0 or 1 items. It will pass the possible emission to `onSuccess()`, and in either case, it will call `onComplete()` when done. `Maybe.just()` can be used to create a `Maybe` emitting a single item. `Maybe.empty()` creates a `Maybe` that emits nothing:

```
import io.reactivex.rxjava3.core.Maybe;

public class Ch2_30a {
    public static void main(String[] args) {
        // has emission
        Maybe<Integer> source = Maybe.just(100);
        source.subscribe(s -> System.out.println("Process 1: " + s),
                e -> System.out.println("Error captured: " + e),
                () -> System.out.println("Process 1 done!"));
        //no emission
        Maybe<Integer> empty = Maybe.empty();
        empty.subscribe(s -> System.out.println("Process 2: " + s),
                e -> System.out.println("Error captured: " + e),
                () -> System.out.println("Process 2 done!"));
    }
}
```

The output is as follows:

```
Process 1: 100
Process 2 done!
```

The message **Process 1 done!** does not come up because there is no ambiguity: the `Maybe` observable cannot emit more than one item, so it is completed implicitly. And `MaybeObserver` does not expect anything else. To prove this point, let's replace `Maybe` with `Observable`:

```
import io.reactivex.rxjava3.core.Observable;

public class Ch2_30b {
    public static void main(String[] args) {
        // has emission
        Observable<Integer> source = Observable.just(100);
        source.subscribe(s -> System.out.println("Process 1:" + s),
                e -> System.out.println("Error captured: " + e),
                () -> System.out.println("Process 1 done!"));
        //no emission
        Observable<Integer> empty = Observable.empty();
        empty.subscribe(s -> System.out.println("Process 2:" + s),
                e -> System.out.println("Error captured: " + e),
                () -> System.out.println("Process 2 done!"));
    }
}
```

The output changes to the following:

```
Process 1: 100
Process 1 done!
Process 2 done!
```

Now, the `onComplete` event was issued to tell the `Observer` that it should not expect anything else.

Certain `Observable` operators that we will discuss later yield a `Maybe`. One example is the `firstElement()` operator, which is similar to `first()`, but returns an empty result if no elements are emitted:

```java
import io.reactivex.rxjava3.core.Observable;

public class Ch2_31 {
    public static void main(String[] args) {
        Observable<String> source =
                Observable.just("Alpha", "Beta");
        source.firstElement()
                .subscribe(s -> System.out.println("RECEIVED " + s),
                    e -> System.out.println("Error captured: " + e),
                    () -> System.out.println("Done!")
                );
    }
}
```

The output is as follows:

```
RECEIVED Alpha
```

Please note that the `onComplete` event was not generated this time because the `Observable` has no idea that the processing has stopped after the first emission.

Completable

`Completable` is simply concerned with an action being executed, but it does not receive any emissions. Logically, it does not have `onNext()` or `onSuccess()` to receive emissions, but it does have `onError()` and `onComplete()`:

```java
interface CompletableObserver<T> {
    void onSubscribe@NonNull Disposable d);
    void onComplete();
    void onError(@NonNull Throwable error);
}
```

`Completable` is something you likely will not use often. You can construct one quickly by calling `Completable.complete()` or `Completable.fromRunnable()`. The former immediately calls `onComplete()` without doing anything, while `fromRunnable()` executes the specified action before calling `onComplete()`:

```
import io.reactivex.rxjava3.core.Completable;

public class Ch2_32 {
    public static void main(String[] args) {
        Completable.fromRunnable(() -> runProcess())
                .subscribe(() -> System.out.println("Done!"));
    }

    private static void runProcess() {
        //run process here
    }
}
```

The output is as follows:

```
Done!
```

Disposing

When you call `subscribe()` to an `Observable` to receive emissions, a stream is created to process those emissions through the `Observable` chain. Of course, this uses resources. When we are done, we want to dispose of these resources so that they can be garbage-collected.

Thankfully, the finite `Observable` that calls `onComplete()` will typically dispose of itself safely when all items are emitted. But if you are working with an infinite or long-running `Observable`, you likely will run into situations where you want to explicitly stop the emissions and dispose of everything associated with that subscription. As a matter of fact, you cannot trust the garbage collector to take care of active subscriptions that you no longer need, and explicit disposal is necessary in order to prevent memory leaks.

`Disposable` is a link between an `Observable` and an active `Observer`. You can call its `dispose()` method to stop emissions and dispose of all resources used for that `Observer`. It also has an `isDisposed()` method, indicating whether it has been disposed of already:

```
public interface Disposable {
    void dispose();
    boolean isDisposed();
}
```

If you look up an `Observable` API, you may have noticed that the `subscribe()` methods that accept lambda expressions (not `Observer`) return a `Disposable`. You can use this object to stop emissions at any time by calling its `dispose()` method.

For instance, we can stop receiving emissions from `Observable.interval()` after 5 seconds:

```
import io.reactivex.rxjava3.core.Observable;
import io.reactivex.rxjava3.disposables.Disposable;
import java.util.concurrent.TimeUnit;

public class Ch2_33 {
    public static void main(String[] args) {
        Observable<Long> seconds =
                            Observable.interval(1, TimeUnit.SECONDS);
        Disposable disposable = seconds
                .subscribe(l -> System.out.println("Received: " + l));
        //sleep 5 seconds
        sleep(5000);
        //dispose and stop emissions
        disposable.dispose();
        //sleep 5 seconds to prove
        //there are no more emissions
        sleep(5000);
    }
}
```

Here, we let `Observable.interval()` run for 5 seconds, but we save the `Disposable` returned from the `subscribe()` method. Then, we call the `dispose()` method to stop the process and free any resources that were being used. Then, we let the main thread sleep for another 5 seconds just to prove that no more emissions are happening.

The output is as follows:

```
Received: 0
Received: 1
Received: 2
Received: 3
Received: 4
```

That is exactly what we would have expected.

Handling a disposable within an Observer

Earlier, we skipped talking about the onSubscribe() method in Observer, but now we will address it. You may have noticed that Disposable is passed in the implementation of an Observer through the onSubscribe() method. This method was added in RxJava 2.0, and it allows the Observer to have the ability to dispose of the subscription at any time.

For instance, you can implement your own Observer and use onNext(), onComplete(), or onError() to have access to the Disposable. This way, these three events can call dispose() if, for whatever reason, the Observer does not want any more emissions:

```
Observer<Integer> myObserver = new Observer<Integer>() {
    private Disposable disposable;
    @Override
    public void onSubscribe(Disposable disposable) {
      this.disposable = disposable;
    }
    @Override
    public void onNext(Integer value) {
      //has access to Disposable
    }
    @Override
    public void onError(Throwable e) {
      //has access to Disposable
    }
    @Override
    public void onComplete() {
      //has access to Disposable
    }
};
```

Disposable is sent from the source all the way down the chain to the Observer, so each step in the Observable chain has access to the Disposable.

Note that the `subscribe()` method that accepts `Observer` returns `void` (not a `Disposable`) since it is assumed that the `Observer` will handle everything. If you do not want to explicitly handle the `Disposable` and want RxJava to handle it for you (which is probably a good idea until you have reason to take control), you can extend `ResourceObserver` as your `Observer`, which uses default `Disposable` handling. Pass the `ResourceObserver` object to `subscribeWith()` instead of `subscribe()`, and you will get the default `Disposable` returned:

```java
import io.reactivex.rxjava3.core.Observable;
import io.reactivex.rxjava3.disposables.Disposable;
import io.reactivex.rxjava3.observers.ResourceObserver;
import java.util.concurrent.TimeUnit;

public class Ch2_34 {
    public static void main(String[] args) {
        Observable<Long> source =
                    Observable.interval(1, TimeUnit.SECONDS);
        ResourceObserver<Long> myObserver = new
                ResourceObserver<Long>() {
                    @Override
                    public void onNext(Long value) {
                        System.out.println(value);
                    }
                    @Override
                    public void onError(Throwable e) {
                        e.printStackTrace();
                    }
                    @Override
                    public void onComplete() {
                        System.out.println("Done!");
                    }
                };
        //capture Disposable
        Disposable disposable = source.subscribeWith(myObserver);
    }
}
```

Using CompositeDisposable

If you have several subscriptions that need to be managed and disposed of, it can be helpful to use `CompositeDisposable`. This implements `Disposable`, but internally holds a collection of `Disposable` objects, which you can add to and then dispose of all at once:

```java
import io.reactivex.rxjava3.core.Observable;
import io.reactivex.rxjava3.disposables.CompositeDisposable;
```

```
import io.reactivex.rxjava3.disposables.Disposable;
import java.util.concurrent.TimeUnit;

public class Ch2_35 {
    private static final CompositeDisposable disposables =
                                    new CompositeDisposable();
    public static void main(String[] args) {
        Observable<Long> seconds =
                            Observable.interval(1, TimeUnit.SECONDS);
        //subscribe and capture disposables
        Disposable disposable1 = seconds
            .subscribe(l -> System.out.println("Observer 1: " + l));
        Disposable disposable2 = seconds
            .subscribe(l -> System.out.println("Observer 2: " + l));
        //put both disposables into CompositeDisposable
        disposables.addAll(disposable1, disposable2);
        //sleep 5 seconds
        sleep(5000);
        //dispose all disposables
        disposables.dispose();
        //sleep 5 seconds to prove
        //there are no more emissions
        sleep(5000);
    }
}
```

The output is as follows:

```
Observer 1: 0
Observer 2: 0
Observer 1: 1
Observer 2: 1
Observer 1: 2
Observer 2: 2
Observer 1: 3
Observer 2: 3
Observer 1: 4
Observer 2: 4
```

As you can see, `CompositeDisposable` is a simple but helpful utility to maintain a collection of `Disposable` objects that you can add to by calling `add()` or `addAll()`. When you no longer want these subscriptions, you can call `dispose()` to dispose of all of them at once.

Handling disposal with Observable.create()

If your `Observable.create()` is returning a long-running or infinite `Observable`, you should ideally check the `isDisposed()` method of `ObservableEmitter` regularly, to see whether you should keep sending emissions. This prevents unnecessary work from being done if the subscription is no longer active.

In this case, you should use `Observable.range()`, but for the sake of the example, let's say we are emitting integers in a `for`-loop in `Observable.create()`. Before emitting each integer, you should make sure that `ObservableEmitter` does not indicate that the `dispose()` method was called:

```
import io.reactivex.rxjava3.core.Observable;

public class Ch2_36 {
    public static void main(String[] args) {
        Observable<Integer> source =
            Observable.create(observableEmitter -> {
                try {
                    for (int i = 0; i < 1000; i++) {
                        while (!observableEmitter.isDisposed()) {
                            observableEmitter.onNext(i);
                        }
                        if (observableEmitter.isDisposed()) {
                            return;
                        }
                    }
                    observableEmitter.onComplete();
                } catch (Throwable e) {
                    observableEmitter.onError(e);
                }
            });
    }
}
```

If your `Observable.create()` is wrapped around a resource, you should also handle the disposal of that resource to prevent leaks. `ObservableEmitter` has the `setCancellable()` and `setDisposable()` methods for that. In our earlier JavaFX example, we should remove `ChangeListener` from our JavaFX `ObservableValue` when disposal occurs. We can provide a lambda to `setCancellable()`, which will execute the following action when `dispose()` is called:

```
Observable<T> valuesOf(final ObservableValue<T> fxObservable) {
    return Observable.create(observableEmitter -> {
        observableEmitter.onNext(fxObservable.getValue());
```

```
final ChangeListener<T> listener =
        (observableValue, prev, current) ->
                        observableEmitter.onNext(current);
fxObservable.addListener(listener);
observableEmitter.setCancellable(() ->
                    fxObservable.removeListener(listener));
    });
}
```

Summary

This was an intense chapter, but it provides a solid foundation for how to use RxJava to tackle real-world work. RxJava, with all of its expressive power, has some nuances that are entirely due to the change of mindset it demands.

It has done an impressive amount of work taking an imperative language like Java and adapting it to become reactive and functional. But this interoperability requires some understanding of the implementations between an Observable and an Observer. We touched on various ways to create an Observable as well as how it interacts with Observer.

Take your time to digest all this information but do not let it stop you from moving on to the next two chapters, where the usefulness of RxJava starts to take form and the pragmatic application of RxJava becomes clear.

3
Basic Operators

In the previous chapter, you learned a lot about the `Observable` and `Observer`. We also covered a small number of operators, particularly `map()` and `filter()`, with a view to understanding the role of operators as well. But there are hundreds of other RxJava operators we can leverage to express business logic and behavior.

We will cover operators comprehensively throughout this book, so you know which ones to use and when. Being aware of the operators available and combining them is critical for using ReactiveX effectively. You should strive to use operators to express business logic so that your code stays as reactive as possible.

This chapter lays the foundation for the study of RxJava operators. A solid understanding of the basic operator is necessary for understanding the more complex operators described in the following chapters. Even if you know some or all of the basic operators, refreshing your knowledge will help you to gain a deeper and more nuanced insight into how RxJava works, which is critical for more complex cases.

It should be noted that RxJava operators produce observables that are observers of the `Observable` they are called on. If you call `map()` on an `Observable`, the returned `Observable` will subscribe to it. It will then transform each emission and, in turn, be a producer for observers downstream, including other operators and the terminal `Observer` itself.

Try not to cheat or get creative by extracting values out of the `Observable` chain, or resort to blocking processes or imperative programming tactics. When you keep algorithms and processes reactive, you can easily leverage the benefits of reactive programming such as lower memory usage, flexible concurrency, and disposability. So, use operators only to process data coming from an `Observable` and to get the result you need from an `Observer` at the end of the processing chain.

In this chapter, we will cover the following topics:

- Conditional operators
- Suppressing operators
- Transforming operators
- Reducing operators
- Boolean operators
- Collection operators
- Error recovery operators
- Action operators
- Utility operators

Conditional operators

Conditional operators emit or transform `Observable` conditionally. This allows a control flow to be organized and the path of execution to be determined, which is especially important for adding decision-making ability to your program.

takeWhile() and skipWhile()

Another variant of the `take()` operator is the `takeWhile()` operator, which takes emissions while a condition derived from each emission is `true`. The following example will keep taking emissions while emissions are less than 5. The moment it encounters one that is not, it will generate the `onComplete` event and dispose of the used resources:

```
import io.reactivex.rxjava3.core.Observable;

public class Ch3_01 {
    public static void main(String[] args) {
        Observable.range(1, 100)
                .takeWhile(i -> i < 5)
                .subscribe(i -> System.out.println("RECEIVED: " + i));
    }
}
```

The output of the preceding code snippet is as follows:

```
RECEIVED: 1
RECEIVED: 2
RECEIVED: 3
RECEIVED: 4
```

Just like the takeWhile() function, there is a skipWhile() function. This keeps skipping emissions while they comply with the condition. The moment that condition produces false, the emissions start flowing through.

In the following code, we skip emissions as long as they are less than or equal to 95. The moment an emission is encountered that makes the condition return false, all subsequent emissions are not skipped anymore and flow downstream:

```java
import io.reactivex.rxjava3.core.Observable;

public class Ch3_02 {
    public static void main(String[] args) {
        Observable.range(1, 100)
                .skipWhile(i -> i <= 95)
                .subscribe(i -> System.out.println("RECEIVED: " + i));
    }
}
```

The output of the preceding code snippet is as follows:

```
RECEIVED: 96
RECEIVED: 97
RECEIVED: 98
RECEIVED: 99
RECEIVED: 100
```

The takeUntil() operator is similar to takeWhile(), but it accepts another Observable as a parameter. It keeps taking emissions until that other Observable pushes an emission. The skipUntil() operator has similar behavior. It also accepts another Observable as an argument but it keeps skipping until the other Observable emits something.

defaultIfEmpty()

If we want to resort to a single emission when a given `Observable` turns out to be empty, we can use `defaultIfEmpty()`. For example, if we have an `Observable<String>` and filter only items that start with `Z`, we can resort to emitting `None`:

```
import io.reactivex.rxjava3.core.Observable;

public class Ch3_03 {
    public static void main(String[] args) {
        Observable<String> items = Observable.just("Alpha", "Beta");
        items.filter(s -> s.startsWith("Z"))
                .defaultIfEmpty("None")
                .subscribe(System.out::println);
    }
}
```

The output of the preceding code snippet is as follows:

None

Of course, if emissions were to occur, we would never see the message **None**. It happens only when the source `Observable` is empty.

switchIfEmpty()

Similar to `defaultIfEmpty()`, `switchIfEmpty()` specifies a different `Observable` to emit values from if the source `Observable` is empty. This allows you to specify a different sequence of emissions in the event that the source is empty rather than emitting just one value, as in the case of `defaultIfEmpty()`.

We could choose to emit three additional strings, for example, if the preceding `Observable` came out empty due to a `filter()` operation:

```
import io.reactivex.rxjava3.core.Observable;

public class Ch3_04 {
    public static void main(String[] args) {
        Observable.just("Alpha", "Beta", "Gamma")
                .filter(s -> s.startsWith("Z"))
                .switchIfEmpty(Observable.just("Zeta", "Eta", "Theta"))
                .subscribe(i -> System.out.println("RECEIVED: " + i),
                        e -> System.out.println("RECEIVED ERROR: " + e));
    }
}
```

The output of the preceding code snippet is as follows:

```
RECEIVED: Zeta
RECEIVED: Eta
RECEIVED: Theta
```

Of course, if the preceding `Observable` is not empty, then `switchIfEmpty()` will have no effect and that second specified `Observable` will not be used.

Suppressing operators

There are operators that suppress emissions that do not meet a specified criterion. These operators work by simply not calling the `onNext()` function downstream for a disqualified emission, and therefore it does not go down the chain to `Observer`. We have already seen the `filter()` operator, which is probably the most common suppressing operator. We will start with this one.

filter()

The `filter()` operator accepts `Predicate<T>` for a given `Observable<T>`. This means that you provide it a lambda that qualifies each emission by mapping it to a `Boolean` value, and emissions with `false` will not go downstream.

For instance, you can use `filter()` to only allow string emissions that are not five characters in length:

```java
import io.reactivex.rxjava3.core.Observable;

public class Ch3_05 {
    public static void main(String[] args) {
        Observable.just("Alpha", "Beta", "Gamma")
                .filter(s -> s.length() != 5)
                .subscribe(s -> System.out.println("RECEIVED: " + s));
    }
}
```

The output of the preceding code snippet is as follows:

```
RECEIVED: Beta
```

The `filter()` operator is probably the most commonly used to suppress emissions.

 Note that if all emissions fail to meet your criteria, the returned `Observable` will be empty, with no emissions occurring before `onComplete()` is called.

take()

The `take()` operator has two overloaded versions. One takes the specified number of emissions and calls `onComplete()` after all of them reach it. It will also dispose of the entire subscription so that no more emissions will occur. For instance, `take(2)` will emit the first two emissions and then call `onComplete()` (this will generate an `onComplete` event):

```
import io.reactivex.rxjava3.core.Observable;

public class Ch3_06 {
    public static void main(String[] args) {
        Observable.just("Alpha", "Beta", "Gamma")
            .take(2)
            .subscribe(s -> System.out.println("RECEIVED: " + s));
    }
}
```

The output of the preceding code snippet is as follows:

```
RECEIVED: Alpha
RECEIVED: Beta
```

Note that if the `take()` operator receives fewer emissions than specified, it will simply emit what it does get and then emit the `onComplete` event.

The other version of the `take()` operator accepts emissions within the specific time duration and then emits `onComplete`. Of course, our cold `Observable` emits so quickly that it would serve as a bad example for this case. Maybe a better example would be to use an `Observable.interval()` function.

Let's emit every `300` milliseconds, but set the `take()` operator to accept emissions for only `2` seconds in the following code snippet:

```
import io.reactivex.rxjava3.core.Observable;
import java.time.LocalDateTime;
import java.time.format.DateTimeFormatter;
```

```
import java.util.concurrent.TimeUnit;

public class Ch3_07 {
    public static void main(String[] args) {
        DateTimeFormatter f = DateTimeFormatter.ofPattern("ss:SSS");
        System.out.println(LocalDateTime.now().format(f));
        Observable.interval(300, TimeUnit.MILLISECONDS)
                .take(2, TimeUnit.SECONDS)
                .subscribe(i -> System.out.println(LocalDateTime.now()
                                    .format(f) + " RECEIVED: " + i));
        sleep(5000);
    }
}
```

The output of the preceding code is as follows:

```
50:644
51:047 RECEIVED: 0
51:346 RECEIVED: 1
51:647 RECEIVED: 2
51:947 RECEIVED: 3
52:250 RECEIVED: 4
52:551 RECEIVED: 5
```

You will likely get output similar to that shown here (with each print happening every 300 milliseconds). The first column is the current time in seconds and milliseconds. As you can see, we can get only 6 emissions in 2 seconds if they are spaced out by 300 milliseconds because the first value is emitted after 300 milliseconds too.

Note that there is also a takeLast() operator, which takes the last specified number of emissions (or time duration) before the onComplete event is generated. Just keep in mind that it internally queues emissions until its onComplete() function is called, and then it can identify and emit the last emissions.

skip()

The skip() operator does the opposite of the take() operator. It ignores the specified number of emissions and then emits the ones that follow. Let's skip the first 90 emissions in the following code snippet:

```
import io.reactivex.rxjava3.core.Observable;

public class Ch3_08 {
    public static void main(String[] args) {
        Observable.range(1, 100)
```

```
                .skip(90)
                .subscribe(i -> System.out.println("RECEIVED: " + i));
        }
    }
```

The output of the following code snippet is as follows:

```
RECEIVED: 91
RECEIVED: 92
RECEIVED: 93
RECEIVED: 94
RECEIVED: 95
RECEIVED: 96
RECEIVED: 97
RECEIVED: 98
RECEIVED: 99
RECEIVED: 100
```

Just as in the case of the `take()` operator, there is also an overloaded version that accepts a time duration.

And there is a `skipLast()` operator, which skips the last specified number of items (or time duration) before the `onComplete` event is generated. Just keep in mind that the `skipLast()` operator queues and delays emissions until it identifies the last specified number of emissions in that scope.

distinct()

The `distinct()` operator emits unique emissions. It suppresses any duplicates that follow. Equality is based on the `hashCode()` and `equals()` methods implemented by the emitted objects. If we want to emit the distinct lengths of strings, this could be done as follows:

```
import io.reactivex.rxjava3.core.Observable;

public class Ch3_09 {
    public static void main(String[] args) {
        Observable.just("Alpha", "Beta", "Gamma")
                .map(String::length)
                .distinct()
                .subscribe(i -> System.out.println("RECEIVED: " + i));
    }
}
```

The output of the preceding code snippet is as follows:

```
RECEIVED: 5
RECEIVED: 4
```

Keep in mind that if you have a wide, diverse spectrum of unique values, `distinct()` can use a bit of memory. Imagine that each subscription results in a `HashSet` that tracks previously captured unique values.

There is an overloaded version of `distinct(Function<T,K> keySelector)` that accepts a function that maps each emission to a key used for equality logic. Then, the uniqueness of each emitted item is based on the uniqueness of this generated key, not the item itself. For instance, we can use string length as the key used for uniqueness:

```java
import io.reactivex.rxjava3.core.Observable;

public class Ch3_10 {
    public static void main(String[] args) {
        Observable.just("Alpha", "Beta", "Gamma")
            .distinct(String::length)
            .subscribe(i -> System.out.println("RECEIVED: " + i));
    }
}
```

The output of the preceding code snippet is as follows:

```
RECEIVED: Alpha
RECEIVED: Beta
```

`Alpha` is five characters, and `Beta` is four. `Gamma` was ignored because `Alpha` was already emitted as a 5-character length value.

If the generated key is an object, then its uniqueness is based on the `equals()` method implemented by that object.

distinctUntilChanged()

The `distinctUntilChanged()` function ignores consecutive duplicate emissions. If the same value is being emitted repeatedly, all the duplicates are ignored until a new value is emitted. Duplicates of the next value will be ignored until it changes again, and so on. Observe the output for the following code to see this behavior in action:

```java
import io.reactivex.rxjava3.core.Observable;

public class Ch3_11 {
```

```
public static void main(String[] args) {
    Observable.just(1, 1, 1, 2, 2, 3, 3, 2, 1, 1)
        .distinctUntilChanged()
        .subscribe(i -> System.out.println("RECEIVED: " + i));
    }
}
```

The output of the preceding code snippet is as follows:

```
RECEIVED: 1
RECEIVED: 2
RECEIVED: 3
RECEIVED: 2
RECEIVED: 1
```

The first emission of 1 gets through to subscribe(). But the next two 1 values are ignored because they are consecutive duplicates. When the item switches to 2, the first 2 is emitted, but the following duplicate is ignored. A 3 is emitted and its following duplicate is ignored as well. Finally, we switch back to a 2, which emits, and then a 1 whose duplicate is ignored.

Just like with distinct(), you can use distinctUntilChanged() with an optional argument – a lambda expression for a key generation. In the following code snippet, we execute the distinctUntilChanged() operation with strings keyed on their lengths:

```
import io.reactivex.rxjava3.core.Observable;

public class Ch3_12 {
    public static void main(String[] args) {
        Observable.just("Alpha", "Beta", "Zeta", "Eta", "Gamma", "Delta")
            .distinctUntilChanged(String::length)
            .subscribe(i -> System.out.println("RECEIVED: " + i));
    }
}
```

The output of the preceding code snippet is as follows:

```
RECEIVED: Alpha
RECEIVED: Beta
RECEIVED: Eta
RECEIVED: Gamma
```

The Zeta value was skipped because it comes right after Beta, which is also four characters. The Delta value is ignored as well because it follows Gamma, which is five characters too.

elementAt()

You can get a specific emission by its index specified by the long value, starting at 0. After the item is found and emitted, onComplete() is called and the subscription is disposed of.

For example, if you want to get the fourth emission coming from an Observable, you can do it as shown in the following code snippet:

```
import io.reactivex.rxjava3.core.Observable;

public class Ch3_13 {
    public static void main(String[] args) {
        Observable.just("Alpha", "Beta", "Zeta", "Eta", "Gamma")
                .elementAt(3)
                .subscribe(i -> System.out.println("RECEIVED: " + i));
    }
}
```

The output of the following code snippet is as follows:

RECEIVED: Eta

You may not have noticed, but elementAt() returns Maybe<T> instead of Observable<T>. This is because it yields one emission, but if there are fewer emissions than the index sought, it will be empty.

There are other flavors of elementAt(), such as elementAtOrError(), which returns a Single and emits an error if an element at that index is not found. singleElement() turns an Observable into a Maybe, but produces an error if there is more than one element. Finally, firstElement() and lastElement() emit the first and the last items, respectively.

Transforming operators

In this section, we'll cover operators that transform emissions. You have already seen `map()`, which is the most obvious operator in this category. We'll start with that one.

map()

For a given `Observable<T>`, the `map()` operator transforms an emitted value of the `T` type into a value of the `R` type (that may or may not be the same type `T`) using the `Function<T, R>` lambda expression provided. We have already used this operator many times, turning `String` objects into integers (their lengths), for example. This time, we will take raw date strings and use the `map()` operator to turn each of them into a `LocalDate` emission, as shown in the following code snippet:

```
import io.reactivex.rxjava3.core.Observable;
import java.time.LocalDate;
import java.time.format.DateTimeFormatter;

public class Ch3_14 {
    public static void main(String[] args) {
        DateTimeFormatter dtf = DateTimeFormatter.ofPattern("M/d/yyyy");
        Observable.just("1/3/2016", "5/9/2016", "10/12/2016")
                .map(s -> LocalDate.parse(s, dtf))
                .subscribe(i -> System.out.println("RECEIVED: " + i));
    }
}
```

The output of the preceding code snippet is as follows:

```
RECEIVED: 2016-01-03
RECEIVED: 2016-05-09
RECEIVED: 2016-10-12
```

We provided the `map()` operator with a function (in the lambda expression form) that turns each `String` object into a `LocalDate` object. The `DateTimeFormatter` format was created in advance in order to assist with the `LocalDate.parse()` processing. Finally, we pushed each `LocalDate` emission into the `Observer` to be printed.

The `map()` operator does a one-to-one conversion of each emitted value. If you need to do a one-to-many conversion (turn one emission into several emissions), you can use `flatMap()` or `concatMap()`, which we will cover in the next chapter.

cast()

`cast()` is a simple, map-like operator that casts each emitted item to another type. If we need to cast each value emitted by `Observable<String>` to an `Object` (and return an `Observable<Object>`), we could use the `map()` operator as shown in the following example:

```
Observable<Object> items = Observable.just("Alpha", "Beta", "Gamma")
                                       .map(s -> (Object) s);
```

Instead, we can use the more specialized shorthand `cast()`, and simply pass the class type we want to cast to, as shown in this code snippet:

```
Observable<Object> items = Observable.just("Alpha", "Beta", "Gamma")
                                       .cast(Object.class);
```

If you find that you are having typing issues due to inherited or polymorphic types being mixed, this is an effective brute-force way to cast everything down to a common base type, but strive to use generics properly and type wildcards appropriately first.

startWithItem()

For a given `Observable<T>`, the `startWithItem()` operator (previously called `startWith()` in RxJava 2.x) allows you to insert a value of type `T` that will be emitted before all the other values. For instance, if we have an `Observable<String>` that emits drink names we would like to print, we can use `startWithItem()` to insert a header as the first value of the stream:

```
import io.reactivex.rxjava3.core.Observable;

public class Ch3_15 {
    public static void main(String[] args) {
        Observable<String> menu =
                Observable.just("Coffee", "Tea", "Espresso", "Latte");
        //print menu
        menu.startWithItem("COFFEE SHOP MENU")
            .subscribe(System.out::println);
    }
}
```

The output of the preceding code snippet is as follows:

```
COFFEE SHOP MENU
Coffee
Tea
Espresso
Latte
```

If you want to start with more than one value emitted first, use `startWithArray()`, which accepts `varargs` (an array or any number of `String` values as parameters). If you need to add a divider between the header and menu items, start with both the header and divider as the values passed into the `startWithArray()` operator, as shown in the following example:

```
import io.reactivex.rxjava3.core.Observable;

public class Ch3_16 {
    public static void main(String[] args) {
        Observable<String> menu =
                Observable.just("Coffee", "Tea", "Espresso", "Latte");
        //print menu
        menu.startWithArray("COFFEE SHOP MENU", "----------------")
                .subscribe(System.out::println);
    }
}
```

The output of the preceding code snippet is as follows:

```
COFFEE SHOP MENU
----------------
Coffee
Tea
Espresso
Latte
```

The same result can be achieved using `startWithIterable()`, which accepts an n object of the iterable type. Here is an example:

```
List<String> list =
        Arrays.asList("COFFEE SHOP MENU", "----------------");
menu.startWithIterable(list).subscribe(System.out::println);
```

The `startWithItem()` operator is helpful for cases like this, where we want to seed an initial value or precede our emissions with one particular value. When more than one value has to be emitted first, before the values from the source `Observable` start flowing, the `startWithArray()` or `startWithIterable()` operator is your friend.

If you want emissions of one `Observable` to precede the emissions of another `Observable`, use `Observable.concat()` or `concatWith()`, which we will cover in the next chapter.

sorted()

If you have a finite `Observable<T>` that emits items that are of a primitive type, `String` type, or objects that implement `Comparable<T>`, you can use `sorted()` to sort the emissions. Internally, it collects all the emissions and then re-emits them in the specified order. In the following code snippet, we sort items coming from `Observable<Integer>` so that they are emitted in their natural order:

```
import io.reactivex.rxjava3.core.Observable;

public class Ch3_17 {
    public static void main(String[] args) {
        Observable.just(6, 2, 5, 7, 1, 4, 9, 8, 3)
                .sorted()
                .subscribe(System.out::print);
    }
}
```

The output of the preceding code snippet is as follows (note that, in order to make the output more compact, we use `print()` in this example, instead of `println()`, which we have used hitherto):

```
123456789
```

Of course, this can have some performance implications and consumes the memory as it collects all emitted values in memory before emitting them again. If you use this against an infinite `Observable`, you may even get an `OutOfMemoryError` exception.

The overloaded version, `sorted(Comparator<T> sortFunction)`, can be used to establish an order other than the natural sort order of the emitted items that are of a primitive type, `String` type, or objects that implement `Comparable<T>`. For example, we can provide `Comparator<T>` to reverse the sorting order, as in the following code snippet:

```
import io.reactivex.rxjava3.core.Observable;
import java.util.Comparator;

public class Ch3_18 {
    public static void main(String[] args) {
        Observable.just(6, 2, 5, 7, 1, 4, 9, 8, 3)
```

```
                    .sorted(Comparator.reverseOrder())
                    .subscribe(System.out::print);
        }
    }
```

The output of the preceding code snippet is as follows:

987654321

This overloaded version, `sorted(Comparator<T> sortFunction)`, can also be used to sort the emitted items that are objects that do not implement `Comparable<T>`.

Since `Comparator` is a single abstract method interface, you can implement it quickly with a lambda expression. Specify the two parameters representing two emissions, `T o1` and `T o2`, and then implement the `Comparator<T>` functional interface by providing the body for its `compare(T o1, T o2)` method. For instance, we can sort the emitted items not according to their implementation of the `compareTo(T o)` method (that is, the `Comparable<T>` interface), but using the comparator provided. For example, we can sort `String` type items not according to their implementation of the `Comparable<T>` interface, but according to their length:

```
import io.reactivex.rxjava3.core.Observable;
import java.util.Comparator;

public class Ch3_19 {
    public static void main(String[] args) {
        Observable.just("Alpha", "Beta", "Gamma")
                  .sorted(Comparator.comparingInt(String::length))
                  .subscribe(System.out::println);
    }
}
```

The output of the preceding code snippet is as follows:

Beta
Alpha
Gamma

Please be aware that the behavior of `sorted(Comparator<T> sortFunction)` in this case is the same as the behavior of the following combination of operators:

```
map(String::length).sorted()
```

scan()

The `scan()` method is a rolling aggregator. It adds every emitted item to the provided accumulator and emits each incremental accumulated value. For instance, let's emit the rolling sum of all of the values emitted so far, including the current one, as follows:

```
import io.reactivex.rxjava3.core.Observable;

public class Ch3_20 {
    public static void main(String[] args) {
        Observable.just(5, 3, 7)
                .scan((accumulator, i) -> accumulator + i)
                .subscribe(s -> System.out.println("Received: " + s));
    }
}
```

The output of the preceding code snippet is as follows:

```
Received: 5
Received: 8
Received: 15
```

As you can see, first, the `scan()` operator emitted the value of 5, which was the first value it received. Then, it received 3 and added it to 5, emitting 8. After that, 7 was received, which was added to 8, thereby emitting 15.

This operator does not have to be used just for rolling sums. You can create many kinds of accumulators, even non-math ones such as `String` concatenations or `boolean` reductions.

Note that `scan()` is very similar to `reduce()`, which we will learn about shortly. Be careful not to confuse them though. The `scan()` operator emits the rolling accumulation for each emission, whereas `reduce()` yields a single result reflecting the final accumulated value after `onComplete()` is called. This means that `reduce()` has to be used with a finite `Observable` only, while the `scan()` operator can be used with an infinite `Observable` too.

You can also provide an initial value for the first argument and aggregate the emitted values into a different type than what is being emitted. If we wanted to emit the rolling count of emissions, we could provide an initial value of 0 and just add 1 to it for every emitted value. Keep in mind that the initial value would be emitted first, so use `skip(1)` after `scan()` if you do not want that initial emission to be included in the accumulator:

```
import io.reactivex.rxjava3.core.Observable;

public class Ch3_21 {
    public static void main(String[] args) {
```

```
Observable.just("Alpha", "Beta", "Gamma")
    .scan(0, (total, next) -> total + 1)
    .subscribe(s -> System.out.println("Received: " + s));
    }
}
```

The output of the preceding code snippet is as follows:

```
Received: 0
Received: 1
Received: 2
Received: 3
```

As you can see, the `scan()` operator emitted 0 first, and then added 1 every time it received another emission, acting effectively as a counter of the received values.

Reducing operators

You will likely have moments when you need to take a series of emitted values and aggregate them into a single value (usually emitted through a `Single`). We will cover a few operators that accomplish this. Note that nearly all of these operators only work on a finite `Observable` that calls `onComplete()` because, typically, we can aggregate only finite datasets. We will explore this behavior as we cover these operators.

count()

The `count()` operator counts the number of emitted items and emits the result through a `Single` once `onComplete()` is called. Here is an example:

```
import io.reactivex.rxjava3.core.Observable;

public class Ch3_22 {
    public static void main(String[] args) {
        Observable.just("Alpha", "Beta", "Gamma")
            .count()
            .subscribe(s -> System.out.println("Received: " + s));
    }
}
```

The output of the preceding code snippet is as follows:

```
Received: 3
```

Like most reduction operators, this should not be used on an infinite `Observable`. It will hang up and work indefinitely, never emitting a count or calling `onComplete()`. If you need to count emissions of an infinite `Observable`, consider using `scan()` to emit a rolling count instead.

reduce()

The `reduce()` operator is syntactically identical to `scan()`, but it only emits the final result when the source `Observable` calls `onComplete()`. Depending on which overloaded version is used, it can yield `Single` or `Maybe`. If you need the `reduce()` operator to emit the sum of all emitted integer values, for example, you can take each one and add it to the rolling total. But it will only emit once—after the last emitted value is processed (and the `onComplete` event is emitted):

```
import io.reactivex.rxjava3.core.Observable;

public class Ch3_23 {
    public static void main(String[] args) {
        Observable.just(5, 3, 7)
                .reduce((total, i) -> total + i)
                .subscribe(s -> System.out.println("Received: " + s));
    }
}
```

The output of the preceding code snippet is as follows:

```
Received: 15
```

Similar to `scan()`, there is a seed argument that you can provide that will serve as the initial value to accumulate on. If we wanted to turn our emissions into a single comma-separated `String` value, we could use `reduce()`, too, as shown in the following example:

```
import io.reactivex.rxjava3.core.Observable;

public class Ch3_24 {
    public static void main(String[] args) {
        Observable.just(5, 3, 7)
                .reduce("", (total, i) ->
                        total + (total.equals("") ? "" : ",") + i)
                .subscribe(s -> System.out.println("Received: " + s));
    }
}
```

The output of the preceding code snippet is as follows:

```
Received: 5,3,7
```

We provided an empty string as our seed value, and we maintained a rolling concatenation and kept adding to it. We also prevented a preceding comma using a ternary operator to check whether the `total` is the seed value, returning an empty string instead of a comma if it is.

Your seed value for the `reduce()` operator should be immutable, such as an integer or `String`. Bad side effects can happen if it is mutable. In such cases, you should use `collect()` (or `seedWith()`), which we will cover in a moment.

> If you want to reduce the emitted values of type `T` into a collection, such as `List<T>`, use `collect()` instead of `reduce()`. Using `reduce()` will have the undesired side effect of using the same list for each subscription, rather than creating a fresh empty one each time.

Boolean operators

There is a sub-category of reducing operators that evaluate the result to a `boolean` value and return a `Single<Boolean>` object.

all()

The `all()` operator verifies that all emissions meet the specified criterion and returns a `Single<Boolean>` object. If they all pass, it returns the `Single<Boolean>` object that contains `true`. If it encounters one value that fails the criterion, it immediately calls `onComplete()` and returns the object that contains `false`. In the following code snippet, we test six (or fewer) integers, verifying that they all are less than `10`:

```java
import io.reactivex.rxjava3.core.Observable;

public class Ch3_25 {
    public static void main(String[] args) {
        Observable.just(5, 3, 7, 11, 2, 14)
                .all(i -> i < 10)
                .subscribe(s -> System.out.println("Received: " + s));
    }
}
```

The output of the preceding code snippet is as follows:

```
Received: false
```

When the `all()` operator encountered 11, it immediately emitted `false` and called `onComplete()`. It did not even receive 2 or 14 because that would be unnecessary work. It has already found an element that fails the test.

 If you call `all()` on an empty `Observable`, it will emit `true` due to the principle of vacuous truth. You can read more about vacuous truth on Wikipedia at `https://en.wikipedia.org/wiki/Vacuous_truth`.

any()

The `any()` method checks whether at least one emission meets a specified criterion and returns a `Single<Boolean>`. The moment it finds an emission that does, it returns a `Single<Boolean>` object with `true` and then calls `onComplete()`. If it processes all emissions and finds that none of them meet the criterion, it returns a `Single<Boolean>` object with `false` and calls `onComplete()`.

In the following code snippet, we emit four date strings, convert them into the `LocalDate` type, and check whether any are in the month of June or later:

```java
import io.reactivex.rxjava3.core.Observable;
import java.time.LocalDate;

public class Ch3_26 {
    public static void main(String[] args) {
        Observable.just("2016-01-01", "2016-05-02",
                                     "2016-09-12", "2016-04-03")
                .map(LocalDate::parse)
                .any(dt -> dt.getMonthValue() >= 6)
                .subscribe(s -> System.out.println("Received: " + s));
    }
}
```

The output of the preceding code snippet is as follows:

```
Received: true
```

When it encountered the `2016-09-12` date, it immediately emitted `true` and called `onComplete()`. It did not proceed to process `2016-04-03`.

If you call `any()` on an empty `Observable`, it will emit `false` due to the principle of vacuous truth. You can read more about vacuous truth on Wikipedia at `https://en.wikipedia.org/wiki/Vacuous_truth`.

isEmpty()

The `isEmpty()` operator checks whether an `Observable` is going to emit more items. It returns a `Single<Boolean>` with `true` if the `Observable` does not emit items anymore.

In the following code snippet, an `Observable` emits strings, and neither contain the letter z. The following filter, however, only allows a downstream flow of those items that do contain the letter z. This means that, after the filter, the `Observable` emits no items (becomes empty), but if the letter z is found in any of the emitted strings, the received result changes to `false`, as demonstrated in the following example:

```
import io.reactivex.rxjava3.core.Observable;

public class Ch3_27 {
    public static void main(String[] args) {
        Observable.just("One", "Two", "Three")
                .filter(s -> s.contains("z"))
                .isEmpty()
                .subscribe(s -> System.out.println("Received1: " + s));

        Observable.just("One", "Twoz", "Three")
                .filter(s -> s.contains("z"))
                .isEmpty()
                .subscribe(s -> System.out.println("Received2: " + s));
    }
}
```

The output of the preceding code snippet is as follows:

```
Received1: true
Received2: false
```

contains()

The `contains()` operator checks whether a specified item (based on the `hashCode()`/`equals()` implementation) has been emitted by the source `Observable`. It returns a `Single<Boolean>` with `true` if the specified item was emitted, and `false` if it was not.

In the following code snippet, we emit the integers 1 through 10000, and we check whether the number 9563 is emitted from it using `contains()`:

```
import io.reactivex.rxjava3.core.Observable;

public class Ch3_28 {
    public static void main(String[] args) {
        Observable.range(1, 10000)
                .contains(9563)
                .subscribe(s -> System.out.println("Received: " + s));
    }
}
```

The output of the preceding code snippet is as follows:

```
Received: true
```

As you have probably guessed, the moment the specified value is found, the operator returns `Single<Boolean>` with `true`, calls `onComplete()`, and disposes of the processing pipeline. If the source calls `onComplete()` and the element was not found, it returns `Single<Boolean>` with `false`.

sequenceEqual()

The `sequenceEqual()` operator checks whether two observables emit the same values in the same order. It returns a `Single<Boolean>` with `true` if the emitted sequences are the same pairwise.

In the following code snippet, we create and then compare observables that emit the same sequence or different (by order or by value) sequences:

```
import io.reactivex.rxjava3.core.Observable;

public class Ch3_29 {
    public static void main(String[] args) {
        Observable<String> obs1 = Observable.just("One","Two","Three");
        Observable<String> obs2 = Observable.just("One","Two","Three");
        Observable<String> obs3 = Observable.just("Two","One","Three");
        Observable<String> obs4 = Observable.just("One","Two");

        Observable.sequenceEqual(obs1, obs2)
                .subscribe(s -> System.out.println("Received: " + s));

        Observable.sequenceEqual(obs1, obs3)
                .subscribe(s -> System.out.println("Received: " + s));
```

```
        Observable.sequenceEqual(obs1, obs4)
                .subscribe(s -> System.out.println("Received: " + s));
    }
}
```

The output of the preceding code snippet is as follows:

```
Received: true
Received: false
Received: false
```

As you can see, the output confirms that the sequence of the values emitted by the observables obs1 and obs2 are equal in size, values, and their order. The observables obs1 and obs3 emit sequences of the same values but in a different order, while the observables obs1 and obs4 have different sizes.

Collection operators

A collection operator accumulates all emissions into a collection such as a List or Map and then returns that entire collection as a single value. It is another form of a reducing operator since it aggregates emitted items into a single one. We will dedicate a section to each of the collection operators and several examples since their usage is slightly more complex than the previous examples.

 Note that you should avoid reducing a stream of items into collections for the sake of it. It can undermine the benefits of reactive programming where items are processed in a beginning-to-end, one-at-a-time sequence. You only want to aggregate the emitted items into a collection when you need to group them logically in some way.

toList()

The toList() is probably the most often used among all the collection operators. For a given Observable<T>, it collects incoming items into a List<T> and then pushes that List<T> object as a single value through Single<List<T>>.

In the following code snippet, we collect `String` values into a `List<String>`. After the preceding `Observable` signals `onComplete()`, that list is pushed into the `Observer` to be printed:

```
import io.reactivex.rxjava3.core.Observable;

public class Ch3_30 {
    public static void main(String[] args) {
        Observable.just("Alpha", "Beta", "Gamma")
                .toList()
                .subscribe(s -> System.out.println("Received: " + s));
    }
}
```

The output of the preceding code snippet is as follows:

```
Received: [Alpha, Beta, Gamma]
```

By default, `toList()` uses an `ArrayList` implementation of the `List` interface. You can optionally specify an integer argument to serve as the `capacityHint` value that optimizes the initialization of the `ArrayList` to expect roughly that number of items:

```
import io.reactivex.rxjava3.core.Observable;

public class Ch3_31 {
    public static void main(String[] args) {
        Observable.range(1, 1000)
                .toList(1000)
                .subscribe(s -> System.out.println("Received: " + s));
    }
}
```

If you want to use a different `List` implementation, you can provide a `Callable` function as an argument to specify one. In the following code snippet, we provide a `CopyOnWriteArrayList` instance to serve as a `List` implementation:

```
import io.reactivex.rxjava3.core.Observable;
import java.util.concurrent.CopyOnWriteArrayList;

public class Ch3_32 {
    public static void main(String[] args) {
        Observable.just("Beta", "Gamma", "Alpha")
                .toList(CopyOnWriteArrayList::new)
                .subscribe(s -> System.out.println("Received: " + s));
    }
}
```

The result of the preceding code appears as follows:

```
Received: [Beta, Gamma, Alpha]
```

If you want to use Google Guava's immutable list, this is a little trickier since it is immutable and uses a builder. We will show you how to do this while discussing the `collect()` operator later in this section.

toSortedList()

A different flavor of `toList()` operator is `toSortedList()`. It collects the emitted values into a `List` object that has the elements sorted in a natural order (based on their `Comparable` implementation). Then, it pushes that `List<T>` object with sorted elements into the `Observer`:

```java
import io.reactivex.rxjava3.core.Observable;

public class Ch3_33 {
    public static void main(String[] args) {
        Observable.just("Beta", "Gamma", "Alpha")
                .toSortedList()
                .subscribe(s -> System.out.println("Received: " + s));
    }
}
```

The output of the preceding code snippet is as follows:

```
Received: [Alpha, Beta, Gamma]
```

As with the `sorted()` operator, you can provide a `Comparator` as an argument to apply a different sorting logic. You can also specify an initial capacity for the backing `ArrayList`, just like in the case of the `toList()` operator.

toMap() and toMultiMap()

For a given `Observable<T>`, the `toMap()` operator collects received values into `Map<K, T>`, where `K` is the key type. The key is generated by the `Function<T, K>` function provided as the argument. For example, if we want to collect strings into `Map<Char, String>`, where each string is keyed off their first character, we can do it like this:

```java
import io.reactivex.rxjava3.core.Observable;

public class Ch3_34 {
```

```
        public static void main(String[] args) {
            Observable.just("Alpha", "Beta", "Gamma")
                    .toMap(s -> s.charAt(0))
                    .subscribe(s -> System.out.println("Received: " + s));
        }
    }
```

The output of the preceding code snippet is as follows:

```
Received: {A=Alpha, B=Beta, G=Gamma}
```

The `s -> s.charAt(0)` lambda argument takes each received `String` value and derives the key to pair it with. In this case, we are making the first character of each `String` value the key.

If we decide to yield a different value other than the received one to associate with the key, we can provide a second lambda argument that maps each received value to a different one. We can, for instance, map each first letter key with the length of the received `String` object:

```
import io.reactivex.rxjava3.core.Observable;

public class Ch3_35 {
    public static void main(String[] args) {
        Observable.just("Alpha", "Beta", "Gamma")
                .toMap(s -> s.charAt(0), String::length)
                .subscribe(s -> System.out.println("Received: " + s));
    }
}
```

The output of the preceding code snippet is as follows:

```
Received: {A=5, B=4, G=5}
```

By default, `toMap()` uses the `HashMap` class as the `Map` interface implementation. You can also provide a third argument to specify a different `Map` implementation. For instance, we can provide `ConcurrentHashMap` instead of `HashMap` as the desired implementation of the `Map` interface:

```
import io.reactivex.rxjava3.core.Observable;
import java.util.concurrent.ConcurrentHashMap;

public class Ch3_36 {
    public static void main(String[] args) {
        Observable.just("Alpha", "Beta", "Gamma")
                .toMap(s -> s.charAt(0), String::length,
                        ConcurrentHashMap::new)
```

```
                    .subscribe(s -> System.out.println("Received: " + s));
        }
    }
```

Note that if there is a key that maps to multiple received values, the last value for that key is going to replace the previous ones. For example, let's make the string length the key for each received value. Then, Alpha is going to be replaced by Gamma:

```
import io.reactivex.rxjava3.core.Observable;

public class Ch3_37 {
    public static void main(String[] args) {
        Observable.just("Alpha", "Beta", "Gamma")
                .toMap(String::length)
                .subscribe(s -> System.out.println("Received: " + s));
    }
}
```

The output of the preceding code snippet is as follows:

Received: {4=Beta, 5=Gamma}

If you want a given key to map to multiple values, you can use toMultiMap() instead, which maintains a list of corresponding values for each key. The items Alpha and Gamma will then all be put in a list that is keyed off the length 5:

```
import io.reactivex.rxjava3.core.Observable;

public class Ch3_38 {
    public static void main(String[] args) {
        Observable.just("Alpha", "Beta", "Gamma")
                .toMultimap(String::length)
                .subscribe(s -> System.out.println("Received: " + s));
    }
}
```

The output of the preceding code snippet is as follows:

Received: {4=[Beta], 5=[Alpha, Gamma]}

collect()

When none of the collection operators can do what you need, you can always use the collect() operator to specify a different type to collect items into.

For instance, there is no `toSet()` operator to collect emissions in a `Set<T>`, but you can quickly use `collect(Callable<U> initialValueSupplier, BiConsumer<U, T> collector)` to effectively do this.

Let's say you need to collect `String` values in a `Set<String>` implementation. To accomplish that, you can specify the first argument—the function that produces an initial value of the `Set<String>` implementation you would like to use, and the second argument—the function that is going to collect the values (whatever you need to collect) in that `Set<String>` implementation you have chosen. Here is the code that uses `HashSet<String>` as the `Set<String>` implementation:

```
import io.reactivex.rxjava3.core.Observable;
import java.util.HashSet;

public class Ch3_39 {
    public static void main(String[] args) {
        Observable.just("Alpha", "Beta", "Gamma", "Beta")
                .collect(HashSet<String>::new, HashSet::add)
                .subscribe(s -> System.out.println("Received: " + s));
    }
}
```

The output of the preceding code snippet is as follows:

```
Received: [Gamma, Alpha, Beta]
```

The `collect()` operator in our example now emits a single `HashSet<String>` object containing all the emitted values, except the duplicates (note that `Beta` was emitted twice by the source `Observable`); that is the nature of the `HashSet` class.

When you need to collect values into a mutable object and you need a new mutable object seed each time, use `collect()` instead of the `reduce()` operator.

You can also use `collect()` for trickier cases that are not straightforward collection implementations. For example, let's assume you have added Google Guava as a dependency (`https://github.com/google/guava`):

```
<dependency>
    <groupId>com.google.guava</groupId>
    <artifactId>guava</artifactId>
    <version>28.2-jre</version>
</dependency>
```

You did it because you want to collect values in
com.google.common.collect.ImmutableList. To create an ImmutableList , you
have to call its builder() factory to yield an ImmutableList.Builder<T>. You then call
its add() method to put items in the builder, followed by a call to build(), which returns
a sealed final ImmutableList<T> that cannot be modified.

To accomplish that, you can supply an ImmutableList.Builder<T> for your first lambda
argument and then add each element through its add() method in the second argument.
This will emit ImmutableList.Builder<T> once it is fully populated, and you can
transform it using the map() operator and its build() method, which produces the
ImmutableList<T> object. Here is the code that does just that:

```
import com.google.common.collect.ImmutableList;
import io.reactivex.rxjava3.core.Observable;

public class Ch3_40 {
    public static void main(String[] args) {
        Observable.just("Alpha", "Beta", "Gamma")
            .collect(ImmutableList::builder, ImmutableList.Builder::add)
            .map(ImmutableList.Builder::build)
            .subscribe(s -> System.out.println("Received: " + s));
    }
}
```

The output of the preceding code snippet is as follows:

```
Received: [Alpha, Beta, Gamma]
```

Again, the collect() operator is helpful to collect emissions into any type, when the
Observable operators do not provide out-of-the-box.

Error recovery operators

Exceptions can occur almost anywhere in the chain of the Observable operators, and we
already know about the onError event that is communicated down the Observable chain
to the Observer. After that, the subscription terminates and no more emissions occur.

But sometimes, we want to intercept exceptions before they get to the Observer and
attempt some form of recovery. We can also pretend that the error never happened and
expect to continue processing the emissions.

However, a more productive approach to error handling would be to attempt resubscribing or switch to an alternate source `Observable`. And if you find that none of the error recovery operators meet your needs, the chances are you can compose one yourself.

For demonstration examples, let's divide `10` by each emitted integer value, where one of the values is `0`. This will result in a `/` `by` `zero` exception being pushed to the `Observer`, as we saw in the *Observable.fromCallable()* section in `Chapter` `2`, *Observable and Observer* (examples `Ch2_26a` and `Ch_26b`). Here is another example:

```
import io.reactivex.rxjava3.core.Observable;

public class Ch3_41 {
    public static void main(String[] args) {
        Observable.just(5, 2, 4, 0, 3)
                .map(i -> 10 / i)
                .subscribe(i -> System.out.println("RECEIVED: " + i),
                    e -> System.out.println("RECEIVED ERROR: " + e));
    }
}
```

The output of the preceding code snippet is as follows:

```
RECEIVED: 2
RECEIVED: 5
RECEIVED: 2
RECEIVED ERROR: java.lang.ArithmeticException: / by zero
```

onErrorReturnItem() and onErrorReturn()

When you want to resort to a default value when an exception occurs, you can use the `onErrorReturnItem()` operator. If we want to emit `-1` when an exception occurs, we can do it like this:

```
import io.reactivex.rxjava3.core.Observable;

public class Ch3_42 {
    public static void main(String[] args) {
        Observable.just(5, 2, 4, 0, 3)
                .map(i -> 10 / i)
                .onErrorReturnItem(-1)
                .subscribe(i -> System.out.println("RECEIVED: " + i),
                    e -> System.out.println("RECEIVED ERROR: " + e));
    }
}
```

The output of the preceding code snippet is as follows:

```
RECEIVED: 2
RECEIVED: 5
RECEIVED: 2
RECEIVED: -1
```

You can see that the emissions stopped after the error anyway, but the error itself did not flow down to the Observer. Instead, the value −1 was received by it as if emitted by the source Observable.

You can also use the onErrorReturn(Function<Throwable,T> valueSupplier) operator to dynamically produce the value using the specified function. This gives you access to a Throwable object, which you can use while calculating the returned value as shown in the following code snippet:

```
import io.reactivex.rxjava3.core.Observable;

public class Ch3_43 {
    public static void main(String[] args) {
        Observable.just(5, 2, 4, 0, 3)
                .map(i -> 10 / i)
                .onErrorReturn(e ->
                        e instanceof ArithmeticException ? -1 : 0)
                .subscribe(i -> System.out.println("RECEIVED: " + i),
                    e -> System.out.println("RECEIVED ERROR: " + e));
    }
}
```

The location of onErrorReturn() in the chain of the operators matters. If we put it before the map() operator in our example, the error would not be caught because it happened downstream. To intercept the emitted error, it must originate upstream from the onErrorReturn() operator.

Note that, again, although we handled the error, the emission was still terminated after that. We did not get the 3 that was supposed to follow. If you want to resume emissions, you can handle the error within the map() operator where the error occurs. You would do this in lieu of onErrorReturn() or onErrorReturnItem():

```
import io.reactivex.rxjava3.core.Observable;

public class Ch3_44 {
    public static void main(String[] args) {
        Observable.just(5, 2, 4, 0, 3)
                .map(i -> {
                    try {
```

```
                    return 10 / i;
                } catch (ArithmeticException e) {
                    return -1;
                }
            })
            .subscribe(i -> System.out.println("RECEIVED: " + i),
                e -> System.out.println("RECEIVED ERROR: " + e));
    }
}
```

The output of the preceding code snippet is as follows:

```
RECEIVED: 2
RECEIVED: 5
RECEIVED: 2
RECEIVED: -1
RECEIVED: 3
```

onErrorResumeWith()

Similar to `onErrorReturn()` and `onErrorReturnItem()`, the `onErrorResumeWith()` operator (previously called `onErrorResuumeNext()` in RxJava 2.x) handles the exception too. The only difference is that it accepts another `Observable` as a parameter to emit potentially multiple values, not a single value, in the event of an exception.

This is somewhat contrived and likely has no business use case, but we can emit three -1 values in the event of an error:

```
import io.reactivex.rxjava3.core.Observable;

public class Ch3_45 {
    public static void main(String[] args) {
        Observable.just(5, 2, 4, 0, 3)
                .map(i -> 10 / i)
                .onErrorResumeWith(Observable.just(-1).repeat(3))
                .subscribe(i -> System.out.println("RECEIVED: " + i),
                    e -> System.out.println("RECEIVED ERROR: " + e));
    }
}
```

The output of the preceding code snippet is as follows:

```
RECEIVED: 2
RECEIVED: 5
RECEIVED: 2
RECEIVED: -1
RECEIVED: -1
RECEIVED: -1
```

We can also provide `Observable.empty()` to quietly stop emissions in the event that there is an error and gracefully call the `onComplete()` function:

```java
import io.reactivex.rxjava3.core.Observable;

public class Ch3_46 {
    public static void main(String[] args) {
        Observable.just(5, 2, 4, 0, 3)
                .map(i -> 10 / i)
                .onErrorResumeWith(Observable.empty())
                .subscribe(i -> System.out.println("RECEIVED: " + i),
                    e -> System.out.println("RECEIVED ERROR: " + e));
    }
}
```

The output of the preceding code snippet is as follows:

```
RECEIVED: 2
RECEIVED: 5
RECEIVED: 2
```

Instead of another `Observable`, you can provide the `Function<Throwable, Observable<T>>` function to produce an `Observable` dynamically from the emitted `Throwable`, as shown in the following code snippet:

```java
import io.reactivex.rxjava3.core.Observable;

public class Ch3_47 {
    public static void main(String[] args) {
        Observable.just(5, 2, 4, 0, 3)
                .map(i -> 10 / i)
                .onErrorResumeNext((Throwable e) ->
                        Observable.just(-1).repeat(3))
                .subscribe(i -> System.out.println("RECEIVED: " + i),
                    e -> System.out.println("RECEIVED ERROR: " + e));
    }
}
```

The output of the preceding code is as follows:

```
RECEIVED: 2
RECEIVED: 5
RECEIVED: 2
RECEIVED: -1
RECEIVED: -1
RECEIVED: -1
```

retry()

Another way to attempt recovery is to use the retry() operator, which has several overloaded versions. It will re-subscribe to the preceding Observable and, hopefully, not have the error again.

If you call retry() with no arguments, it will resubscribe an infinite number of times for each error. You need to be careful with retry() without parameters as it can have chaotic effects. Using it with our example will cause it to emit these integers infinitely and repeatedly:

```
import io.reactivex.rxjava3.core.Observable;

public class Ch3_48 {
    public static void main(String[] args) {
        Observable.just(5, 2, 4, 0, 3)
  .map(i -> 10 / i)
  .retry()
  .subscribe(i -> System.out.println("RECEIVED: " + i),
  e -> System.out.println("RECEIVED ERROR: " + e));
    }
}
```

The output of the preceding code snippet is as follows:

```
RECEIVED: 5
RECEIVED: 2
RECEIVED: 2
RECEIVED: 5
RECEIVED: 2
RECEIVED: 2
RECEIVED: 5
RECEIVED: 2
   . . .
```

It might be safer to specify `retry()` a fixed number of times before it gives up and just emits the error to the `Observer`. In the following code snippet, we retry two times:

```
import io.reactivex.rxjava3.core.Observable;

public class Ch3_49 {
    public static void main(String[] args) {
        Observable.just(5, 2, 4, 0, 3, 2, 8)
                .map(i -> 10 / i)
                .retry(2)
                .subscribe(i -> System.out.println("RECEIVED: " + i),
                        e -> System.out.println("RECEIVED ERROR: " + e));
    }
}
```

The output of the preceding code snippet is as follows:

```
RECEIVED: 2
RECEIVED: 5
RECEIVED: 2
RECEIVED: 2
RECEIVED: 5
RECEIVED: 2
RECEIVED: 2
RECEIVED: 5
RECEIVED: 2
RECEIVED ERROR: java.lang.ArithmeticException: / by zero
```

You can also provide the `Predicate<Throwable>` or `BiPredicate<Integer, Throwable>` function to conditionally control when `retry()` is attempted.

The `retryUntil(BooleanSupplier stop)` operator allows retries as long as the specified `BooleanSupplier` function returns `false`.

There is also an advanced `retryWhen()` operator that supports advanced composition for tasks such as delaying retries.

Action operators

The following are some helpful operators that can assist in debugging as well as getting visibility into an Observable chain. These are the action or doOn operators. They do not modify the Observable, but use it for side effects.

doOnNext() and doAfterNext()

The three operators, doOnNext(), doOnComplete(), and doOnError(), are like putting a mini Observer right in the middle of the Observable chain.

The doOnNext() operator allows a peek at each received value before letting it flow into the next operator. The doOnNext() operator does not affect the processing or transform the emission in any way. We can use it just to create a side effect for each received value. For instance, we can perform an action with each String object before it is mapped to its length. In this case, we just print them by providing a Consumer<T> function as a lambda expression:

```
import io.reactivex.rxjava3.core.Observable;

public class Ch3_50 {
    public static void main(String[] args) {
        Observable.just("Alpha", "Beta", "Gamma")
                .doOnNext(s -> System.out.println("Processing: " + s))
                .map(String::length)
                .subscribe(i -> System.out.println("Received: " + i));
    }
}
```

The output of the preceding code snippet is as follows:

```
Processing: Alpha
Received: 5
Processing: Beta
Received: 4
Processing: Gamma
Received: 5
```

You can also leverage `doAfterNext()`, which performs the action after the item is passed downstream rather than before. The demo code of `doAfterNext()` appears as follows:

```
import io.reactivex.rxjava3.core.Observable;

public class Ch3_51 {
    public static void main(String[] args) {
        Observable.just("Alpha", "Beta", "Gamma")
                .doAfterNext(s -> System.out.println("After: " + s))
                .map(String::length)
                .subscribe(i -> System.out.println("Received: " + i));
    }
}
```

The output is as follows:

```
Received: 5
After: Alpha
Received: 4
After: Beta
Received: 5
After: Gamma
```

doOnComplete() and doOnError()

The `onComplete()` operator allows you to fire off an action when an `onComplete` event is emitted at the point in the `Observable` chain. This can be helpful in seeing which points of the `Observable` chain have completed, as shown in the following code snippet:

```
import io.reactivex.rxjava3.core.Observable;

public class Ch3_52 {
    public static void main(String[] args) {
        Observable.just("Alpha", "Beta", "Gamma")
                .doOnComplete(() ->
                        System.out.println("Source is done emitting!"))
                .map(String::length)
                .subscribe(i -> System.out.println("Received: " + i));
    }
}
```

The output of the preceding code snippet is as follows:

```
Received: 5
Received: 4
Received: 5
Source is done emitting!
```

And, of course, onError() will peek at the error being emitted up the chain, and you can perform an action with it. This can be helpful to put between operators to see which one is to blame for an error:

```java
import io.reactivex.rxjava3.core.Observable;

public class Ch3_53 {
    public static void main(String[] args) {
        Observable.just(5, 2, 4, 0, 3, 2, 8)
            .doOnError(e -> System.out.println("Source failed!"))
            .map(i -> 10 / i)
            .doOnError(e -> System.out.println("Division failed!"))
            .subscribe(i -> System.out.println("RECEIVED: " + i),
                e -> System.out.println("RECEIVED ERROR: " + e));
    }
}
```

The output of the preceding code snippet is as follows:

```
RECEIVED: 2
RECEIVED: 5
RECEIVED: 2
Division failed!
RECEIVED ERROR: java.lang.ArithmeticException: / by zero
```

We used doOnError() in two places to see where the error first appeared. Since we did not see Source failed! printed, but we saw Division failed!, we can deduce that the error occurred in the map() operator.

Use these three operators together to get an insight into what your Observable operation is doing or to quickly create side effects.

 There is also a doOnTerminate() operator, which fires for an onComplete or onError event (but *before* the event), and the doAfterTerminate(), which fires for an onComplete or onError event too, but only *after* the event.

doOnEach()

The `doOnEach()` operator is very similar to `doOnNext()`. The only difference is that in `doOnEach()`, the emitted item comes wrapped inside a `Notification` that also contains the type of the event. This means you can check which of the three events—`onNext()`, `onComplete()`, or `onError()`—has happened and select an appropriate action.

The `subscribe()` method accepts these three actions as lambda arguments or an entire `Observer<T>`. So, using `doOnEach()` is like putting `subscribe()` right in the middle of your `Observable` chain! Here is an example:

```
import io.reactivex.rxjava3.core.Observable;

public class Ch3_54 {
    public static void main(String[] args) {
        Observable.just("One", "Two", "Three")
                .doOnEach(s -> System.out.println("doOnEach: " + s))
                .subscribe(i -> System.out.println("Received: " + i));
    }
}
```

The output is as follows:

```
doOnEach: OnNextNotification[One]
Received: One
doOnEach: OnNextNotification[Two]
Received: Two
doOnEach: OnNextNotification[Three]
Received: Three
doOnEach: OnCompleteNotification
```

As you can see, the event is wrapped inside `OnNextNotification` in this case. You can check the event type, as shown in the following code:

```
import io.reactivex.rxjava3.core.Observable;

public class Ch3_55 {
    public static void main(String[] args) {
        Observable.just("One", "Two", "Three")
                .doOnEach(s -> System.out.println("doOnEach: " +
                        s.isOnNext() + ", " + s.isOnError() +
                                ", " + s.isOnComplete()))
                .subscribe(i -> System.out.println("Received: " + i));
    }
}
```

The output looks like this:

```
doOnEach: true, false, false
Received: One
doOnEach: true, false, false
Received: Two
doOnEach: true, false, false
Received: Three
doOnEach: false, false, true
```

The error and the value (the emitted item) can be extracted from `Notification` in the same way as shown in the following code snippet:

```java
import io.reactivex.rxjava3.core.Observable;

public class Ch3_56 {
    public static void main(String[] args) {
        Observable.just("One", "Two", "Three")
                .doOnEach(s -> System.out.println("doOnEach: " +
                                 s.getError() + ", " + s.getValue()))
                .subscribe(i -> System.out.println("Received: " + i));
    }
}
```

The output looks like this:

```
doOnEach: null, One
Received: One
doOnEach: null, Two
Received: Two
doOnEach: null, Three
Received: Three
doOnEach: null, null
```

doOnSubscribe() and doOnDispose()

Two other helpful action operators are `doOnSubscribe()` and `doOnDispose()`. `doOnSubscribe(Consumer<Disposable> onSubscribe)` executes the function provided at the moment subscription occurs. It provides access to the `Disposable` object in case you want to call `dispose()` in that action. The `doOnDispose(Action onDispose)` operator performs the specified action when disposal is executed.

We use both operators to print when subscription and disposal occur, as shown in the following code snippet. Then, the emitted values go through, and then disposal is finally fired.

Let's now try and see how these operators are called:

```
import io.reactivex.rxjava3.core.Observable;

public class Ch3_57 {
    public static void main(String[] args) {
        Observable.just("Alpha", "Beta", "Gamma")
                .doOnSubscribe(d -> System.out.println("Subscribing!"))
                .doOnDispose(() -> System.out.println("Disposing!"))
                .subscribe(i -> System.out.println("RECEIVED: " + i));
    }
}
```

The output of the preceding code snippet is as follows:

```
Subscribing!
RECEIVED: Alpha
RECEIVED: Beta
RECEIVED: Gamma
```

As you could predict, we set the subscribe event to fire off first, but doOnDispose() was not called. That is because the dispose() method was not called. Let's do this then:

```
import io.reactivex.rxjava3.core.Observable;
import io.reactivex.rxjava3.disposables.Disposable;
import java.util.concurrent.TimeUnit;

public class Ch3_58 {
    public static void main(String[] args) {
        Disposable disp = Observable.interval(1, TimeUnit.SECONDS)
                .doOnSubscribe(d -> System.out.println("Subscribing!"))
                .doOnDispose(() -> System.out.println("Disposing!"))
                .subscribe(i -> System.out.println("RECEIVED: " + i));

        sleep(3000);
        disp.dispose();
        sleep(3000);
    }
}
```

This time, we see that doOnDispose() was called:

```
Subscribing!
RECEIVED: Alpha
RECEIVED: Beta
RECEIVED: Gamma
Disposing!
```

Another option is to use the doFinally() operator, which will fire after either onComplete() or onError() is called or disposed of by the chain. We will demonstrate how this works shortly.

doOnSuccess()

Remember that Maybe and Single types do not have an onNext() event, but rather an onSuccess() operator to pass a single emission. The doOnSuccess() operator usage should effectively feel like doOnNext():

```
import io.reactivex.rxjava3.core.Observable;

public class Ch3_59 {
    public static void main(String[] args) {
        Observable.just(5, 3, 7)
                .reduce((total, next) -> total + next)
                .doOnSuccess(i -> System.out.println("Emitting: " + i))
                .subscribe(i -> System.out.println("Received: " + i));
    }
}
```

The output of the preceding code snippet is as follows:

```
Emitting: 15
Received: 15
```

doFinally()

The doFinally() operator is executed when onComplete(), onError(), or disposal happens. It is executed under the same conditions as doAfterTerminate(), plus it is also executed after the disposal. For example, look at the following code:

```
import io.reactivex.rxjava3.core.Observable;

public class Ch3_60 {
    public static void main(String[] args) {
        Observable.just("One", "Two", "Three")
                .doFinally(() -> System.out.println("doFinally!"))
                .doAfterTerminate(() ->
                        System.out.println("doAfterTerminate!"))
                .subscribe(i -> System.out.println("Received: " + i));
    }
}
```

The output is as follows:

```
Received: One
Received: Two
Received: Three
doAfterTerminate!
doFinally!
```

Now, let's see how they work when `dispose()` is called:

```
import io.reactivex.rxjava3.core.Observable;
import io.reactivex.rxjava3.disposables.Disposable;
import java.util.concurrent.TimeUnit;

public class Ch3_61 {
    public static void main(String[] args) {
        Disposable disp = Observable.interval(1, TimeUnit.SECONDS)
                .doOnSubscribe(d -> System.out.println("Subscribing!"))
                .doOnDispose(() -> System.out.println("Disposing!"))
                .doFinally(() -> System.out.println("doFinally!"))
                .doAfterTerminate(() ->
                            System.out.println("doAfterTerminate!"))
                .subscribe(i -> System.out.println("RECEIVED: " + i));

        sleep(3000);
        disp.dispose();
        sleep(3000);
    }
}
```

The output is as follows:

```
Subscribing!
RECEIVED: 0
RECEIVED: 1
RECEIVED: 2
Disposing!
doFinally!
```

The `doFinally()` operator guarantees that the action is executed exactly once per subscription.

And, by the way, the location of these operators in the chain does not matter, because they are driven by the events, not by the emitted data. For example, we can put them in the chain in the opposite order:

```
import io.reactivex.rxjava3.core.Observable;
import io.reactivex.rxjava3.disposables.Disposable;
```

```
import java.util.concurrent.TimeUnit;

public class Ch3_62 {
    public static void main(String[] args) {
        Disposable disp = Observable.interval(1, TimeUnit.SECONDS)
                .doAfterTerminate(() ->
System.out.println("doAfterTerminate!"))
                .doFinally(() -> System.out.println("doFinally!"))
                .doOnDispose(() -> System.out.println("Disposing!"))
                .doOnSubscribe(d -> System.out.println("Subscribing!"))
                .subscribe(i -> System.out.println("RECEIVED: " + i));

        sleep(3000);
        disp.dispose();
        sleep(3000);
    }
}
```

Yet, the output remains the same:

```
Subscribing!
RECEIVED: 0
RECEIVED: 1
RECEIVED: 2
Disposing!
doFinally!
```

Utility operators

To close this chapter, we will cover some helpful operators that have diverse functionality that cannot be captured under the specific functional title.

delay()

We can postpone emissions using the delay() operator. It will hold any received emissions and delay each one for the specified time period. If we wanted to delay emissions by 3 seconds, we could do it like this:

```
import io.reactivex.rxjava3.core.Observable;
import java.util.concurrent.TimeUnit;

public class Ch3_63 {
    public static void main(String[] args) {
        DateTimeFormatter f = DateTimeFormatter.ofPattern("MM:ss");
```

```
System.out.println(LocalDateTime.now().format(f));
Observable.just("Alpha", "Beta", "Gamma")
        .delay(3, TimeUnit.SECONDS)
        .subscribe(s -> System.out.println(LocalDateTime.now()
                            .format(f) + " Received: " + s));
sleep(5000);
    }
}
```

The output of the preceding code snippet is as follows (the first column is the current time of the hour in minutes and seconds):

```
02:26
02:29 Received: Alpha
02:29 Received: Beta
02:29 Received: Gamma
```

As you can see, the emission from the source `Observable` was delayed by 3 seconds. You can pass an optional third `boolean` argument indicating whether you want to delay error notifications as well.

Because `delay()` operates on a different scheduler (such as `Observable.interval()`), we need to use the `sleep(long ms)` method to keep the application alive long enough to see this happen (5 seconds in our case). We described the implementation of the `sleep(long ms)` method in the *Observable.interval()* section of Chapter 2, *Observable and Observer*.

For more advanced cases, you can pass another `Observable` as your `delay()` argument, and this will delay emissions until that other `Observable` emits something.

> Note that there is a `delaySubscription()` operator, which will delay subscribing to the `Observable` preceding it rather than delaying each individual emission.

repeat()

The `repeat()` operator will repeat subscription after `onComplete()` a specified number of times. For instance, we can repeat the emissions twice for the given `Observable` by passing 2 as an argument for `repeat()`, as shown in the following code snippet:

```
import io.reactivex.rxjava3.core.Observable;

public class Ch3_64 {
```

```
        public static void main(String[] args) {
            Observable.just("Alpha", "Beta", "Gamma")
                    .repeat(2)
                    .subscribe(s -> System.out.println("Received: " + s));
        }
    }
```

The output of the preceding code snippet is as follows:

```
Received: Alpha
Received: Beta
Received: Gamma
Received: Alpha
Received: Beta
Received: Gamma
```

If you do not specify a number, it will repeat infinitely, forever re-subscribing after every onComplete(). There is also a repeatUntil() operator that accepts a BooleanSupplier function and continues repeating until the provided function returns true.

single( )

The single() operator returns a Single that emits the item emitted by this Observable. If the Observable emits more than one item, the single() operator throws an exception. If the Observable emits no item, the Single, produced by the single() operator, emits the item passed to the operator as a parameter. Here is an example:

```
import io.reactivex.rxjava3.core.Observable;

public class Ch3_65 {
    public static void main(String[] args) {
        Observable.just("One")
                .single("Four")
                .subscribe(i -> System.out.println("Received: " + i));
    }
}
```

The output is as follows:

```
Received: One
```

Now, let's make sure that nothing gets to the `single()` operator by filtering out all the items using the following code:

```
import io.reactivex.rxjava3.core.Observable;

public class Ch3_66 {
    public static void main(String[] args) {
        Observable.just("One", "Two", "Three")
                .filter(s -> s.contains("z"))
                .single("Four")
                .subscribe(i -> System.out.println("Received: " + i));
    }
}
```

The output is as follows:

Received: Four

 There is also a `singleElement()` operator that returns `Maybe` when the `Observable` emits one item or nothing and throws an exception otherwise. And there is a `singleOrError()` operator that returns `Single` when the `Observable` emits one item only and throws an exception otherwise.

timestamp( )

The `timestamp()` operator attaches a timestamp to every item emitted by an `Observable`, as shown in the following code:

```
import io.reactivex.rxjava3.core.Observable;
import java.util.concurrent.TimeUnit;

public class Ch3_67 {
    public static void main(String[] args) {
        Observable.just("One", "Two", "Three")
                .timestamp(TimeUnit.SECONDS)
                .subscribe(i -> System.out.println("Received: " + i));
    }
}
```

The output is as follows:

```
Received: Timed[time=1561694750, unit=SECONDS, value=One]
Received: Timed[time=1561694750, unit=SECONDS, value=Two]
Received: Timed[time=1561694750, unit=SECONDS, value=Three]
```

As you can see, the results are wrapped inside the object of the `Timed` class, which provide accessors to the values that we can unwrap as follows:

```java
import io.reactivex.rxjava3.core.Observable;
import java.util.concurrent.TimeUnit;

public class Ch3_68 {
    public static void main(String[] args) {
        Observable.just("One", "Two", "Three")
                .timestamp(TimeUnit.SECONDS)
                .subscribe(i -> System.out.println("Received: " +
                    i.time() + " " + i.unit() + " " + i.value()));
    }
}
```

The output will then show the values in a more user-friendly format:

```
Received: 1561736795 SECONDS One
Received: 1561736795 SECONDS Two
Received: 1561736795 SECONDS Three
```

timeInterval()

The `timeInterval()` operator emits the time lapses between the consecutive emissions of a source `Observable`. Here is an example:

```java
import io.reactivex.rxjava3.core.Observable;
import java.util.concurrent.TimeUnit;

public class Ch3_69 {
    public static void main(String[] args) {
        Observable.interval(2, TimeUnit.SECONDS)
                .doOnNext(i -> System.out.println("Emitted: " + i))
                .take(3)
                .timeInterval(TimeUnit.SECONDS)
                .subscribe(i -> System.out.println("Received: " + i));
        sleep(7000);
    }
}
```

The output is as follows:

```
Emitted: 0
Received: Timed[time=2, unit=SECONDS, value=0]
Emitted: 1
Received: Timed[time=2, unit=SECONDS, value=1]
Emitted: 2
Received: Timed[time=2, unit=SECONDS, value=2]
```

And we can unwrap the values the same way we did for the timestamp() operator:

```java
import io.reactivex.rxjava3.core.Observable;
import java.util.concurrent.TimeUnit;

public class Ch3_70 {
    public static void main(String[] args) {
        Observable.interval(2, TimeUnit.SECONDS)
                .doOnNext(i -> System.out.println("Emitted: " + i))
                .take(3)
                .timeInterval(TimeUnit.SECONDS)
                .subscribe(i -> System.out.println("Received: " +
                        i.time() + " " + i.unit() + " " + i.value()));
        sleep(7000);
    }
}
```

The output is as follows:

```
Emitted: 0
Received: 2 SECONDS 0
Emitted: 1
Received: 2 SECONDS 1
Emitted: 2
Received: 2 SECONDS 2
```

As you can see, this output essentially is the same as the previous one. The only difference is that we have extracted the values from the object of the Timed class.

Summary

We covered a lot of ground in this chapter, and hopefully, by now, you are starting to see that RxJava has a lot of practical applications. We covered various operators that suppress and transform emissions as well as reducing them to a single emission in some form. You learned how RxJava provides robust ways to recover from errors as well as to get visibility into what the `Observable` chain is doing with action operators.

If you want to learn more about RxJava operators, there are many resources online. Marble diagrams are a popular form of Rx documentation, visually showing how each operator works. The *rxmarbles.com* (`http://rxmarbles.com`) site is a popular, interactive web app that allows you to drag marble emissions and see the affected behavior with each operator. There is also an *RxMarbles* Android App (`https://play.google.com/store/apps/details?id=com.moonfleet.rxmarbles`) that you can use on your Android device. Of course, you can also see a comprehensive list of operators on the ReactiveX website (`http://reactivex.io/documentation/operators.html`).

Believe it or not, we have barely gotten started. This chapter only covered the basic operators. In the coming chapters, we will cover operators that provide powerful behavior, such as concurrency and multicasting. But before we do that, let's move on to operators that combine observables.

Section 2: Reactive Operators

2

This module takes the reader into the heart of Java reactive programming where the power of RxJava shines. You will learn how to combine streams of emissions; cache, replay, and share them across several receivers; how to process the emitted data concurrently; switch, throttle, and buffer the stream; how to deal with backpressure; and how to create new operators.

The following chapters are included in this module:

4
Combining Observables

We have covered many operators that suppress, transform, reduce, and collect emissions. These operators can do a lot of work, but what about combining multiple observables and consolidating them into one? If we want to accomplish more with ReactiveX, we need to take multiple streams of data and events and make them work together, and there are operators and factories to achieve this. These combining operators and factories also work safely with observables occurring on different threads (discussed in `Chapter 6`, *Concurrency and Parallelization*).

In this chapter, we start the transition from making RxJava useful to making it powerful. We will cover the following types of operators that allow observables to be combined:

- Merging factories and operators
- Concatenating factories and operators
- Ambiguous operators
- Zipping operators
- Combining the latest operators
- Grouping operators

Merging factories and operators

A common task done in ReactiveX is taking two or more `Observable<T>` instances and merging them into one `Observable<T>`. This merged `Observable<T>` subscribes to all of its merged sources simultaneously, making it effective for merging both finite and infinite observables. We can leverage this merging behavior principally in two ways – using factories or using operators. We can use both in the same processing chain too, as described in this section.

Observable.merge() factory and mergeWith() operator

The `Observable.merge()` factory will take two or more `Observable<T>` sources emitting the same type `T` and then consolidate them into a single `Observable<T>`.

If we have only two to four `Observable<T>` sources to merge, you can pass each one as an argument to the `Observable.merge()` factory. In the following code snippet, I have merged two `Observable<String>` instances into one `Observable<String>`:

```
import io.reactivex.rxjava3.core.Observable;

public class Ch4_01 {
    public static void main(String[] args) {
        Observable<String> src1 = Observable.just("Alpha", "Beta");
        Observable<String> src2 = Observable.just("Zeta", "Eta");
        Observable.merge(src1, src2)
                .subscribe(i -> System.out.println("RECEIVED: " + i));
    }
}
```

The output of the preceding program is as follows:

```
RECEIVED: Alpha
RECEIVED: Beta
RECEIVED: Zeta
RECEIVED: Eta
```

Alternatively, you can use `mergeWith()`, which is the operator version of `Observable.merge()`:

```
import io.reactivex.rxjava3.core.Observable;

public class Ch4_01a {
    public static void main(String[] args) {
        Observable<String> src1 = Observable.just("Alpha", "Beta");
        Observable<String> src2 = Observable.just("Zeta", "Eta");
        src1.mergeWith(src2)
            .subscribe(i -> System.out.println("RECEIVED: " + i));
    }
}
```

The output of the preceding example is exactly the same as that of the previous one.

The `Observable.merge()` factory and the `mergeWith()` operator will subscribe to all the specified sources simultaneously, but will likely fire the emissions in order if they are cold and on the same thread. This is just an implementation detail that is not guaranteed to work the same way every time. If you want to fire elements of each `Observable` sequentially and keep their emissions in sequential order, you should use `Observable.concat()`.

 You should not rely on ordering when using merge factories and operators, even if ordering seems to be preserved. Having said that, the order of emissions from each source `Observable` is maintained. The way the sources are merged is an implementation detail, so use concatenation factories and operators if you want to guarantee order.

If you have more than four `Observable<T>` sources, you can use `Observable.mergeArray()` to pass an array of `Observable` instances that you want to merge, as shown in the following code snippet. Since RxJava 2.0 was written for JDK 6+ and has no access to a `@SafeVarargs` annotation, you may get a safety warning:

```java
import io.reactivex.rxjava3.core.Observable;

public class Ch4_02 {
    public static void main(String[] args) {
        Observable<String> src1 = Observable.just("Alpha", "Beta");
        Observable<String> src2 = Observable.just("Gamma", "Delta");
        Observable<String> src3 = Observable.just("Epsilon", "Zeta");
        Observable<String> src4 = Observable.just("Eta", "Theta");
        Observable<String> src5 = Observable.just("Iota", "Kappa");
        Observable.mergeArray(src1, src2, src3, src4, src5)
                .subscribe(i -> System.out.println("RECEIVED: " + i));
    }
}
```

The output of the preceding code is as follows:

```
RECEIVED: Alpha
RECEIVED: Beta
RECEIVED: Gamma
RECEIVED: Delta
RECEIVED: Epsilon
RECEIVED: Zeta
RECEIVED: Eta
RECEIVED: Theta
RECEIVED: Iota
RECEIVED: Kappa
```

There is also an overloaded version of `Observable.merge()` that accepts `Iterable<Observable<T>>` and produces the same results in a more type-safe manner:

```
import io.reactivex.rxjava3.core.Observable;
import java.util.Arrays;
import java.util.List;

public class Ch4_03 {
    public static void main(String[] args) {
        Observable<String> src1 = Observable.just("Alpha", "Beta");
        Observable<String> src2 = Observable.just("Gamma", "Delta");
        Observable<String> src3 = Observable.just("Epsilon", "Zeta");
        Observable<String> src4 = Observable.just("Eta", "Theta");
        Observable<String> src5 = Observable.just("Iota", "Kappa");
        List<Observable<String>> sources =
                Arrays.asList(src1, src2, src3, src4, src5);
        Observable.merge(sources)
                .subscribe(i -> System.out.println("RECEIVED: " + i));
    }
}
```

It merges all the `Observable<T>` instances from the `Iterable` into one.

The reason `mergeArray()` gets its own method and is not a `merge()` overload instead is to avoid ambiguity. This is true for all the `xxxArray()` operators.

Note that `Observable.merge()` works with infinite observables. Since it will subscribe to all observables and fire their emissions as soon as they are available, you can merge multiple infinite sources into a single stream.

In the following example, we merge two `Observable.interval()` sources that emit at 1-second and 300-millisecond intervals, respectively. But before we merge, we do some math with the emitted index to figure out how much time has elapsed and emit it with the source name included in the `String` value. We let this process run for three seconds:

```
import io.reactivex.rxjava3.core.Observable;
import java.util.concurrent.TimeUnit;

public class Ch4_04 {
    public static void main(String[] args) {
        //emit every second
        Observable<String> src1 = Observable.interval(1,
                TimeUnit.SECONDS)
                .map(l -> l + 1) // emit elapsed seconds
```

```
                .map(l -> "Source1: " + l + " seconds");
        //emit every 300 milliseconds
        Observable<String> src2 =
            Observable.interval(300, TimeUnit.MILLISECONDS)
                .map(l -> (l + 1) * 300) // emit elapsed milliseconds
                .map(l -> "Source2: " + l + " milliseconds");
        //merge and subscribe
        Observable.merge(src1, src2)
                .subscribe(System.out::println);
        //keep alive for 3 seconds
        sleep(3000);
    }
}
```

The output of the preceding code is as follows:

```
Source2: 300 milliseconds
Source2: 600 milliseconds
Source2: 900 milliseconds
Source1: 1 seconds
Source2: 1200 milliseconds
Source2: 1500 milliseconds
Source2: 1800 milliseconds
Source1: 2 seconds
Source2: 2100 milliseconds
Source2: 2400 milliseconds
Source2: 2700 milliseconds
Source1: 3 seconds
Source2: 3000 milliseconds
```

To summarize, `Observable.merge()` combines multiple `Observable<T>` sources emitting the same type `T` and consolidates them into a single `Observable<T>`. It works on infinite `Observable` instances and does not necessarily guarantee that the emissions come in any order. If you care about the emissions being strictly ordered by having each `Observable` source fired sequentially, consider using `Observable.concat()`, which we will cover shortly.

flatMap()

The `flatMap()` operator is one of, if not *the*, most powerful operators in RxJava. If you have to invest time in understanding any RxJava operator, this is the one. It performs a dynamic `Observable.merge()` by taking each emission and mapping it to an `Observable`. Then, it merges the resulting observables into a single stream.

The simplest application of `flatMap()` is to map *one emission to many emissions*. Let's say we want to emit the letters from each string coming from `Observable<String>`. We can use `flatMap(Function<T,Observable<R>> mapper)` to provide a function (implemented using a lambda expression) that maps each string to `Observable<String>`. Note that the mapped `Observable<R>` can emit any type `R`, different from the source `T` emissions. In this example, it just happened to be `String`, like the source:

```
import io.reactivex.rxjava3.core.Observable;

public class Ch4_05 {
    public static void main(String[] args) {
        Observable<String> source =
                Observable.just("Alpha", "Beta", "Gamma");
        source.flatMap(s -> Observable.fromArray(s.split("")))
                .subscribe(System.out::println);
    }
}
```

The output of the preceding code is as follows:

```
A
l
p
h
a
B
e
t
a
G
a
m
m
a
```

We have taken those five `String`-type emitted values and mapped them (through `flatMap()`) to emit the letters from each one. We did this by calling each string's `split()` method, and we passed into it an empty `String` argument `""` as the letters' separator. This returns an array, `String[]`, containing all the letters, which we passed into `Observable.fromArray()` to emit each letter. The `flatMap()` expects each emission to yield an `Observable`, and it merges all the resulting observables and emits their values in a single stream.

Here is another example: let's take a sequence of `String` values (each a concatenated series of values separated by "`/`"), use `flatMap()` on them, and filter only numeric values before converting them into `Integer` emissions:

```
import io.reactivex.rxjava3.core.Observable;

public class Ch4_06 {
    public static void main(String[] args) {
        Observable<String> source =
                Observable.just("521934/2342/FOXTROT",
                                        "21962/12112/TANGO/78886");
        source.flatMap(s -> Observable.fromArray(s.split("/")))
            //use regex to filter integers
            .filter(s -> s.matches("[0-9]+"))
            .map(Integer::valueOf)
            .subscribe(System.out::println);
    }
}
```

The output of the preceding code is as follows:

```
521934
2342
21962
12112
78886
```

We broke up each `String` by means of the / character, which yielded an array. We turned that into an `Observable` and used `flatMap()` on it to emit each `String`. We filtered only the `String` values that are numeric using a regular expression `[0-9]+` (eliminating FOXTROT and TANGO) and then turned each emission into an `Integer`.

Just like `Observable.merge()`, `flatMap()` can also map emissions to infinite instances of `Observable` and merge them. For instance, it can receive simple `Integer` values from `Observable<Integer>` but use `flatMap()` on them to drive an `Observable.interval()`, where each `Integer` value serves as the period argument.

In the following code example, the source `Observable` emits the values 2, 3, 10, and 7, each transformed by `flatMap()` to an interval `Observable` that emits a value every 2, 3, 10, and 7 seconds, respectively. The four `Observable` instances produced by `flatMap()` are then merged into a single stream:

```
import io.reactivex.rxjava3.core.Observable;
import java.util.concurrent.TimeUnit;

public class Ch4_07 {
```

```
public static void main(String[] args) {
    Observable.just(2, 3, 10, 7)
        .flatMap(i -> Observable.interval(i, TimeUnit.SECONDS)
                    .map(i2 -> i + "s interval: " +
                                ((i + 1) * i) + " seconds elapsed"))
        .subscribe(System.out::println);
    sleep(12000);
    }
}
```

Note that `i -> Observable.interval(...).map(...)` represents the
`Function<T,Observable<R>> mapper` function passed as the parameter into
`flatMap()`. The output of this code is as follows:

```
2s interval: 2 seconds elapsed
3s interval: 3 seconds elapsed
2s interval: 4 seconds elapsed
2s interval: 6 seconds elapsed
3s interval: 6 seconds elapsed
7s interval: 7 seconds elapsed
2s interval: 8 seconds elapsed
3s interval: 9 seconds elapsed
2s interval: 10 seconds elapsed
10s interval: 10 seconds elapsed
2s interval: 12 seconds elapsed
3s interval: 12 seconds elapsed
```

The `Observable.merge()` operator accepts a fixed number of `Observable` sources.
However, `flatMap()` dynamically adds new `Observable` sources for each value that
comes in. This means that you can keep merging new incoming `Observable` sources all the
time.

Another quick note about `flatMap()` is that it can be used in many clever ways. For
example, you can evaluate each received value within `flatMap()` and figure out what kind
of `Observable` you want to return. If the previous example emitted a value of 0 to
`flatMap()`, this would force `Observable.interval()` to emit continuously an infinite
number of values. To avoid this issue, we can add an `if` statement to check whether the
incoming value is 0 and return `Observable.empty()` when it is. Here's how the code may
appear:

```
import io.reactivex.rxjava3.core.Observable;
import java.util.concurrent.TimeUnit;

public class Ch4_07a {
    public static void main(String[] args) {
        Observable.just(2, 0, 3, 10, 7)
```

```
                    .flatMap(i -> {
                        if (i == 0) {
                            return Observable.empty();
                        } else {
                            return Observable.interval(i, TimeUnit.SECONDS)
                                    .map(l -> i + "s interval: " +
                                            ((l + 1) * i) + " seconds elapsed");

                        }
                    })
                    .subscribe(System.out::println);
            sleep(12000);
        }
    }
```

The output of the preceding example is the same as the output of the previous one. Replacing the `Observable` with an empty one in the case of value 0 has the effect of skipping this value.

Of course, this is probably too clever as you can just put `filter()` before `flatMap()` and filter out values that are equal to 0. But the point is that you can evaluate an emission in `flatMap()` and determine what kind of `Observable` you want to return.

`flatMap()` is also a great way to take a hot `Observable` with a UI event stream (such as JavaFX or Android button clicks) and `flatMap()` each of those events to an entire process within `flatMap()`. Failure and error recovery can be handled entirely within that `flatMap()`, so each item does not disrupt future button clicks.

If you do not want rapid button clicks to produce several redundant instances of a process, you can disable the button using `doOnNext()` or leverage `switchMap()` to kill previous processes, which we will discuss in `Chapter 7`, *Switching, Throttling, Windowing, and Buffering*.

Note that there are many overloads and variants of `flatMap()` that we will not get into deeply for the sake of brevity. We will just demonstrate one of them, as it has a certain complexity of usage.

flatMap() with combiner

The `flatMap()` operator has an overloaded version,
`flatMap(Function<T,Observable<R>> mapper, BiFunction<T,U,R> combiner)`,
that allows the provision of a *combiner* along with the mapper function. This second
combiner function associates the originally emitted `T` value with each flat-mapped `U` value
and turns both into an `R` value. We can modify our earlier example of emitting letters from
each string and associate each letter with the original string emission it was mapped from:

```
import io.reactivex.rxjava3.core.Observable;

public class Ch4_08 {
    public static void main(String[] args) {
        Observable.just("Alpha", "Beta", "Gamma")
                .flatMap(s -> Observable.fromArray(s.split("")),
                                        (s, r) -> s + "-" + r)
                .subscribe(System.out::println);
    }
}
```

The output of the preceding code is as follows:

```
Alpha-A
Alpha-l
Alpha-p
Alpha-h
Alpha-a
Beta-B
Beta-e
Beta-t
Beta-a
Gamma-G
    . . .
```

We can also use `flatMapIterable()` to map each `T` value into an `Iterable<R>` instead of
an `Observable<R>`. It will then emit all the `R` values for each `Iterable<R>`, saving us the
step and overhead of converting it into an `Observable`.

There is also `flatMapSingle()` that maps the input to `Single`, `flatMapMaybe()` that
maps to `Maybe`, and `flatMapCompletable()` that maps to `Completable`.

A lot of these overloads also apply to `concatMap()`, which we will cover next.

Concatenating factories and operators

Concatenation is remarkably similar to merging, but with an important nuance: it emits items of each provided `Observable` sequentially and in the order specified. It does not move on to the next `Observable` until the current one calls `onComplete()`. This makes it great to ensure that the merged `Observable` starts emitting in a guaranteed order. However, it is often a poor choice for infinite `Observable`, as it will indefinitely hold up the queue and forever leave the `Observable` that is next in line waiting.

We will cover the factories and operators used for concatenation. You will find that they are much like the merging ones, except that they have sequential behavior.

 You should prefer concatenation when you want to guarantee that the concatenated `Observable` instances fire their emissions in the specified order. If you do not care about ordering, use merging instead.

Observable.concat() factory and concatWith() operator

The `Observable.concat()` factory is the concatenation equivalent to `Observable.merge()`. It will combine the emitted values of multiple observables, but will fire each one sequentially and only move to the next after `onComplete()` is called.

In the following code, we have two source observables emitting strings. We can use `Observable.concat()` to fire the emissions from the first one and then fire the emissions from the second one:

```
import io.reactivex.rxjava3.core.Observable;

public class Ch4_09 {
    public static void main(String[] args) {
        Observable<String> src1 = Observable.just("Alpha", "Beta");
        Observable<String> src2 = Observable.just("Zeta", "Eta");
        Observable.concat(src1, src2)
                .subscribe(i -> System.out.println("RECEIVED: " + i));
    }
}
```

The output of the preceding code is as follows:

```
RECEIVED: Alpha
RECEIVED: Beta
RECEIVED: Zeta
RECEIVED: Eta
```

This is the same output as from our `Observable.merge()` example earlier. But, as discussed in the merging section, we should use `Observable.concat()` to guarantee emission ordering, as merging does not guarantee it.

You can also use the `concatWith()` operator to accomplish the same thing, as shown in the following code:

```
import io.reactivex.rxjava3.core.Observable;

public class Ch4_09a {
    public static void main(String[] args) {
        Observable<String> src1 = Observable.just("Alpha", "Beta");
        Observable<String> src2 = Observable.just("Zeta", "Eta");
        src1.concatWith(src2)
            .subscribe(i -> System.out.println("RECEIVED: " + i));
    }
}
```

The output of the preceding code example is the same as the output of the previous example.

If we use `Observable.concat()` with infinite observables, it will forever emit from the first one it encounters and prevent any following `Observable` from firing. If we ever want to put an infinite `Observable` anywhere in a concatenation operation, it should be listed last. This ensures that it does not hold up any `Observable` following it because there are none. We can also use `take()` operators to make an infinite `Observable` finite.

Here, we fire an `Observable` that emits every second, but only take two emissions from it. After that, it calls `onComplete()` and disposes the source `Observable`. Then, a second `Observable` concatenated after it will emit forever (or in this case, when the application quits after five seconds). Since this second `Observable` is the last one specified in `Observable.concat()`, it will not hold up any subsequent observables by being infinite:

```
import io.reactivex.rxjava3.core.Observable;

public class Ch4_10 {
    public static void main(String[] args) {
        //emit every second, but only take 2 emissions
        Observable<String> src1 =
```

```
            Observable.interval(1, TimeUnit.SECONDS)
                    .take(2)
                    .map(l -> l + 1) // emit elapsed seconds
                    .map(l -> "Source1: " + l + " seconds");
    //emit every 300 milliseconds
    Observable<String> src2 =
        Observable.interval(300, TimeUnit.MILLISECONDS)
                    .map(l -> (l + 1) * 300) // emit elapsed millis
                    .map(l -> "Source2: " + l + " milliseconds");
    Observable.concat(src1, src2)
            .subscribe(i -> System.out.println("RECEIVED: " + i));
    //keep application alive for 5 seconds
    sleep(5000);
    }
  }
```

The output of the preceding code is as follows:

```
RECEIVED: Source1: 1 seconds
RECEIVED: Source1: 2 seconds
RECEIVED: Source2: 300 milliseconds
RECEIVED: Source2: 600 milliseconds
RECEIVED: Source2: 900 milliseconds
RECEIVED: Source2: 1200 milliseconds
RECEIVED: Source2: 1500 milliseconds
```

There are concatenation counterparts for arrays and `Iterable<Observable<T>>` inputs as well, just like there are in the case of merging. The `Observable.concatArray()` factory fires off each `Observable` sequentially in an `Observable[]` array. The `Observable.concat()` factory also accepts an `Iterable<Observable<T>>` and fires off each `Observable<T>` in the same manner.

Note that there are a few variants of `concatMap()`. Use `concatMapIterable()` when you want to map each emission to an `Iterable<T>` instead of an `Observable<T>`. It emits all T values for each `Iterable<T>`, saving you the step and overhead of turning each one into an `Observable<T>`. There is also a `concatMapEager()` operator that eagerly subscribes to all `Observable` sources it receives and caches the emissions until it is their turn to emit.

concatMap()

Just as there is `flatMap()`, which dynamically merges observables, there is a concatenation counterpart called `concatMap()`. Use this operator if you care about ordering and want each `Observable` being mapped from each emission before starting the next one.

More specifically, `concatMap()` merges each mapped `Observable` sequentially and fires them one at a time. It moves to the next `Observable` when the current one calls `onComplete()`. If source emissions produce observables faster than `concatMap()` can emit from them, those observables are queued.

Our earlier `flatMap()` examples would be better suited for `concatMap()` if we explicitly cared about emission order. Although our example here has the same output as the `flatMap()` example, we should use `concatMap()` when we explicitly care about maintaining ordering and want to process each mapped `Observable` sequentially:

```
import io.reactivex.rxjava3.core.Observable;

public class Ch4_11 {
    public static void main(String[] args) {
        Observable<String> source =
                    Observable.just("Alpha", "Beta", "Gamma");
        source.concatMap(s -> Observable.fromArray(s.split("")))
            .subscribe(System.out::println);
    }
}
```

The output will be as follows:

```
A
l
p
h
a
B
e
t
a
G
a
m
m
a
```

Again, it is unlikely that you will ever use `concatMap()` to map to an infinite `Observable`. As you can guess, this would result in a subsequent `Observable` never firing. You will likely want to use `flatMap()` instead, and we will see it used in concurrency examples in `Chapter 6`, *Concurrency and Parallelization*.

Ambiguous operators

After covering merging and concatenation, let's get an easy combining operation out of the way. The `Observable.amb()` factory (**amb** stands for **ambiguous**) accepts an `Iterable<Observable<T>>` object as a parameter and emits the values of the first `Observable` that emits, while the others are disposed of. This is helpful when there are multiple sources of the same data or events and you want the fastest one to win.

Here, we have two interval sources and we combine them with the `Observable.amb()` factory. If one emits every second while the other emits every 300 milliseconds, the latter is going to win because it emits more often:

```
import io.reactivex.rxjava3.core.Observable;

public class Ch4_12 {
    public static void main(String[] args) {
        //emit every second
        Observable<String> src1 =
            Observable.interval(1, TimeUnit.SECONDS)
                    .take(2)
                    .map(l -> l + 1) // emit elapsed seconds
                    .map(l -> "Source1: " + l + " seconds");
        //emit every 300 milliseconds
        Observable<String> src2 =
            Observable.interval(300, TimeUnit.MILLISECONDS)
                    .map(l -> (l + 1) * 300) // emit elapsed millis
                    .map(l -> "Source2: " + l + " milliseconds");
        //emit Observable that emits first
        Observable.amb(Arrays.asList(src1, src2))
                    subscribe(i -> System.out.println("RECEIVED: " + i));
        //keep application alive for 5 seconds
        sleep(5000);
    }
}
```

The output of this example looks as follows:

```
RECEIVED: Source2: 300 milliseconds
RECEIVED: Source2: 600 milliseconds
RECEIVED: Source2: 900 milliseconds
RECEIVED: Source2: 1200 milliseconds
RECEIVED: Source2: 1500 milliseconds
RECEIVED: Source2: 1800 milliseconds
RECEIVED: Source2: 2100 milliseconds
...
```

You can also use an `ambWith()` operator, which will accomplish the same result:

```
//emit Observable that emits first
src1.ambWith(src2)
    .subscribe(i -> System.out.println("RECEIVED: " + i));
```

You can also use `Observable.ambArray()` to specify a `varargs` array rather than `Iterable<Observable<T>>`.

Zipping operators

Zipping allows you to take an emitted value from each `Observable` source and combine them into a single emission. Each `Observable` can emit a different type, but you can combine these different emitted types into a single emission. Here is an example. If we have an `Observable<String>` and an `Observable<Integer>`, we can `zip` each `String` and `Integer` together in a one-to-one pairing. Then, we can combine them using the `BiFunction<String,Integer,String>` `zipper` function. This function is implemented in this example as `(s,i) -> s + "-" + i`, which concatenates the received two input values into one `String` value with a separator, `"-"`, in the middle:

```
import io.reactivex.rxjava3.core.Observable;

public class Ch4_13 {
    public static void main(String[] args) {
        Observable<String> src1 =
                Observable.just("Alpha", "Beta", "Gamma");
        Observable<Integer> src2 = Observable.range(1, 6);
        Observable.zip(src1, src2, (s, i) -> s + "-" + i)
                .subscribe(System.out::println);
    }
}
```

The output is as follows:

```
Alpha-1
Beta-2
Gamma-3
```

The `zip()` function received both `Alpha` and a `1` and then paired them up into a concatenated string separated by a dash, –, and pushed it forward. Then, it received `Beta` and `2` and emitted them forward as a concatenation, and so on.

An emission from one `Observable` must wait to get paired with an emission from the other `Observable`. If one `Observable` calls `onComplete()` and the other still has emissions waiting to get paired, those emissions will simply be dropped, since they have nothing to be paired with. This happened to the values `4`, `5`, and `6` of the `src2` since we only had `3` values emitted from the `src1`.

You can also accomplish this using a `zipWith()` operator, as shown here:

```
src1.zipWith(src2, (s,i) -> s + "-" + i)
```

You can pass up to nine `Observable` instances to the `Observable.zip()` factory. If you need more than that, you can pass an `Iterable<Observable<T>>` or use `zipArray()` to provide an `Observable[]` array. Note that if one or more sources are producing emissions faster than another, `zip()` will queue up those rapid emissions as they wait on the slower source to provide emissions. This could cause undesirable performance issues as each source queues in memory. If you only care about zipping the latest emission from each source rather than catching up an entire queue, you will want to use `combineLatest()`, which we will cover later in this section.

 Use `Observable.zipIterable()` to pass a `boolean delayError` argument to delay errors until all sources terminate and `int bufferSize` to hint at an expected number of elements from each source for queue size optimization. You may specify the latter to increase performance in certain scenarios by buffering emissions before they are zipped.

Zipping can also be helpful in slowing down emissions using `Observable.interval()`. Here, we zip each string with a one-second interval. This will slow each string emission by one second, but keep in mind the fact that five-string emissions will likely be queued as they wait for an interval emission to pair with:

```
import io.reactivex.rxjava3.core.Observable;
import java.time.LocalTime;
import java.util.concurrent.TimeUnit;

public class Ch4_14 {
    public static void main(String[] args) {
        Observable<String> strings =
                        Observable.just("Alpha", "Beta", "Gamma");
        Observable<Long> seconds =
                        Observable.interval(1, TimeUnit.SECONDS);
```

```
Observable.zip(strings, seconds, (s, l) -> s)
        .subscribe(s -> System.out.println("Received " + s +
                                " at " + LocalTime.now()));
sleep(4000);
    }
}
```

In this example, while combining the streams in the `zip()` method, we ignore values emitted by `Observable<Long> seconds`. We use it just to demonstrate how the `zip()` method waits until values from all the observables are emitted. The output is as follows:

```
Received Alpha at 13:15:07.038857
Received Beta at 13:15:08.023963
Received Gamma at 13:15:09.018764
```

Combining the latest operators

The `Observable.combineLatest()` factory is somewhat similar to `zip()`, but for every emission that fires from one of the sources, it will immediately couple up with the latest emission from every other source. It will not queue up unpaired emissions for each source, but rather cache and pair the latest one.

Here, let's use `Observable.combineLatest()` between two interval observables, the first emitting at 300 milliseconds and the other every second:

```java
import io.reactivex.rxjava3.core.Observable;
import java.util.concurrent.TimeUnit;

public class Ch4_15 {
    public static void main(String[] args) {
        Observable<Long> source1 =
                Observable.interval(300, TimeUnit.MILLISECONDS);
        Observable<Long> source2 =
                Observable.interval(1, TimeUnit.SECONDS);
        Observable.combineLatest(source1, source2, (l1, l2) ->
                        "SOURCE 1: " + l1 + " SOURCE 2: " + l2)
                .subscribe(System.out::println);
        sleep(3000);
    }
}
```

The output is as follows:

```
SOURCE 1: 2    SOURCE 2: 0
SOURCE 1: 3    SOURCE 2: 0
SOURCE 1: 4    SOURCE 2: 0
SOURCE 1: 5    SOURCE 2: 0
SOURCE 1: 5    SOURCE 2: 1
SOURCE 1: 6    SOURCE 2: 1
SOURCE 1: 7    SOURCE 2: 1
SOURCE 1: 8    SOURCE 2: 1
SOURCE 1: 9    SOURCE 2: 1
SOURCE 1: 9    SOURCE 2: 2
```

There is a lot going on here, but let's try to break it down:

1. `Observable<Long> source1` is emitting every 300 milliseconds, but the first two emissions do not yet have anything to pair with from `Observable<Long> source2`, which emits every second, and no emission has occurred yet.

2. Finally, after 1 second, `source2` pushes its first emission, `0`, and it pairs with the latest emission, `2` (the third emission), from `source1`. Note that the two previous emissions, `0` and `1`, from `source1` were completely forgotten because the third emission, `2`, is now the latest emission.

3. `source1` then pushes `3`, `4`, and then `5` at 300-millisecond intervals, but `0` is still the latest emission from `source2`, so all three pair with it.

4. Then, `source2` emits its second emission, `1`, and it pairs with `5`, the latest emission from `source2`.

In simpler terms, when one source fires, it couples with the latest emissions from the others. The `Observable.combineLatest()` operator is especially helpful in combining UI inputs, as previous user inputs are frequently irrelevant and only the latest is of concern.

withLatestFrom()

Similar to `Observable.combineLatest()`, but not exactly the same, is the `withLatestFrom()` operator. This will map each `T` emission with the latest values from other observables and combine them, but it will only take *one* emission from each of the other observables:

```java
import io.reactivex.rxjava3.core.Observable;
import java.util.concurrent.TimeUnit;

public class Ch4_16 {
```

```
public static void main(String[] args) {
    Observable<Long> source1 =
                Observable.interval(300, TimeUnit.MILLISECONDS);
    Observable<Long> source2 =
                    Observable.interval(1, TimeUnit.SECONDS);
    source2.withLatestFrom(source1, (l1, l2) ->
                    "SOURCE 2: " + l1 + " SOURCE 1: " + l2)
        .subscribe(System.out::println);
    sleep(3000);
    }
}
```

The output is as follows:

SOURCE 2: 0   SOURCE 1: 2
SOURCE 2: 1   SOURCE 1: 5
SOURCE 2: 2   SOURCE 1: 9

As you can see here, `source2` emits every second while `source1` emits every 300 milliseconds. When the `withLatestFrom()` operator is called on `source2` and receives `source1` as a parameter, it combines the `source2` emission with the latest emission from `source1`, but it does not care about any previous or subsequent emissions.

You can pass up to four `Observable` instances of any type to `withLatestFrom()`. If you need more than that, you can pass them as `Iterable<Observable<T>>`.

Grouping operators

To group emissions by a specified key into separate observables is a powerful operation. This can be achieved by calling the `groupBy(Function<T,K> keySelector)` operator, which accepts a function that maps each emission to a key. It will then return an `Observable<GroupedObservable<K,T>>`, which emits a special type of `Observable` called `GroupedObservable`. The `GroupedObservable<K,T>` class is just like any other `Observable`, but it has the key `K` value accessible as a property. It emits `T` type values that are mapped for that given key.

For instance, we can use the `groupBy()` operator to group emissions for an `Observable<String>` by each string's length. We will subscribe to it in a moment, but here is how we declare it:

```
import io.reactivex.rxjava3.core.Observable;
import io.reactivex.rxjava3.observables.GroupedObservable;
```

```
public class Ch4_17 {
    public static void main(String[] args) {
        Observable<String> source = Observable.just("Alpha", "Beta",
                                        "Gamma", "Delta", "Epsilon");
        Observable<GroupedObservable<Integer, String>> byLengths =
                                        source.groupBy(s -> s.length());
    }
}
```

We will likely need to use `flatMap()` on each `GroupedObservable`, but within that `flatMap()` operation, we may want to reduce or collect those common-key emissions (since this will return a `Single`, we will need to use `flatMapSingle()`). Let's call `toList()` so that we can emit the emissions as lists grouped by their lengths:

```
import io.reactivex.rxjava3.core.Observable;
import io.reactivex.rxjava3.observables.GroupedObservable;

public class Ch4_18 {
    public static void main(String[] args) {
        Observable<String> source = Observable.just("Alpha", "Beta",
                                        "Gamma", "Delta", "Epsilon");
        Observable<GroupedObservable<Integer, String>> byLengths =
                                        source.groupBy(s -> s.length());
        byLengths.flatMapSingle(grp -> grp.toList())
                .subscribe(System.out::println);
    }
}
```

The output is as follows:

```
[Beta]
[Alpha, Gamma, Delta]
[Epsilon]
```

`Beta` is the only emission whose length equals 4, so it is the only element in the list for that length key. The values `Alpha`, `Beta`, and `Gamma` all have lengths of 5, so they were emitted from the same `GroupedObservable` emitting items for a length of 5 and were collected in the same list. `Epsilon` was the only emission with a length of 7, so it was the only element in its list.

Keep in mind that GroupedObservable also has a getKey() method, which returns the key value identified with that GroupedObservable. If we wanted to simply concatenate the String emissions for each GroupedObservable and then concatenate the length key in front of it, we could do it as follows:

```
import io.reactivex.rxjava3.core.Observable;
import io.reactivex.rxjava3.observables.GroupedObservable;

public class Ch4_19 {
    public static void main(String[] args) {
        Observable<String> source = Observable.just("Alpha", "Beta",
                                    "Gamma", "Delta", "Epsilon");
        Observable<GroupedObservable<Integer, String>> byLengths =
                            source.groupBy(s -> s.length());
        byLengths.flatMapSingle(grp -> grp.reduce("", (x, y) ->
                    x.equals("") ? y : x + ", " + y).map(s ->
                                grp.getKey() + ": " + s))
                .subscribe(System.out::println);
    }
}
```

The output is as follows:

```
4: Beta
5: Alpha, Gamma, Delta
7: Epsilon
```

Note that GroupedObservable is a weird combination of a hot and cold Observable. It is not cold as it does not replay missed emissions to a second Observer, but it caches emissions and flushes them to the first Observer, ensuring that none are missed. If you need to replay the emissions, collect them in a list, as we did earlier, and perform your operations against that list. You can also use caching operators, which we will learn about in the next chapter.

Summary

In this chapter, we covered combining observables, which can be useful in a variety of ways. Merging is helpful in combining and simultaneously firing multiple observables and combining their emissions into a single stream.

The `flatMap()` operator is especially critical to know, as dynamically merging observables derived from emissions opens up a lot of useful functionality in RxJava.

Concatenation is similar to merging, but it fires off the source observables sequentially rather than all at once. Combining with ambiguous allows us to select the first `Observable` to emit and fire its emissions.

Zipping combines emissions from multiple observables, whereas `combineLatest()` combines the latest emissions from each source every time one of them fires.

Finally, grouping splits up an `Observable` into several `GroupedObservable` objects, each with emissions that have a common key.

Take time to explore combining observables and experiment to see how they work. They are critical for unlocking functionalities in RxJava and quickly express event and data transformations. We will look at some powerful applications with `flatMap()` when we cover concurrency in `Chapter 6`, *Concurrency and Parallelization*.

In the next chapter, you will learn more about hot and cold observables and discuss how to implement multicasting with `ConnectableObservable`. You will also practice how to replay and cache data using `ConnectableObservable`.

Finally, you will learn about `Subject`, which is useful for decoupling while multicasting. You will also see how and when to use it and when not to.

5
Multicasting, Replaying, and Caching

We have seen the hot and cold `Observable` in action throughout this book, although most of our examples have been for a cold `Observable` (even ones using `Observable.interval()`). As a matter of fact, there are a lot of subtleties in the hotness and coldness of an `Observable`, which we will look at in this chapter.

When you have more than one `Observer`, the default behavior is to create a separate stream for each one. This may or may not be desirable, and we need to be aware of when to force an `Observable` to be hot by multicasting using a `ConnectableObservable`. We got a brief introduction to the `ConnectableObservable` in `Chapter 2`, *Observable and Observer*, but we will look at it in greater detail – go the entire chain of the operators and learn about multicasting with `ConnectableObservable`. It will uncover some subtleties of `ConnectableObservable` functionality and usage. We will also learn about replaying and caching, both of which leverage the `ConnectableObservable` too.

Finally, we will learn about `Subject`, a utility that can be useful for decoupling while multicasting, but that should be used conservatively only in certain situations. We will cover the different flavors of subjects as well as when to use them and when to avoid them.

Here is a broad outline of what to expect:

- Understanding multicasting
- Automatic connection
- Replaying and caching
- Subjects

Understanding multicasting

We have used the `ConnectableObservable` earlier in `Chapter 2`, *Observable and Observer*. Remember how a cold `Observable`, such as the one created by `Observable.range()`, regenerates emissions for each subscribed `Observer`? Let's take a look at the following code:

```
import io.reactivex.rxjava3.core.Observable;

public class Ch5_01 {
    public static void main(String[] args) {
        Observable<Integer> ints = Observable.range(1, 3);
        ints.subscribe(i -> System.out.println("Observer One: " + i));
        ints.subscribe(i -> System.out.println("Observer Two: " + i));
    }
}
```

The output obtained is as follows:

```
Observer One: 1
Observer One: 2
Observer One: 3
Observer Two: 1
Observer Two: 2
Observer Two: 3
```

Here, `Observer One` received all three emissions and called `onComplete()`. After that, `Observer Two` received the three emissions (that were regenerated again) and called `onComplete()`. These were two separate streams of data generated for two separate subscriptions. If we wanted to consolidate them into a single stream of data that pushes each emission to both subscribed observers simultaneously, we can call `publish()` on `Observable`, which will return a `ConnectableObservable`.

Let's set up the observers in advance and then call `connect()` to start firing the emissions:

```
import io.reactivex.rxjava3.core.Observable;
import io.reactivex.rxjava3.observables.ConnectableObservable;

public class Ch5_02 {
    public static void main(String[] args) {
        ConnectableObservable<Integer> ints =
                            Observable.range(1, 3).publish();
        ints.subscribe(i -> System.out.println("Observer One:" + i));
        ints.subscribe(i -> System.out.println("Observer Two:" + i));
```

```
            ints.connect();
        }
    }
```

The output obtained is as follows:

```
    Observer One: 1
    Observer Two: 1
    Observer One: 2
    Observer Two: 2
    Observer One: 3
    Observer Two: 3
```

Using `ConnectableObservable` forces emissions from the source to become hot, pushing a single stream of emissions to all observers at the same time, rather than giving a separate stream to each `Observer`. This idea of stream consolidation is known as multicasting, but there are nuances to it, especially when operators become involved. Even when you call `publish()` and use a `ConnectableObservable`, any operator added before `subscribe()` can create a new stream. We will take a look at this behavior and how to manage it next.

Multicasting with operators

To see how multicasting works within a chain of operators, we are going to use `Observable.range()` and then map each emission to a random integer. Since these random values will be non-deterministic and different for each subscription, it will provide a good way to see whether our multicasting is working because each `Observer` should receive the same value.

Let's start with emitting the numbers 1 through 3 and map each one to a random integer between 0 and 100,000. If we have two observers, we can expect different integers for each one. Note that your output will be different to that presented due to the random nature of number generation. Just note that both observers are receiving different random integers:

```java
import io.reactivex.rxjava3.core.Observable;
import java.util.concurrent.ThreadLocalRandom;

public class Ch5_03 {
    public static void main(String[] args) {
        Observable<Integer> ints = Observable.range(1, 3)
                                        .map(i -> randomInt());
        ints.subscribe(i -> System.out.println("Observer 1: " + i));
        ints.subscribe(i -> System.out.println("Observer 2: " + i));
    }
```

```
public static int randomInt() {
    return ThreadLocalRandom.current().nextInt(100000);
}
}
```

Note the `randomInt()` method we have implemented to generate a random integer. We will use it throughout other examples, but do not show its source code anymore so as to save space.

The output obtained is as follows:

```
Observer 1: 38895
Observer 1: 36858
Observer 1: 82955
Observer 2: 55957
Observer 2: 47394
Observer 2: 16996
```

What happens here is that the `Observable.range()` source yields two separate emission generators, with each coldly emitting a separate stream for each `Observer`. Each stream also has its own separate `map()` instance, hence, each `Observer` gets different random integers. You can visually see this structure of two separate streams in the following diagram:

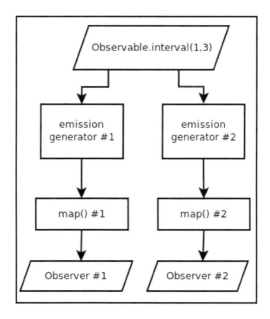

But what if you need to emit the same three random integers to both observers? Your first instinct might be to call `publish()` after `Observable.range()` to yield a `ConnectableObservable`. Then, you may call the `map()` operator on it, followed by the subscribing and a `connect()` call.

However, you will see that this does not achieve the desired result. Each `Observer` still gets three separate random integers:

```
import io.reactivex.rxjava3.core.Observable;
import io.reactivex.rxjava3.observables.ConnectableObservable;
import java.util.concurrent.ThreadLocalRandom;

public class Ch5_04 {
    public static void main(String[] args) {
        ConnectableObservable<Integer> ints =
                                Observable.range(1, 3).publish();
        Observable<Integer> rInts = ints.map(i -> randomInt());
        rInts.subscribe(i -> System.out.println("Observer 1: " + i));
        rInts.subscribe(i -> System.out.println("Observer 2: " + i));
        ints.connect();
    }
}
```

The output obtained is as follows:

```
Observer 1: 99350
Observer 2: 96343
Observer 1: 4155
Observer 2: 75273
Observer 1: 14280
Observer 2: 97638
```

This occurred because we performed the multicast before the `map()` operator. Even though we consolidated both streams to one set of emissions coming from `Observable.range()`, each `Observer` is still going to get a separate stream at `map()`.

Everything before `publish()` was consolidated into a single stream (or, more technically, a single proxy `Observer`). But after `publish()`, it creates a separate stream for each `Observer` again, as shown in the following diagram:

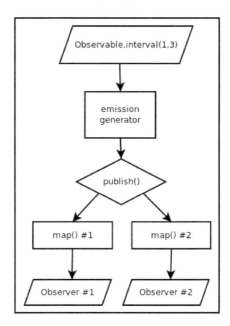

If we want to prevent the `map()` operator from yielding a separate stream for each `Observer`, we need to call `publish()` after `map()` instead:

```java
import io.reactivex.rxjava3.core.Observable;
import io.reactivex.rxjava3.observables.ConnectableObservable;
import java.util.concurrent.ThreadLocalRandom;

public class Ch5_05 {
    public static void main(String[] args) {
        ConnectableObservable<Integer> rInts =
            Observable.range(1, 3).map(i -> randomInt()).publish();
        rInts.subscribe(i -> System.out.println("Observer 1: " + i));
        rInts.subscribe(i -> System.out.println("Observer 2: " + i));
        rInts.connect();
    }
}
```

The output obtained is as follows:

```
Observer 1: 90125
Observer 2: 90125
Observer 1: 79156
Observer 2: 79156
Observer 1: 76782
Observer 2: 76782
```

That's better! Each `Observer` got the same three random integers, and we have effectively multicast the entire operation right before the two observers, as shown in the following diagram. We now have a single stream throughout the entire chain:

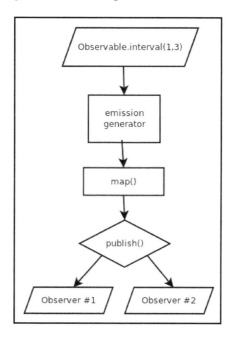

When to multicast

Multicasting is helpful when you need to send the same data to several observers. If the emitted data has to be processed the same way for each of these observers, do it before calling `publish()`. This prevents redundant work being done by multiple observers. You may do this to increase performance, to reduce memory and CPU usage, or simply because your business logic requires pushing the same emissions to all observers.

Make cold observables multicast only when you are doing so for performance reasons and have multiple observers receiving the same data simultaneously. Remember that multicasting creates hot `ConnectableObservables`, and you have to be careful and time the `connect()` call so data is not missed by some observers. Typically in your API, keep your cold observables cold and call `publish()` when you need to make them hot.

Even if your source `Observable` is hot (such as a UI event in JavaFX or Android), putting operators against that `Observable` can cause redundant work in observers. Do not multicast when there is only one `Observer` because multicasting can cause an overhead. However, if there are multiple observers, you need to find the proxy point where you can multicast and consolidate the upstream operations. This point is typically the boundary where observers have common operations upstream and diverge into different operations downstream.

For instance, you may have one `Observer` that prints the random integers but another one that finds the sum with `reduce()`. At this point, that single stream should, in fact, fork into two separate streams because they are no longer redundant and doing different work, as shown in the following code snippet:

```
import io.reactivex.rxjava3.core.Observable;
import io.reactivex.rxjava3.observables.ConnectableObservable;
import java.util.concurrent.ThreadLocalRandom;

public class Ch5_06 {
    public static void main(String[] args) {
        ConnectableObservable<Integer> rInts =
            Observable.range(1, 3).map(i -> randomInt()).publish();
        //Observer 1 - print each random integer
        rInts.subscribe(i -> System.out.println("Observer 1: " + i));

        //Observer 2 - sum the random integers, then print
        rInts.reduce(0, (total, next) -> total + next)
            .subscribe(i -> System.out.println("Observer 2: " + i));
        rInts.connect();
    }
}
```

The output obtained is as follows:

```
Observer 1: 40021
Observer 1: 78962
Observer 1: 46146
Observer 2: 165129
```

Here is a visual diagram showing the common operations being multicasted:

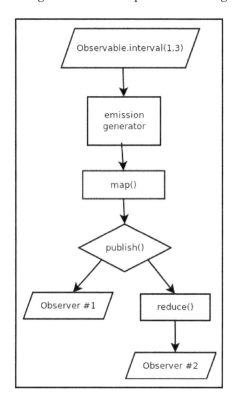

With a thorough understanding of ConnectableObservable and multicasting under our belts, we can move on to some convenient operators that help streamline multicasting.

Automatic connection

There are definitely times you would want to manually call connect() on ConnectableObservable to precisely control when the emissions start firing. There are also operators that automatically call connect() for you, but with this convenience, it is important to have an awareness of their timing behavior. Allowing an Observable to dynamically connect can backfire if you are not careful, as emissions can be missed by observers.

autoConnect()

The `autoConnect(int numberOfSubscribers)` operator on `ConnectableObservable` can be quite handy. For a given `ConnectableObservable<T>`, calling `autoConnect(int numberOfSubscribers)` will return an `Observable<T>` that will automatically call `connect()` after a specified number of observers are subscribed. Since our previous example had two observers, we can streamline it by calling `autoConnect(2)` immediately after `publish()`:

```
import io.reactivex.rxjava3.core.Observable;
import java.util.concurrent.ThreadLocalRandom;

public class Ch5_07 {
    public static void main(String[] args) {
        Observable<Integer> rInts =
            Observable.range(1, 3).map(i -> randomInt()).publish()
                                          .autoConnect(2);
        //Observer 1 - prints each random integer
        rInts.subscribe(i -> System.out.println("Observer 1: " + i));

        //Observer 2 - sums the random integers, then prints
         rInts.reduce(0, (total, next) -> total + next)
              .subscribe(i -> System.out.println("Observer 2: " + i));
    }
}
```

The output obtained is as follows:

```
Observer 1: 83428
Observer 1: 77336
Observer 1: 64970
Observer 2: 225734
```

This saved us the trouble of having to save `ConnectableObservable` and call its `connect()` method later. Instead, it will start firing when it gets 2 subscriptions, which we have planned and specified as an argument in advance. Obviously, this does not work well when you have an unknown number of observers and you want all of them to receive all emissions.

Even when all observers finish or have been disposed of, the `autoConnect()` method persists its subscription to the source. If the source is finite and disposed of, `autoConnect()` does not subscribe to source again when a new `Observer` subscribes downstream. To demonstrate it, we can add a third `Observer` to our example but keep `autoConnect(2)` instead of `autoConnect(3)`. The third `Observer` is going to miss the emissions:

```
import io.reactivex.rxjava3.core.Observable;
import java.util.concurrent.ThreadLocalRandom;

public class Ch5_08 {
    public static void main(String[] args) {
        Observable<Integer> rInts =
            Observable.range(1, 3).map(i -> randomInt()).publish()
                                           .autoConnect(2);
        //Observer 1 - prints each random integer
        rInts.subscribe(i -> System.out.println("Observer 1: " + i));
        //Observer 2 - sums the random integers, then print
        rInts.reduce(0, (total, next) -> total + next)
            .subscribe(i -> System.out.println("Observer 2: " + i));
        //Observer 3 - receives nothing
        rInts.subscribe(i -> System.out.println("Observer 3:" + i));
    }
```

The output obtained is as follows:

```
Observer 1: 8198
Observer 1: 31718
Observer 1: 97915
Observer 2: 137831
```

An overloaded version of `autoConnect()` (without argument) defaults to one subscriber only. This can be helpful if you want it to start firing on the first subscription and do not care about any subsequent observers missing previous emissions. In the following example, we call `publish()` and `autoConnect()` on the `Observable.interval()` observable. The first `Observer` starts firing off the emissions every second, so the emitted integer represents the number of seconds since the first subscription. Then, 3 seconds later, another `Observer` subscribes and misses the first few emissions:

```
import io.reactivex.rxjava3.core.Observable;
import java.util.concurrent.TimeUnit;

public class Ch5_09 {
    public static void main(String[] args) {
        Observable<Long> ints =
                Observable.interval(1, TimeUnit.SECONDS).publish()
```

```
                                                         .autoConnect();
    //Observer 1
    ints.subscribe(i -> System.out.println("Observer 1: " + i));
    sleep(3000);
    //Observer 2
    ints.subscribe(i -> System.out.println("Observer 2: " + i));
    sleep(3000);
  }
}
```

The output obtained is as follows:

```
Observer 1: 0
Observer 1: 1
Observer 1: 2
Observer 1: 3
Observer 2: 3
Observer 1: 4
Observer 2: 4
Observer 1: 5
Observer 2: 5
```

If you pass 0 to autoConnect() for the numberOfSubscribers argument, it will start firing immediately and not wait for any Observers. This can be handy to start firing emissions without waiting for any subscription.

refCount() and share()

The refCount() operator on ConnectableObservable is similar to autoConnect(1), which fires after getting one subscription, with one important difference: after all its observers have been disposed of, it disposes of itself and starts over when a new subscription comes in. It does not persist the subscription to the source when it has no subscribers. When another subscription happens, it essentially **starts over**.

Look at the following example: we have Observable.interval() emitting every second, and it multicasts with refCount(). Observer 1 takes five emissions, and Observer 2 takes two emissions. We stagger their subscriptions with our sleep() function to put a three-second pause between subscriptions. Because these two subscriptions are finite due to the take() operators, they are terminated by the time Observer 3 subscribes. Note how Observer 3 starts over with a fresh set of intervals starting at 0:

```
import io.reactivex.rxjava3.core.Observable;
import java.util.concurrent.TimeUnit;
```

```
public class Ch5_10 {
    public static void main(String[] args) {
        Observable<Long> ints =
                Observable.interval(1, TimeUnit.SECONDS).publish()
                                                        .refCount();
        //Observer 1
        ints.take(5)
            .subscribe(l -> System.out.println("Observer 1: " + l));
        sleep(3000);
        //Observer 2
        ints.take(2)
            .subscribe(l -> System.out.println("Observer 2: " + l));
        sleep(3000);
        //There should be no more subscribers at this point

        //Observer 3
        ints.subscribe(l -> System.out.println("Observer 3: " + l));
        sleep(3000);
    }
}
```

The output obtained is as follows:

```
Observer 1: 0
Observer 1: 1
Observer 1: 2
Observer 1: 3
Observer 2: 3
Observer 1: 4
Observer 2: 4
Observer 3: 0
Observer 3: 1
Observer 3: 2
```

Using `refCount()` can be helpful to multicast between multiple observers, but dispose of the upstream connection when no downstream observers are present anymore. You can also use an alias for `publish().refCount()` using the `share()` operator. This will accomplish the same result:

```
Observable<Long> ints =
                Observable.interval(1, TimeUnit.SECONDS).share();
```

Replaying and caching

Multicasting also allows caching values that are shared across multiple observers. This may sound surprising, but when you think about it long enough, you may realize this makes sense. If we are sharing data across multiple observers, it makes sense that any caching feature would be shared across observers too.

Replaying and caching data is a multicasting activity, and we will explore now how to do it safely and efficiently with RxJava.

Replaying

The `replay()` operator is a powerful way to hold onto previous emissions and re-emit them when a new `Observer` comes in. It returns `ConnectableObservable`, which both multicasts emissions and emits previous emissions. It emits the cached values immediately when a new `Observer` subscribes so it is caught up, and then it fires current emissions from that point forward.

Let's start with a `replay()` with no arguments. This will replay all previous emissions to tardy observers and then emit current emissions as soon as the tardy `Observer` is caught up. If we use `Observable.interval()` to emit every second, we can call `replay()` on it to multicast and replay previous integer emissions. Since `replay()` returns `ConnectableObservable`, let's use `autoConnect()` so that it starts firing on the first subscription. After three seconds, we bring in a second `Observer`:

```
import io.reactivex.rxjava3.core.Observable;
import java.util.concurrent.TimeUnit;

public class Ch5_11 {
    public static void main(String[] args) {
        Observable<Long> ints =
            Observable.interval(1, TimeUnit.SECONDS).replay()
                                                    .autoConnect();
        //Observer 1
        ints.subscribe(l -> System.out.println("Observer 1: " + l));
        sleep(3000);

        //Observer 2
        ints.subscribe(l -> System.out.println("Observer 2: " + l));
        sleep(3000);
    }
}
```

The output obtained is as follows:

```
Observer 1: 0
Observer 1: 1
Observer 1: 2
Observer 2: 0
Observer 2: 1
Observer 2: 2
Observer 1: 3
Observer 2: 3
Observer 1: 4
Observer 2: 4
Observer 1: 5
Observer 2: 5
```

Did you see that? After three seconds, `Observer 2` came in and immediately received the first three emissions it missed: 0, 1, and 2. After that, it receives the same emissions as `Observer 1` going forward. Just note that this can get expensive with memory, as `replay()` will keep caching all the emissions it receives.

If the source is infinite or you only care about the last few emissions, you might want to specify a buffer size by using an overloaded version of the `replay()` method, `replay(int bufferSize)`, to limit it to replaying only a certain number of last emissions. If we call `replay(2)` on our second `Observer` to cache the last two emissions, it will not get 0, but it will receive 1 and 2. The 0 was released from the cache as soon as 2 came in.

The output obtained is as follows:

```
Observer 1: 0
Observer 1: 1
Observer 1: 2
Observer 2: 1
Observer 2: 2
Observer 1: 3
Observer 2: 3
Observer 1: 4
Observer 2: 4
Observer 1: 5
Observer 2: 5
```

Note that if you always want to persist the cached values in your `replay()` even if there are no subscriptions, use it in conjunction with `autoConnect()`, not `refCount()`.

In the following example, the source `Observable` emits "Alpha", "Beta", and "Gamma" strings. Then, we use `replay(1).autoConnect()` to hold on to the last value. The second `Observer` receives only the last value, as expected:

```
import io.reactivex.rxjava3.core.Observable;

public class Ch5_12 {
    public static void main(String[] args) {
        Observable<String> src =
            Observable.just("Alpha", "Beta", "Gamma").replay(1)
                                                .autoConnect();
        //Observer 1
        src.subscribe(l -> System.out.println("Observer 1: " + l));

        //Observer 2
        src.subscribe(l -> System.out.println("Observer 2: " + l));
    }
}
```

The output obtained is as follows:

```
Observer 1: Alpha
Observer 1: Beta
Observer 1: Gamma
Observer 2: Gamma
```

Let's now try and use `refCount()` instead of `autoConnect()`:

```
Observable<String> source = Observable.just("Alpha", "Beta", "Gamma")
                    .replay(1)
                    .refCount();
```

The output obtained is as follows:

```
Observer 1: Alpha
Observer 1: Beta
Observer 1: Gamma
Observer 2: Alpha
Observer 2: Beta
Observer 2: Gamma
```

What happened here is that `refCount()` causes the cache (and the entire chain) to be disposed of and reset the moment `Observer 1` is done, as there are no more observers. When `Observer 2` comes in, it starts all over and emits everything just like `Observer 1` did, and another cache is built. This may not be desirable, so you may consider using `autoConnect()` to persist the state of `replay()` and not have it disposed when no observers are subscribed anymore.

There are other overloads for `replay()`, particularly a version that allows specification of a time-based window. In the following example, we construct an `Observable.interval()` that emits every 300 milliseconds and subscribe to it. We also map each emitted consecutive integer to the elapsed milliseconds. Then, we replay only the last one second of emissions for each new `Observer`, which we add after two seconds:

```
import io.reactivex.rxjava3.core.Observable;
import java.util.concurrent.TimeUnit;

public class Ch5_13 {
    public static void main(String[] args) {
        Observable<Long> seconds =
            Observable.interval(300, TimeUnit.MILLISECONDS)
                    .map(l -> (l + 1) * 300) // map to elapsed millis
                    .replay(1, TimeUnit.SECONDS)
                    .autoConnect();
        //Observer 1
        seconds.subscribe(l -> System.out.println("Observer 1: " + l));
        sleep(2000);

        //Observer 2
        seconds.subscribe(l -> System.out.println("Observer 2: " + l));
        sleep(1000);
    }
}
```

The output obtained is as follows:

```
Observer 1: 300
Observer 1: 600
Observer 1: 900
Observer 1: 1200
Observer 1: 1500
Observer 1: 1800
Observer 2: 1500
Observer 2: 1800
Observer 1: 2100
Observer 2: 2100
Observer 1: 2400
```

```
Observer 2: 2400
Observer 1: 2700
Observer 2: 2700
Observer 1: 3000
Observer 2: 3000
```

Look closely at the output. You can see that when `Observer 2` comes in, it immediately receives emissions that happened in the last second, which were `1500` and `1800`. After these two values are replayed, it receives the same emissions as `Observer 1` from that point on.

In another overloaded version of the `replay()` method, you can also specify a `bufferSize` argument in addition to a time interval, so only a certain number of last emissions are buffered within that time period. If we modify our example to only replay one emission that occurred within the last second, it should only replay `1800` to `Observer 2`:

```
Observable<Long> seconds =
        Observable.interval(300, TimeUnit.MILLISECONDS)
                .map(l -> (l + 1) * 300) // map to elapsed millis
                .replay(1, 1, TimeUnit.SECONDS)
                .autoConnect();
```

The output obtained is as follows:

```
Observer 1: 300
Observer 1: 600
Observer 1: 900
Observer 1: 1200
Observer 1: 1500
Observer 1: 1800
Observer 2: 1800
Observer 1: 2100
Observer 2: 2100
Observer 1: 2400
Observer 2: 2400
Observer 1: 2700
Observer 2: 2700
Observer 1: 3000
Observer 2: 3000
```

Caching

When you want to cache all emissions indefinitely for the long term and do not need to control the subscription behavior to the source with `ConnectableObservable`, you can use the `cache()` operator. This will subscribe to the source on the first downstream `Observer` that subscribes and hold all values indefinitely. This makes it a candidate for an infinite `Observable` or a large amount of data that could exhaust the memory. The following is an example of `ConnectableObservable` usage:

```
import io.reactivex.rxjava3.core.Observable;

public class Ch5_14 {
    public static void main(String[] args) {
        Observable<Integer> cachedRollingTotals =
                Observable.just(6, 2, 5, 7, 1, 4, 9, 8, 3)
                        .scan(0, (total, next) -> total + next)
                        .cache();
        cachedRollingTotals.subscribe(System.out::println);
    }
}
```

You can also call `cacheWithInitialCapacity()` and specify the number of elements to be expected in the cache. This will optimize the buffer for that size of elements in advance:

```
        Observable<Integer> cachedRollingTotals =
                Observable.just(6, 2, 5, 7, 1, 4, 9, 8, 3)
                        .scan(0, (total,next) -> total + next)
                        .cacheWithInitialCapacity(9);
```

 Again, do not use `cache()` unless you really want to hold all elements indefinitely and do not have plans to dispose of it at any point. Otherwise, favor `replay()` so that you can more finely control cache sizing and windows as well as disposal policies.

Subjects

As you will learn, a `Subject` is both an `Observer` and an `Observable`, acting as a proxy multicasting device (similar to an event bus). Subjects have their place in reactive programming, but you should strive to exhaust your other options before utilizing them because, if used under the wrong conditions, they can be very difficult to debug. Erik Meijer, the creator of ReactiveX, described them as the "*mutable variables of reactive programming*".

Just like a mutable variable is necessary at times even though you should strive for immutability, a `Subject` is sometimes a necessary tool to reconcile an imperative paradigm with a reactive one.

But before we discuss when and when not to use the `Subject` class, let's take a look at what it does exactly.

PublishSubject

There are a couple of extensions of the `Subject` abstract class that extend the `Observable` abstract class and implement the `Observer` interface. This means that you can manually call `onNext()`, `onComplete()`, and `onError()` on a `Subject`, and it will, in turn, pass those events downstream to the `Observer` objects that subscribe to it.

The simplest `Subject` type is `PublishSubject`, which, like all `Subject` classes, hotly broadcasts to the `Observer` objects that subscribe to it. Other `Subject` types add more behavior, but `PublishSubject` is the most basic `Subject` extension.

We can declare a `Subject<String>`, create an `Observer` object that maps the `String` value to its length, and subscribes to it. Then, we can call `onNext()` on the `Subject<String>` object and a `String` value to it. We can also call `onComplete()` to communicate that no more events will be passed through this `Subject<String>` object, as follows:

```
import io.reactivex.rxjava3.subjects.PublishSubject;
import io.reactivex.rxjava3.subjects.Subject;

public class Ch5_15 {
    public static void main(String[] args) {
        Subject<String> subject = PublishSubject.create();
        subject.map(String::length)
                .subscribe(System.out::println);

        subject.onNext("Alpha");
        subject.onNext("Beta");
        subject.onNext("Gamma");
        subject.onComplete();
    }
}
```

The output of the preceding snippet provides the following results:

```
5
4
5
```

This shows a `Subject` acting like a bridge between imperative programming and reactive programming.

Next, let's look at cases of when and when not to use the `Subject` type.

When to use Subject

More likely, you will use a `Subject` to eagerly subscribe to an unknown number of multiple source observables and consolidate their emissions in a single `Observable` object. Since a `Subject` is an `Observer` too, you can pass it to a `subscribe()` method. This can be helpful in the modularized code where decoupling between observables and observers takes place and executing `Observable.merge()` is not that easy. Here, for example, we use `Subject` to merge and multicast two `Observable` interval sources as follows:

```java
import io.reactivex.rxjava3.core.Observable;
import io.reactivex.rxjava3.subjects.PublishSubject;
import io.reactivex.rxjava3.subjects.Subject;
import java.util.concurrent.TimeUnit;

public class Ch5_16 {
    public static void main(String[] args) {
        Observable<String> source1 =
            Observable.interval(1, TimeUnit.SECONDS)
                    .map(l -> (l + 1) + " seconds");
        Observable<String> source2 =
            Observable.interval(300, TimeUnit.MILLISECONDS)
                    .map(l -> ((l + 1) * 300) + " milliseconds");
        Subject<String> subject = PublishSubject.create();
        subject.subscribe(System.out::println);
        source1.subscribe(subject);
        source2.subscribe(subject);
        sleep(3000);
    }
}
```

The output obtained is as follows:

```
300 milliseconds
600 milliseconds
900 milliseconds
1 seconds
1200 milliseconds
1500 milliseconds
1800 milliseconds
2 seconds
2100 milliseconds
2400 milliseconds
2700 milliseconds
3 seconds
3000 milliseconds
```

Of course, we could use `Observable.merge()` to accomplish this (and technically, for this case, we should). But when you have modularized code managed through dependency injection or other decoupling mechanisms, you may not have your `Observable` sources prepared in advance to put in `Observable.merge()`.

For example, a JavaFX application may have a refresh event coming from a menu bar, button, or a keystroke combination. In this case, it is possible to declare these event sources as `Observable` objects and subscribe them to a `Subject` in a backing class to consolidate the event streams without any hard coupling.

Another note to make is that the first `Observable` to call `onComplete()` on `Subject` is going to cease the other `Observable` objects from pushing their emissions, and downstream cancellation requests are ignored. This means that you will most likely use a `Subject` for infinite, event-driven (that is, user action-driven) observables.

That being said, we will next look at cases where a `Subject` object becomes prone to abuse.

When a Subject goes wrong

Our preceding `Subject` example emitting `Alpha`, `Beta`, and `Gamma` is probably counterintuitive and backward, considering how we have architected our reactive applications. We did not define the source emissions until the end—after all the observers were set up. With such a layout, the process no longer reads from left to right, and from top to bottom.

Since `Subject` is hot, executing the `onNext()` calls before an `Observer` is set up would result in these emissions being missed with our `Subject`. For example, if you move the `onNext()` calls as shown in the following example, you will not get any output because the `Observer` will miss these emissions:

```
import io.reactivex.rxjava3.subjects.PublishSubject;
import io.reactivex.rxjava3.subjects.Subject;

public class Ch5_17 {
    public static void main(String[] args) {
        Subject<String> subject = PublishSubject.create();
        subject.onNext("Alpha");
        subject.onNext("Beta");
        subject.onNext("Gamma");
        subject.onComplete();
        subject.map(String::length)
                .subscribe(System.out::println);
    }
}
```

This shows that a `Subject` object can be somewhat haphazard and dangerous, especially if you expose them to your entire code base and any external code can call `onNext()` to pass emissions. For instance, let's say a `Subject` object was exposed to an external API and something can arbitrarily pass the emission `Puppy` on top of `Alpha`, `Beta`, and `Gamma`. If we want our source to only emit these Greek letters, it should not be prone to receiving accidental or unwanted emissions.

Reactive programming only maintains integrity when a source `Observable` is derived from a well-defined and predictable source. A `Subject` object is not disposable either, as it has no public `dispose()` method and does not release its sources in the event that the `dispose()` method is called downstream.

if you want to make a source `Observable` object hot, it is much better to keep it cold and to multicast using `publish()` or `replay()`. When you need to use `Subject`, cast it down to `Observable` or just do not expose it at all. You can also wrap a `Subject` object inside a class of some sort and have methods pass the events to it.

Serializing a Subject object

A critical **gotcha** to note with `Subjects` is this: the `onSubscribe()`, `onNext()`, `onError()`, and `onComplete()` calls are not threadsafe! If you have multiple threads calling these four methods, emissions could start to overlap and break the `Observable` contract, which demands that emissions happen sequentially. If this happens, a good practice to adopt is to call `toSerialized()` on the `Subject` object to produce a safely serialized `Subject` implementation (backed by the private `SerializedSubject`). This will safely sequentialize concurrent event calls so that no train wreck occurs downstream. The serialization can be done as follows:

```
Subject<String> subject =
PublishSubject.<String>create().toSerialized();
```

 Unfortunately, due to limitations with the Java compiler (including Java 8), we have to explicitly declare the type parameter `String` for our `create()` factory we used earlier. The compiler's type inference does not cascade beyond more than one method invocation, so having two invocations as previously demonstrated would have a compilation error without an explicit type declaration.

BehaviorSubject

There are a few other flavors of a `Subject`. One of them is the `BehaviorSubject` class. It behaves almost the same way as `PublishSubject`, but it also replays the last emitted item to each new `Observer` downstream. This is somewhat like putting `replay(1).autoConnect()` after `PublishSubject`, but it consolidates these operations into a single optimized `Subject` implementation that subscribes eagerly to the source, as demonstrated by the following example:

```
import io.reactivex.rxjava3.subjects.BehaviorSubject;
import io.reactivex.rxjava3.subjects.Subject;

public class Ch5_18 {
    public static void main(String[] args) {
        Subject<String> subject = BehaviorSubject.create();
        subject.subscribe(s -> System.out.println("Observer 1: " + s));
        subject.onNext("Alpha");
        subject.onNext("Beta");
        subject.onNext("Gamma");
        subject.subscribe(s -> System.out.println("Observer 2: " + s));
    }
}
```

The output obtained is as follows:

```
Observer 1: Alpha
Observer 1: Beta
Observer 1: Gamma
Observer 2: Gamma
```

In the preceding example, you can see that `Observer 2` received the last emission `Gamma` even though it missed the three emissions that `Observer 1` received. If you find yourself needing a `Subject` and want to cache the last emission for every new observer, you can use the `BehaviorSubject` class.

ReplaySubject

The `ReplaySubject` class behaves similar to `PublishSubject` followed by a `cache()` operator. It immediately captures emissions regardless of the presence of a downstream `Observer` and optimizes the caching to occur inside the `Subject` itself. Here is an example:

```java
import io.reactivex.rxjava3.subjects.ReplaySubject;
import io.reactivex.rxjava3.subjects.Subject;

public class Ch5_19 {
    public static void main(String[] args) {
        Subject<String> subject = ReplaySubject.create();
        subject.subscribe(s -> System.out.println("Observer 1: " + s));
        subject.onNext("Alpha");
        subject.onNext("Beta");
        subject.onNext("Gamma");
        subject.onComplete();
        subject.subscribe(s -> System.out.println("Observer 2: " + s));
    }
}
```

The output obtained is as follows:

```
Observer 1: Alpha
Observer 1: Beta
Observer 1: Gamma
Observer 2: Alpha
Observer 2: Beta
Observer 2: Gamma
```

Obviously, just like using a parameter-less `replay()` or `cache()` operator, you need to be wary of using this with a large volume of emissions or infinite sources because it will cache them all and take up memory.

AsyncSubject

The `AsyncSubject` class has a highly tailored, finite-specific behavior: it pushes only the last value it receives, followed by an `onComplete()` event. The following snippet demonstrates this behavior:

```
import io.reactivex.rxjava3.subjects.AsyncSubject;
import io.reactivex.rxjava3.subjects.Subject;

public class Ch5_20 {
    public static void main(String[] args) {
        Subject<String> subject = AsyncSubject.create();
        subject.subscribe(s -> System.out.println("Observer 1: " + s),
                        Throwable::printStackTrace,
                        () -> System.out.println("Observer 1 done!")
        );
        subject.onNext("Alpha");
        subject.onNext("Beta");
        subject.onNext("Gamma");
        subject.onComplete();
        subject.subscribe(s -> System.out.println("Observer 2: " + s),
                        Throwable::printStackTrace,
                        () -> System.out.println("Observer 2 done!")
        );
    }
}
```

The output obtained is as follows:

```
Observer 1: Gamma
Observer 1 done!
Observer 2: Gamma
Observer 2 done!
```

As you can tell from the preceding example, the last value to be pushed to `AsyncSubject` was `Gamma` before `onComplete()` was called. Therefore, the `AsyncSubject` emitted only `Gamma` to all observers. This is a `Subject` object that you do not want to use with infinite sources since it only emits when `onComplete()` is called.

AsyncSubject resembles CompletableFuture from Java 8 as it performs a computation that you can choose to observe for completion and get the value. You can also imitate AsyncSubject using takeLast(1).replay(1) on an Observable. Try to use this approach first before resorting to AsyncSubject.

UnicastSubject

An interesting and possibly helpful kind of Subject is the UnicastSubject class. Like any Subject, it can be used to observe and subscribe to the sources. In addition, it buffers all the emissions it receives until an Observer subscribes to it, and then it releases all the emissions to the Observer and clears its cache. The following snippet demonstrates the behavior described:

```
import io.reactivex.rxjava3.core.Observable;
import io.reactivex.rxjava3.subjects.Subject;
import io.reactivex.rxjava3.subjects.UnicastSubject;
import java.util.concurrent.TimeUnit;

public class Ch5_21 {
    public static void main(String[] args) {
        Subject<String> subject = UnicastSubject.create();
        Observable.interval(300, TimeUnit.MILLISECONDS)
                .map(l -> ((l + 1) * 300) + " milliseconds")
                .subscribe(subject);
        sleep(2000);
        subject.subscribe(s -> System.out.println("Observer 1: " + s));
        sleep(2000);
    }
}
```

The output obtained is as follows:

```
Observer 1: 300 milliseconds
Observer 1: 600 milliseconds
Observer 1: 900 milliseconds
Observer 1: 1200 milliseconds
Observer 1: 1500 milliseconds
Observer 1: 1800 milliseconds
Observer 1: 2100 milliseconds
Observer 1: 2400 milliseconds
Observer 1: 2700 milliseconds
Observer 1: 3000 milliseconds
Observer 1: 3300 milliseconds
```

```
Observer 1: 3600 milliseconds
Observer 1: 3900 milliseconds
```

When you run this code, you will see all these results after two seconds. The first six emissions are released immediately to the Observer when it subscribes. Then, it will receive live emissions from that point on. But there is one important property of UnicastSubject; it works with only one Observer and throws an error for any subsequent one.

Logically, this makes sense because it is designed to release buffered emissions from its internal queue once it gets an Observer. But when the cached emissions are released, they cannot be released again to a second Observer since they are already gone. If you want a second Observer to receive missed emissions, you might as well use ReplaySubject. The benefit of UnicastSubject is that, once it gets the first Observer, it clears its buffer and hence frees the memory used by that buffer.

If you want to support more than one Observer and let them receive the live emissions without receiving the missed emissions, you can call publish() to create a single Observer proxy that multicasts to more than one Observer, as shown in the following code snippet:

```
import io.reactivex.rxjava3.core.Observable;
import io.reactivex.rxjava3.subjects.Subject;
import io.reactivex.rxjava3.subjects.UnicastSubject;
import java.util.concurrent.TimeUnit;

public class Ch5_22 {
    public static void main(String[] args) {
        Subject<String> subject = UnicastSubject.create();
        Observable.interval(300, TimeUnit.MILLISECONDS)
                .map(l -> ((l + 1) * 300) + " milliseconds")
                .subscribe(subject);
        sleep(2000);
        //multicast to support multiple Observers
        Observable<String> multicast = subject.publish().autoConnect();
        //bring in first Observer
        multicast.subscribe(s -> System.out.println("Observer 1:
                            "+ s));
        sleep(2000);
        //bring in second Observer
        multicast.subscribe(s -> System.out.println("Observer 2:
                            "+ s));
        sleep(1000);
    }
}
```

The output obtained is as follows:

```
Observer 1:  300 milliseconds
Observer 1:  600 milliseconds
Observer 1:  900 milliseconds
Observer 1: 1200 milliseconds
Observer 1: 1500 milliseconds
Observer 1: 1800 milliseconds
Observer 1: 2100 milliseconds
Observer 1: 2400 milliseconds
Observer 1: 2700 milliseconds
Observer 1: 3000 milliseconds
Observer 1: 3300 milliseconds
Observer 1: 3600 milliseconds
Observer 1: 3900 milliseconds
Observer 1: 4200 milliseconds
Observer 2: 4200 milliseconds
Observer 1: 4500 milliseconds
Observer 2: 4500 milliseconds
Observer 1: 4800 milliseconds
Observer 2: 4800 milliseconds
```

Summary

In this chapter, you have learned about multicasting using `ConnectableObservable` and `Subject`. The biggest takeaway is that `Observable` operators result in separate streams of events for each `Observer` that subscribes to it. If you want to consolidate these multiple streams into a single stream to prevent redundant work, the best way is to call `publish()` on an `Observable` to yield `ConnectableObservable`. You can then manually call `connect()` to fire emissions once your observers are set up or automatically trigger a connection using `autoConnect()` or `refCount()`.

Multicasting also enables replaying and caching, so a tardy `Observer` can receive missed emissions. A `Subject` object provides a way to multicast and cache emissions as well, but you should only utilize it if existing operators cannot achieve what you want.

In the next chapter, we will start working with concurrency. This is where RxJava truly shines and is often the selling point of reactive programming.

Concurrency and Parallelization

6

The need for concurrency has grown rapidly in the past 10 years and has become a necessity for every professional Java programmer. Concurrency (also called **multithreading**) is essentially **multitasking**, where you have several processes executing at the same time. If you want to fully utilize your hardware's computing power (whether it is a phone, server, laptop, or desktop computer), you need to learn how to multithread and leverage concurrency. Thankfully, RxJava makes concurrency much easier and safer to achieve.

In this chapter, we will cover the following topics:

- Why concurrency is necessary
- Concurrency in a nutshell
- Introducing RxJava concurrency
- Understanding schedulers
- Understanding `subscribeOn()`
- Understanding `observeOn()`
- Parallelization
- Understanding `unsubscribeOn()`

Why concurrency is necessary

In olden days, computers had only one CPU, each much slower than any CPU today, and this made concurrency very limited. Hardware manufacturers successfully found ways to make CPUs faster, and this made single-threaded programs faster and the time-sharing of CPU more productive. But eventually, this had a diminishing return, and manufacturers found they could increase computational power by putting multiple CPUs in a device. From desktops and laptops to servers and smartphones, most hardware nowadays sports multiple CPUs, or cores.

For developers, this is a major disruption in building software and how coding is done. Single-threaded software is easier to code. It works fine on a single-core device, but a single-threaded program on a multi-core device will only use one core, leaving the others not utilized. If you want your program to scale, it needs to be coded in a way that utilizes all available cores.

However, concurrency is traditionally not easy to implement. If you have several independent processes that do not interact with each other, it is easier to accomplish. But when resources, especially mutable objects, are shared across different threads and processes, chaos can ensue if locking and synchronization are not carefully implemented. Not only can threads race each other chaotically to read and change an object's properties, but a thread may simply not notice a value change made by another thread! This is why you should strive to make your objects immutable and make as many properties and variables `final` as possible, while anything that is mutable should be synchronized or at least utilize the `volatile` keyword. Such measures ensure that properties and variables are thread-safe.

Thankfully, RxJava makes concurrency and multithreading much easier and safer. There are ways you can undermine the safety it provides, but generally, RxJava handles concurrency safely for you mainly using two operators: `subscribeOn()` and `observeOn()`. As we will find out in this chapter, other operators such as `flatMap()` can be combined with these two operators to create powerful concurrent dataflows.

 While RxJava can help you make safe and powerful concurrent applications with little effort, be aware of the traps and pitfalls in multithreading. Joshua Bloch's famous book, *Effective Java*, is an excellent resource that every Java developer should have, and it succinctly covers best practices for concurrent applications. If you require an in-depth knowledge of Java concurrency, ensure that you read Brian Goetz's *Java Concurrency in Practice* as well.

Concurrency in a nutshell

Concurrency can be applied in a variety of ways. Usually, the motivation behind concurrency is to run more than one task simultaneously in order to get work done faster. As we discussed at the beginning of this book, concurrency can also help our code resemble the real world more, where multiple activities occur at the same time.

First, let's cover some fundamental concepts behind concurrency.

One common application of concurrency is to run different tasks simultaneously. Imagine that you have three chores: mow the lawn, trim the trees, and pull the weeds. If you do these three chores by yourself, you can only do one chore at a time. You cannot mow the lawn and trim the trees simultaneously. You have to sequentially mow the lawn first, then trim the trees, and then pull the weeds. But if you have a friend to help you, one of you can mow the lawn while the other trims the trees. The first one of you to get done can then move on to the third task: pulling the weeds. This way, these three tasks can be done much more quickly.

Metaphorically, you and your friend are **threads**. You both work at the same time, concurrently. Collectively, you both are a **thread pool** ready to execute tasks. The chores are tasks that are queued for the thread pool, which you can execute two at a time. If you have more threads, your thread pool will have more bandwidth to take on more tasks concurrently.

However, depending on how many cores your computer has (as well as the nature of the tasks), you can only have so many threads. Threads are expensive to create, maintain, and destroy, and there is a diminishing return in performance if you create them excessively. That is why it is better to have a thread pool to *reuse* threads and have them get tasks from a queue.

Understanding parallelization

Parallelization (also called parallelism) is a broad term that could encompass the preceding scenario. In effect, you and your friend are executing two tasks at the same time and are thus processing in parallel. But let's apply parallelization to processing multiple identical tasks at the same time. Take, for example, a grocery store that has 10 customers waiting in a line for checkout. These 10 customers represent 10 tasks that are identical. They each need to check out their groceries. If a cashier represents a thread, we can have multiple cashiers to process these customers more quickly. But like threads, cashiers are expensive. We do not want to create a cashier for each customer, but rather pool a fixed number of cashiers and reuse them. If we have five cashiers, we can process five customers at a time while the rest wait in the queue. The moment a cashier finishes a customer, they can process the next one.

This is essentially what parallelization achieves. If you have 1,000 objects and you need to perform an expensive calculation on each one, you can use five threads to process five objects at a time and potentially finish this process five times quicker. It is critical to pool these threads and reuse them because creating 1,000 threads to process these 1,000 objects could overwhelm your memory and crash your program.

With a conceptual understanding of concurrency, we will move on to discussing how it is achieved in RxJava.

Introducing RxJava concurrency

Concurrency in RxJava is simple to execute, but somewhat abstract to understand. By default, an `Observable` executes on the immediate thread, which is the thread that declared the `Observer` and subscribed it. In many of our earlier examples, this was the main thread that kicked off our `main()` method.

However, as hinted in a few other examples, not every `Observable` fires on the immediate thread. Remember those times we used `Observable.interval()`, as shown in the following code? Let's take a look:

```
import io.reactivex.rxjava3.core.Observable;
import java.time.LocalDateTime;
import java.time.format.DateTimeFormatter;
import java.util.concurrent.TimeUnit;

public class Ch6_01 {
    public static void main(String[] args) {
        DateTimeFormatter f = DateTimeFormatter.ofPattern("MM:ss");
        System.out.println(LocalDateTime.now().format(f));
        Observable.interval(1, TimeUnit.SECONDS)
                .map(i -> LocalDateTime.now().format(f) + " " +
                                        i + " Mississippi")
                .subscribe(System.out::println);
        sleep(5000);
    }
}
```

The output is as follows (the first column is the current time in minutes and seconds):

```
02:50
02:52 0 Mississippi
02:53 1 Mississippi
02:54 2 Mississippi
02:55 3 Mississippi
02:56 4 Mississippi
```

This `Observable` fires on a thread other than the main one. Effectively, the main thread kicks-off `Observable.interval()`, but does not wait for it to complete because it is operating on its own separate thread now. This, in fact, makes it a concurrent application because it is leveraging two threads now. If we do not call a `sleep()` method to pause the main thread, it will charge to the end of the `main()` method and quit the application before the intervals have a chance to fire.

Usually, concurrency is useful only when you have long-running or calculation-intensive processes. To help us learn concurrency without creating noisy examples, we will create a helper method called `intenseCalculation()` to emulate a long-running process. It will simply accept any value, sleep for 0-3 seconds, and then return the same value. Here is this method:

```
import java.util.concurrent.ThreadLocalRandom;

private static <T> T intenseCalculation(T value) {
    sleep(ThreadLocalRandom.current().nextInt(3000));
    return value;
}
public static void sleep(long millis) {
    try {
        Thread.sleep(millis);
    } catch (InterruptedException e) {
        e.printStackTrace();
    }
}
```

Let's now create two observables with two observers subscribing to them. In each operation, we map each emission to the `intenseCalculation()` method in order to slow down the processing, as follows:

```
import io.reactivex.rxjava3.core.Observable;

public class Ch6_02 {
    public static void main(String[] args) {
        Observable.just("Alpha", "Beta", "Gamma")
                .map(s -> intenseCalculation((s)))
                .subscribe(System.out::println);
        Observable.range(1, 3)
                .map(s -> intenseCalculation((s)))
                .subscribe(System.out::println);

    }
}
```

The output is as follows:

```
Alpha
Beta
Gamma
1
2
3
```

Note how both observables fire emissions as each one is slowed by 0-3 seconds in the map() operation. More importantly, note how the first Observable firing Alpha, Beta, and Gamma must finish first and call onComplete() before firing the second Observable emitting the numbers 1 through 3. If we fire both observables at the same time rather than waiting for one to complete before starting the other, we could get this operation done much quicker.

We can achieve this using the subscribeOn() operator, which suggests to the source to fire emissions on a specified Scheduler (separate thread). In this case, let's use Schedulers.computation(), which pools a fixed number of threads appropriate for computation operations. It will provide a thread to push emissions for each Observer. When onComplete() is called, the thread will be given back to Scheduler so it can be reused elsewhere:

```java
import io.reactivex.rxjava3.core.Observable;
import io.reactivex.rxjava3.schedulers.Schedulers;

public class Ch6_03 {
    public static void main(String[] args) {
        Observable.just("Alpha", "Beta", "Gamma")
                .subscribeOn(Schedulers.computation())
                .map(s -> intenseCalculation((s)))
                .subscribe(System.out::println);
        Observable.range(1, 3)
                .subscribeOn(Schedulers.computation())
                .map(s -> intenseCalculation((s)))
                .subscribe(System.out::println);
        sleep(20000);
    }
}
```

The output is as follows (yours may be different):

```
1
Alpha
2
3
```

```
Beta
Gamma
```

Your output will likely be different from this one due to the random sleeping times in the `intenseCalculation()` method. But note how both observables are firing simultaneously now, allowing the program to finish much quicker. Rather than the main thread executing emissions for the first `Observable` before moving onto the second, it now fires off both observables immediately and moves on. It will not wait for either `Observable` to complete. That is why we had to add another `sleep()` method call at the end, in order to give both threads time to finish.

Having multiple processes occurring at the same time is what makes an application concurrent. It can result in much greater efficiency as it utilizes more cores. Concurrency also makes code models more powerful and more representative of how our world works, where multiple activities occur simultaneously.

Something else that is exciting about RxJava is its operators, at least the official ones and the custom ones built properly. They can work with observables on different threads safely. Even operators and factories that combine multiple observables, such as `merge()` and `zip()`, combine safely the emissions pushed by different threads. For instance, we can use `zip()` on our two observables in the preceding example even if they are emitting on two separate computation threads:

```java
import io.reactivex.rxjava3.core.Observable;
import io.reactivex.rxjava3.schedulers.Schedulers;

public class Ch6_04 {
    public static void main(String[] args) {
        Observable<String> source1 =
                Observable.just("Alpha", "Beta", "Gamma")
                        .subscribeOn(Schedulers.computation())
                        .map(s -> intenseCalculation((s)));
        Observable<Integer> source2 =
                Observable.range(1, 3)
                        .subscribeOn(Schedulers.computation())
                        .map(s -> intenseCalculation((s)));
        Observable.zip(source1, source2, (s, i) -> s + "-" + i)
                .subscribe(System.out::println);
        sleep(20000);
    }

}
```

The output is as follows:

```
Alpha-1
Beta-2
Gamma-3
```

Being able to split and combine observables emitting on different threads is a powerful feature that eliminates the pain points of callbacks. Observables are agnostic to the thread they work on, making concurrency easy to implement, configure, and evolve at any time.

 When you start making reactive applications concurrent, a subtle complication can creep in. By default, a non-concurrent application will have one thread doing all the work from the source to the final `Observer`. But having multiple threads can cause emissions to be produced faster than the `Observer` can consume. For instance, the `zip()` operator may have one source producing emissions faster than the other. This can overwhelm the program and memory can run out as backlogged emissions are cached by certain operators. When you are working with a high volume of emissions (more than 10,000) and leveraging concurrency, you will likely want to use Flowable instead of Observable, which we will cover in `Chapter 8`, *Flowable and Backpressure*.

Keeping an application alive

Up until this point, we have used a `sleep()` method to keep concurrent reactive applications from quitting prematurely, just long enough for an `Observable` to complete all emissions. If you are using Android, JavaFX, or other frameworks that manage their own non-daemon threads, this is not a concern as the application will be kept alive for you. But if you are simply firing off a program with a `main()` method and you want to kick off a long-running or infinite `Observable`, you may have to keep the main thread alive for a period of longer than 5-20 seconds. Sometimes, you may want to keep it alive indefinitely.

One way to keep an application alive indefinitely is to simply pass `Long.MAX_VALUE` to the `Thread.sleep()` method, as shown in the following code, where we have `Observable.interval()` firing emissions forever:

```java
import io.reactivex.rxjava3.core.Observable;

public class Ch6_05 {
    public static void main(String[] args) {
        Observable.interval(1, TimeUnit.SECONDS)
                .map(l -> intenseCalculation((l)))
                .subscribe(System.out::println);
```

```
        sleep(Long.MAX_VALUE);
    }
}
```

Okay, sleeping your main thread for 9,223,372,036,854,775,807 milliseconds is not forever, but that is the equivalent to 292,471,208.7 years. For the purposes of pausing a thread, that might as well be forever!

There are ways to keep an application alive only long enough for a subscription to finish. With the classical concurrency tools discussed in Brian Goetz's book *Java Concurrency in Practice,* you can keep an application alive using `CountDownLatch` to wait for two subscriptions to finish. But an easier way is to use blocking operators in RxJava.

Blocking operators stop the declaring thread and wait for emissions. Usually, blocking operators are used for unit testing (as we will discuss in Chapter 10, *Testing and Debugging*), and they can attract antipatterns if used improperly in production. However, keeping an application alive based on the life cycle of a finite `Observable` subscription is a valid case to use a blocking operator. As shown here, `blockingSubscribe()` can be used in place of `subscribe()` to stop and wait for `onComplete()` to be called before the main thread is allowed to proceed and exit the application:

```
import io.reactivex.rxjava3.schedulers.Schedulers;
import io.reactivex.rxjava3.core.Observable;

public class Ch6_06 {
    public static void main(String[] args) {
        Observable.just("Alpha", "Beta", "Gamma", "Delta", "Epsilon")
                .subscribeOn(Schedulers.computation())
                .map(Ch6_6::intenseCalculation)
                .blockingSubscribe(System.out::println,
                        Throwable::printStackTrace,
                        () -> System.out.println("Done!"));
    }
}
```

The output is as follows:

```
Alpha
Beta
Gamma
Delta
Epsilon
Done!
```

We will discuss blocking operators in further detail in `Chapter 10`, *Testing and Debugging*. For the remainder of this chapter, we will explore concurrency in detail using the `subscribeOn()` and `observeOn()` operators. But first, we will cover the different `Scheduler` types available in RxJava.

Understanding schedulers

As discussed earlier, thread pools are a collection of threads. Depending on the policy of that thread pool, threads may be persisted and maintained so they can be reused. A queue of tasks is then executed by the threads from that pool.

Some thread pools hold a fixed number of threads (such as a thread created by the `computation()` method we used earlier), while others dynamically create and destroy threads as needed.

Typically, in Java, you use an `ExecutorService` as a thread pool. However, RxJava implements its own concurrency abstraction called `Scheduler`. This defines methods and rules that an actual concurrency provider such as an `ExecutorService` or actor system must obey. The construct flexibly renders RxJava non-opinionated regarding the source of concurrency.

Many of the default `Scheduler` implementations can be found in the `Schedulers` static factory class. For a given `Observer`, a `Scheduler` provides a thread from a pool that will push the emissions from the `Observable`. When `onComplete()` is called, the operation will be disposed of and the thread will be given back to the pool, where it may be persisted and reused by another `Observer`.

 To keep this book practical, we will only look at a `Scheduler` in the Rx context, used with the `subscribeOn()` or `observeOn()` method. If you want to learn how a `Scheduler` works in isolation, refer to the Appendix *Understanding Schedulers*

The following subsections present a few `Scheduler` types in RxJava. There are also third-party ones available in other libraries such as RxAndroid (covered in `Chapter 11`, *RxJava for Android*) and RxJavaFX (covered later in this chapter).

Computation

We already saw the computation `Scheduler` that is created by the factory `Schedulers.computation()` method. Such a `Scheduler` maintains a fixed number of threads based on processor availability for your Java session, making it appropriate for computational tasks. Computational tasks (such as math, algorithms, and complex logic) may utilize cores to their fullest extent. Therefore, there is no benefit in having more worker threads than available cores to perform such work, and the computational `Scheduler` ensures that. The following is an example of a computational `Scheduler` usage:

```
Observable.just("Alpha", "Beta", "Gamma", "Delta", "Epsilon")
        .subscribeOn(Schedulers.computation());
```

When you are unsure how many tasks will be executed concurrently or are simply unsure which `Scheduler` is the right one to use, prefer the computation one by default.

> A number of operators and factories will use the computation `Scheduler` by default unless you specify a different one as an argument. These include one or more overloads for `interval()`, `delay()`, `timer()`, `timeout()`, `buffer()`, `take()`, `skip()`, `takeWhile()`, `skipWhile()`, `window()`, and a few others.

I/O

I/O tasks, such as reading from and writing to databases, web requests, and disk storage use little CPU power and often have idle time waiting for the data to be sent or received. This allows threads to be created more liberally, and `Schedulers.io()` is appropriate for this. It maintains as many threads as there are tasks and dynamically grows the number of threads, caches them, and discards the threads when they are not needed.

For instance, you may use `Schedulers.io()` to perform SQL operations using RxJava-JDBC (`https://github.com/davidmoten/rxjava2-jdbc`):

```
Database db = Database.from(conn);
Observable<String> customerNames =
        db.select("select name from customer")
            .getAs(String.class)
            .subscribeOn(Schedulers.io());
```

But you have to be careful! As a rule of thumb, assume that each subscription results in a new thread.

New thread

The `Schedulers.newThread()` factory returns a `Scheduler` that does not pool threads at all. It creates a new thread for each `Observer` and then destroys the thread when it is not needed anymore. This is different to `Schedulers.io()` because it does not attempt to persist and cache threads for reuse. The following is an example of the `Schedulers.newThread()` factory method usage:

```
Observable.just("Alpha", "Beta", "Gamma", "Delta", "Epsilon")
        .subscribeOn(Schedulers.newThread());
```

This may be helpful in cases where you want to create, use, and then destroy a thread immediately so that it does not take up memory. But for complex applications generally, you will want to use `Schedulers.io()` so that there is some attempt to reuse threads if possible. You also have to be careful as `Schedulers.newThread()` can run amok in a complex application (as can `Schedulers.io()`) and create a high volume of threads, which could crash the application.

Single

When you want to run tasks sequentially on a single thread, you can use `Schedulers.single()` to create a `Scheduler`. This is backed by a single-threaded implementation appropriate for event looping. It can also be helpful to isolate fragile, non-thread-safe operations to a single thread. The following is an example of the `Schedulers.single()` factory method usage:

```
Observable.just("Alpha", "Beta", "Gamma", "Delta", "Epsilon")
        .subscribeOn(Schedulers.single());
```

Trampoline

A `Scheduler` created by `Schedulers.trampoline()` is an interesting one. Most probably, you will not use it often as it is used primarily in RxJava's internal implementation. Its pattern is also borrowed for UI schedulers such as RxJavaFX and RxAndroid. It is just like default scheduling on the immediate thread, but it prevents cases of recursive scheduling where a task schedules a task while on the same thread. Instead of causing a stack overflow error, it allows the current task to finish first and to execute that new scheduled task only afterward.

ExecutorService

It is also possible to build a `Scheduler` from a standard Java `ExecutorService` pool. You may choose to do this in order to have more custom and fine-tuned control over your thread management policies. For example, say we want to create a `Scheduler` that uses 20 threads. We can create a new fixed `ExecutorService` pool with the specified number of threads. Then, you can wrap it inside a `Scheduler` implementation by calling `Schedulers.from()`, as demonstrated in the following example:

```
import io.reactivex.rxjava3.core.Observable;
import io.reactivex.rxjava3.core.Scheduler;
import io.reactivex.rxjava3.schedulers.Schedulers;
import java.util.concurrent.ExecutorService;
import java.util.concurrent.Executors;

public class Ch6_07 {
    public static void main(String[] args) {
        int numberOfThreads = 20;
        ExecutorService executor =
                Executors.newFixedThreadPool(numberOfThreads);
        Scheduler scheduler = Schedulers.from(executor);
        Observable.just("Alpha", "Beta", "Gamma", "Delta", "Epsilon")
                .subscribeOn(scheduler)
                .doFinally(executor::shutdown)
                .subscribe(System.out::println);
    }
}
```

`ExecutorService` will likely keep your program alive indefinitely, so you have to manage its disposal if its activity is supposed to be finite. If you want to support the life cycle of only one `Observable` subscription, you need to call its `shutdown()` method. That is why, in the preceding example, the `shutdown()` method is called after the processing terminates or is disposed of via the `doFinally()` operator.

Starting and shutting down schedulers

Each default `Scheduler` is lazily instantiated. The `Scheduler` created by the `computation()`, `io()`, `newThread()`, `single()`, or `trampoline()` factory method can be disposed of at any time by calling its `shutdown()` method. Alternatively, all created schedulers can be disposed of by calling `Schedulers.shutdown()`. This stops all their threads and forbids new tasks from coming in and throws an error if you try otherwise. You can also call their `start()` method, or `Schedulersers.start()`, to reinitialize the schedulers so that they can accept tasks again.

In desktop and mobile app environments, you should not run into many cases where you have to start and stop the schedulers. On the server side, however, Java EE-based applications (for example, servlets) may get unloaded and reloaded and use a different classloader, causing the old `Scheduler` instances to leak. To prevent this from occurring, the `Servlet` should shut down the `Schedulers` in its `destroy()` method.

Manage the life cycle of schedulers only if you absolutely have to. It is better to let the schedulers dynamically manage their usage of resources and keep them initialized and available so tasks can quickly be executed at a moment's notice. Note carefully that it is better to ensure that all outstanding tasks are completed or disposed of before you shut down the schedulers, or else you may leave the processing sequences in an inconsistent state.

Understanding subscribeOn()

We have touched on using `subscribeOn()` already, but in this section, we will explore it in more detail and look at how it works.

The `subscribeOn()` operator suggests to the source `Observable` which `Scheduler` to use and how to execute operations on one of its threads. If that source is not already tied to a particular `Scheduler`, it will use the specified `Scheduler`. It will then push emissions *all the way* to the final `Observer` using that thread (unless you add `observeOn()` calls, which we will cover later). You can put `subscribeOn()` anywhere in the `Observable` chain, and it will suggest to the source `Observable` which thread to execute emissions with.

In the following example, it makes no difference whether you put this `subscribeOn()` right after `Observable.just()` or after one of the operators. The `subscribeOn()` operator communicates upstream to `Observable.just()` which `Scheduler` to use no matter where you put it. For clarity, though, you should place it as close to the source as possible, as in the following code:

```
//All three accomplish the same effect with subscribeOn()

Observable.just("Alpha", "Beta", "Gamma", "Delta", "Epsilon")
        .subscribeOn(Schedulers.computation()) //preferred
        .map(String::length)
        .filter(i -> i > 5)
        .subscribe(System.out::println);

Observable.just("Alpha", "Beta", "Gamma", "Delta", "Epsilon")
        .map(String::length)
```

```
            .subscribeOn(Schedulers.computation())
            .filter(i -> i > 5)
            .subscribe(System.out::println);

Observable.just("Alpha", "Beta", "Gamma", "Delta", "Epsilon")
            .map(String::length)
            .filter(i -> i > 5)
            .subscribeOn(Schedulers.computation())
            .subscribe(System.out::println);
```

Having multiple observers to the same `Observable` with `subscribeOn()` results in each one getting its own thread (or have them waiting for an available thread if none are available). In the `Observer`, you can print the executing thread's name by calling `Thread.currentThread().getName()`. In the following example, the thread name is printed with each emission, which shows that two threads, in fact, are being used, one for each `Observer`:

```java
import io.reactivex.rxjava3.core.Observable;
import io.reactivex.rxjava3.schedulers.Schedulers;

public class Ch6_08 {
  public static void main(String[] args) {
      Observable<Integer> lengths =
         Observable.just("Alpha", "Beta", "Gamma", "Delta", "Epsilon")
                     .subscribeOn(Schedulers.computation())
                     .map(Ch6_8::intenseCalculation)
                     .map(String::length);
      lengths.subscribe(i -> System.out.println("Received " + i +
                  " on thread " + Thread.currentThread().getName()));
      lengths.subscribe(i -> System.out.println("Received " + i +
                  " on thread " + Thread.currentThread().getName()));
      sleep(10000);
   }
}
```

The output shows that two threads, in fact, are being used, one for each `Observer`, as follows:

```
Received 5 on thread RxComputationThreadPool-2
Received 4 on thread RxComputationThreadPool-2
Received 5 on thread RxComputationThreadPool-2
Received 5 on thread RxComputationThreadPool-2
Received 5 on thread RxComputationThreadPool-1
Received 7 on thread RxComputationThreadPool-2
```

```
Received 4 on thread RxComputationThreadPool-1
Received 5 on thread RxComputationThreadPool-1
Received 5 on thread RxComputationThreadPool-1
```

In this example, one `Observer` is using a thread named `RxComputationThreadPool-2`, while the other is using `RxComputationThreadPool-1`. These names indicate which `Scheduler` they came from (which is the `Computation` one) and what their index is. As shown here, if we want only one thread to serve both observers, we can multicast this operation. Just make sure that `subscribeOn()` is placed before the multicast operators, as in the following example:

```java
import io.reactivex.rxjava3.core.Observable;
import io.reactivex.rxjava3.schedulers.Schedulers;

public class Ch6_09 {
    public static void main(String[] args) {
        Observable<Integer> lengths =
            Observable.just("Alpha", "Beta", "Gamma", "Delta", "Epsilon")
                        .subscribeOn(Schedulers.computation())
                        .map(Ch6_9::intenseCalculation)
                        .map(String::length)
                        .publish()
                        .autoConnect(2);
        lengths.subscribe(i -> System.out.println("Received " + i +
                    " on thread " + Thread.currentThread().getName()));
        lengths.subscribe(i -> System.out.println("Received " + i +
                    " on thread " + Thread.currentThread().getName()));
        sleep(10000);
    }
```

The output is as follows:

```
Received 5 on thread RxComputationThreadPool-1
Received 5 on thread RxComputationThreadPool-1
Received 4 on thread RxComputationThreadPool-1
Received 4 on thread RxComputationThreadPool-1
Received 5 on thread RxComputationThreadPool-1
Received 5 on thread RxComputationThreadPool-1
Received 5 on thread RxComputationThreadPool-1
```

Most `Observable` factories, such as `Observable.fromIterable()` and `Observable.just()`, create an `Observable` that emits items on the `Scheduler` specified by `subscribeOn()`. For factories such as `Observable.fromCallable()` and `Observable.defer()`, the initialization of these sources also runs on the specified `Scheduler` when using `subscribeOn()`.

For instance, if you use `Observable.fromCallable()` to wait on a URL response, you can make it work on the I/O `Scheduler` so that the main thread is not blocking and waiting for it, as in the following example:

```
import io.reactivex.rxjava3.core.Observable;
import io.reactivex.rxjava3.schedulers.Schedulers;
import java.net.URL;
import java.util.Scanner;

public class Ch6_10 {
    public static void main(String[] args) {
      String href = "https://api.github.com/users/thomasnield/starred";
      Observable.fromCallable(() -> getResponse(href))
                .subscribeOn(Schedulers.io())
                .subscribe(System.out::println);
        sleep(10000);
    }

    private static String getResponse(String path) {
        try {
            return new Scanner(new URL(path).openStream(), "UTF-8")
                                    .useDelimiter("\\A").next();
        } catch (Exception e) {
            return e.getMessage();
        }
    }
}
```

The output is as follows (yours may be different):

```
[{"id":23095928,"name":"RxScala","full_name":"ReactiveX/RxScala","o...
```

Nuances of subscribeOn()

It is important to note that the `subscribeOn()` operator has no practical effect with certain sources (and keeps a worker thread unnecessarily on standby until that operation terminates). This might be because an `Observable` already uses a `Scheduler`. For example, `Observable.interval()` will use `Schedulers.computation()` and will ignore any `subscribeOn()` you specify, as shown here:

```
import io.reactivex.rxjava3.core.Observable;
import io.reactivex.rxjava3.schedulers.Schedulers;

public class Ch6_11 {
    public static void main(String[] args) {
```

```
        Observable.interval(1, TimeUnit.SECONDS)
                .subscribeOn(Schedulers.newThread())
                .subscribe(i -> System.out.println("Received " + i +
                    " on thread " + Thread.currentThread().getName()));
        sleep(5000);
    }
}
```

The output is as follows:

```
Received 0 on thread RxComputationThreadPool-1
Received 1 on thread RxComputationThreadPool-1
Received 2 on thread RxComputationThreadPool-1
Received 3 on thread RxComputationThreadPool-1
Received 4 on thread RxComputationThreadPool-1
```

As you can see, the thread used is a `Computation` one, and not a `newThread`. If you want to change it, you can provide a `Scheduler` as a third argument to specify a different `Scheduler` to use. Here, `Observable.interval()` is set to use the `Scheduler` created by the `Schedulers.newThread()` factory method:

```
import io.reactivex.rxjava3.core.Observable;
import io.reactivex.rxjava3.schedulers.Schedulers;

public class Ch6_12 {
    public static void main(String[] args) {
        Observable.interval(1, TimeUnit.SECONDS, Schedulers.newThread())
                .subscribe(i -> System.out.println("Received " + i +
                    " on thread " + Thread.currentThread().getName()));
        sleep(5000);
    }
}
```

The output is as follows:

```
Received 0 on thread RxNewThreadScheduler-1
Received 1 on thread RxNewThreadScheduler-1
Received 2 on thread RxNewThreadScheduler-1
Received 3 on thread RxNewThreadScheduler-1
Received 4 on thread RxNewThreadScheduler-1
```

As was expected, the used thread is `NewThread` now.

This brings up the following point: if you have multiple `subscribeOn()` calls on a given `Observable` chain, the top-most one, or the one closest to the source, will win and cause any subsequent ones to have no practical effect (other than unnecessary resource usage). If `subscribeOn()` is used with `Schedulers.computation()` and downstream, another `subscribeOn()` with `Schedulers.io()` (or any other `Scheduler` factory method) is used, the `Computation` thread remains in use, as the following code demonstrates:

```
import io.reactivex.rxjava3.core.Observable;
import io.reactivex.rxjava3.schedulers.Schedulers;

public class Ch6_13 {
    public static void main(String[] args) {
        Observable.just("Alpha", "Beta", "Gamma", "Delta", "Epsilon")
                .subscribeOn(Schedulers.computation())
                .filter(s -> s.length() == 5)
                .subscribeOn(Schedulers.io())
                .subscribe(i -> System.out.println("Received " + i +
                    " on thread " + Thread.currentThread().getName()));
        sleep(5000);
    }
}
```

The output is as follows:

```
Received Alpha on thread RxComputationThreadPool-1
Received Gamma on thread RxComputationThreadPool-1
Received Delta on thread RxComputationThreadPool-1
```

It can happen that an API returns an `Observable` already preset with a `Scheduler` via `subscribeOn()`, although the consumer of the API wants a different `Scheduler`. That's why API designers are encouraged to provide methods or overloads that allow parameterizing which `Scheduler` to use, just like RxJava's scheduler-dependent factory (for example, `Observable.interval()`) does.

In summary, `subscribeOn()` specifies which `Scheduler` the source `Observable` should use, and it will use a worker from this `Scheduler` to push emissions all the way to the final `Observer`. But watch out if there is a `subscribeOn()` operator already in use upstream and this does not allow an override.

Next, we will learn about `observeOn()`, which switches to a different `Scheduler` at that point in the `Observable` chain.

Understanding observeOn()

The `subscribeOn()` operator instructs the source `Observable` which `Scheduler` to emit emissions on. If `subscribeOn()` is the only concurrent operation in an `Observable` chain, the thread from that `Scheduler` will work the entire `Observable` chain, pushing emissions from the source all the way to the final `Observer`. The `observeOn()` operator, however, will intercept emissions at that point in the `Observable` chain and switch them to a different `Scheduler` going forward.

Unlike `subscribeOn()`, the placement of `observeOn()` matters. It leaves all operations upstream on the default or `subscribeOn()`-defined `Scheduler`, but switches to a different `Scheduler` downstream. In the following example, an `Observable` emits a series of strings (that are /-separated values), which are then split on an I/O `Scheduler`. But after that, the `observeOn()` operator switches to a computation `Scheduler` to filter only numbers and calculate their sum:

```java
import io.reactivex.rxjava3.core.Observable;
import io.reactivex.rxjava3.schedulers.Schedulers;

public class Ch6_14 {
   public static void main(String[] args) {
      Observable.just("WHISKEY/27653/TANGO",
                            "6555/BRAVO","232352/5675675/FOXTROT")
            .subscribeOn(Schedulers.io())      //Starts on I/O scheduler
            .flatMap(s -> Observable.fromArray(s.split("/")))
            .observeOn(Schedulers.computation()) //Switches to
                                           // computation scheduler
            .filter(s -> s.matches("[0-9]+"))
            .map(Integer::valueOf)
            .reduce((total, next) -> total + next)
            .subscribe(i -> System.out.println("Received " + i +
                  " on thread " + Thread.currentThread().getName()));
      sleep(1000);
   }
}
```

The output is as follows:

```
Received 5942235 on thread RxComputationThreadPool-1
```

Of course, this example is not computationally intensive, and in real life, it should be done on a single thread. The overhead of concurrency that we introduced is not warranted, but let's pretend it is a long-running process.

Again, the observeOn() operator intercepts each emission and pushes it forward on a different Scheduler. In the preceding example, operators before observeOn() are executed on Scheduler.io(), but the ones after it are executed by Schedulers.computation(). Upstream operators before observeOn() are not impacted, but downstream ones are.

You might use observeOn() for a situation like the one emulated earlier. If you want to read one or more data sources and wait for the response to come back, you will want to do that part on Schedulers.io() and will likely leverage subscribeOn() since that is the initial operation. But once you have that data, you may want to execute intensive computations with it, and Scheduler.io() may no longer be appropriate. You will want to constrain these operations to a few threads that will fully utilize the CPU. Therefore, you use observeOn() to redirect data to Schedulers.computation().

You can actually use multiple observeOn() operators to switch Schedulers more than once. Continuing with our earlier example, let's say we want to write our computed sum to a disk and write it in a file. Let's pretend this was a lot of data rather than a single number and we want to get this disk-writing operation off the computation Scheduler and put it back in the I/O Scheduler. We can achieve this by introducing a second observeOn(). Let's also add the doOnNext() and doOnSuccess() (due to the Maybe) operators to take a peek at which thread each operation is using:

```java
public class Ch6_15 {
    public static void main(String[] args) {
        //Happens on I/O scheduler
        Observable.just("WHISKEY/27653/TANGO",
                    "6555/BRAVO", "232352/5675675/FOXTROT")
            .subscribeOn(Schedulers.io())
            .flatMap(s -> Observable.fromArray(s.split("/")))
            .doOnNext(s -> System.out.println("Split out " + s +
                    " on thread " + Thread.currentThread().getName()))
            .observeOn(Schedulers.computation()) //Happens on
                                                 //computation scheduler
            .filter(s -> s.matches("[0-9]+"))
            .map(Integer::valueOf)
            .reduce((total, next) -> total + next)
            .doOnSuccess(i -> System.out.println("Calculated sum" + i +
                    " on thread " + Thread.currentThread().getName()))
            .observeOn(Schedulers.io()) //Switches back to I/O scheduler
            .map(i -> i.toString())
```

```
            .doOnSuccess(s -> System.out.println("Writing " + s +
                " to file on thread " + Thread.currentThread().getName()))
            .subscribe(s -> write(s, "/home/thomas/Desktop/output.txt"));
        sleep(1000);
    }
  }
```

The implementation of the `write()` method looks as follows:

```
public static void write(String text, String path) {
    BufferedWriter writer = null;
    try {
        //create a temporary file
        File file = new File(path);
        writer = new BufferedWriter(new FileWriter(file));
        writer.append(text);
    } catch (Exception e) {
        e.printStackTrace();
    } finally {
        try {
            writer.close();
        } catch (Exception e) {}
    }
}
```

The output is as follows:

```
Split out WHISKEY on thread RxCachedThreadScheduler-1
Split out 27653 on thread RxCachedThreadScheduler-1
Split out TANGO on thread RxCachedThreadScheduler-1
Split out 6555 on thread RxCachedThreadScheduler-1
Split out BRAVO on thread RxCachedThreadScheduler-1
Split out 232352 on thread RxCachedThreadScheduler-1
Split out 5675675 on thread RxCachedThreadScheduler-1
Split out FOXTROT on thread RxCachedThreadScheduler-1
Calculated sum 5942235 on thread RxComputationThreadPool-1
Writing 5942235 to file on thread RxCachedThreadSchedule
```

If you look closely at the output, you will see that the `String` emissions were initially pushed and split on the I/O `Scheduler` via the `RxCachedThreadScheduler-1` thread. After that, each emission was switched to the computation `Scheduler` and pushed into a sum calculation, which was all done on the `RxComputationThreadPool-1` thread. That sum was then switched to the I/O `Scheduler` to be written to a text file (which is specified to output on the Linux Mint desktop), and that work was done on `RxCachedThreadScheduler-1` (which happened to be the thread that pushed the initial emissions and was reused!).

Using observeOn() for UI event threads

When it comes to building mobile apps, desktop applications, and other user-facing programs, users have little patience for interfaces that hang up or freeze while work is being done. The visual updating of user interfaces is often done by a single dedicated UI thread, and changes to the user interface must be done on that thread. User input events are typically fired on the UI thread as well. If a user input triggers work, and that work is not moved to another thread, that UI thread becomes busy. This is what makes the user interface unresponsive, and today's users expect better than this. They want to continue interacting with the application while work is happening in the background, so concurrency is a must-have.

Thankfully, RxJava comes to the rescue! You can use `observeOn()` to move UI events to a computation or I/O `Scheduler` to do the work, and when the result is ready, move it back to the UI thread with another `observeOn()`. This second usage of `observeOn()` puts emissions on a UI thread, using a custom `Scheduler` that wraps around the UI thread. RxJava extension libraries such as RxAndroid (https://github.com/ReactiveX/RxAndroid), RxJavaFX (https://github.com/ReactiveX/RxJavaFX), and RxSwing (https://github.com/ReactiveX/RxSwing) come with these custom `Scheduler` implementations.

For instance, say we have a simple JavaFX application that displays a `ListView<String>` of the 50 U.S. states every time a button is clicked on. We can create `Observable<ActionEvent>` off the button and then switch to an I/O `Scheduler` with `observeOn()` (`subscribeOn()` will have no effect on UI event sources). We can load the 50 states from a text web response while on the I/O `Scheduler`. Once the states are returned, we can use another `observeOn()` to put them back on `JavaFxScheduler`, and safely populate them in `ListView<String>` on the JavaFX UI thread, as follows:

```
public final class Ch6_16 extends Application {
    @Override
    public void start(Stage stage) throws Exception {
        VBox root = new VBox();
        ListView<String> listView = new ListView<>();
        Button refreshButton = new Button("REFRESH");
        JavaFxObservable.actionEventsOf(refreshButton)
                    .observeOn(Schedulers.io())
                    .flatMapSingle(a -> Observable
                        .fromArray(getResponse("https://goo.gl/S0xuOi")
                        .split("\\r?\\n")).toList())
                    .observeOn(JavaFxScheduler.platform())
                    .subscribe(list -> listView.getItems()
                                            .setAll(list));
        root.getChildren().addAll(listView, refreshButton);
        stage.setScene(new Scene(root));
```

```
        stage.show();
    }
}
```

The `getResponse()` method is implemented as follows:

```
private static String getResponse(String path) {
    try {
        return new Scanner(new URL(path).openStream(),
                            "UTF-8").useDelimiter("\\A").next();
    } catch (Exception e) { return e.getMessage(); }
}
```

Please note that this code is not for RxJava 3.0 because JavaFX does not support it yet. Nevertheless, this code is successfully building and executing with RxJava 3.0, too. Here are some import statements for your reference:

```
import io.reactivex.Observable;
import io.reactivex.schedulers.Schedulers;
import io.reactivex.rxjavafx.observables.JavaFxObservable;
import io.reactivex.rxjavafx.schedulers.JavaFxScheduler;
import javafx.application.Application;
import javafx.scene.Scene;
import javafx.scene.control.Button;
import javafx.scene.control.ListView;
import javafx.scene.layout.VBox;
import javafx.stage.Stage;
import java.net.URL;
import java.util.Scanner;
```

If you run this JavaFX application, you will get the following screen first:

Clicking the **REFRESH** button will emit an event but switch it to an I/O `Scheduler` where the work is done to retrieve the U.S. states. When the response is ready, it emits a `List<String>` and puts it back on the JavaFX `Scheduler` to be displayed in a `ListView`, as follows:

These concepts apply to Android development as well, where all operations affecting the app user interface are run on `AndroidSchedulers.mainThread()` rather than `JavaFxScheduler.platform()`. We will cover Android development in `Chapter 11`, *RxJava for Android*.

Nuances of observeOn()

The `observeOn()` operator comes with nuances to be aware of, especially when it comes to performance implications due to a lack of backpressure, which we will cover in `Chapter 8`, *Flowable and Backpressure*.

Let's say you have a chain of `Observable` operators with two sets of operations, Operation A and Operation B. Let's not worry what operators each one is using. If you do not have any `observeOn()` between them, the operation will pass emissions strictly one at a time from the source to Operation A, then to Operation B, and finally to the `Observer`. Even with `subscribeOn()`, the source will not pass the next emission down the chain until the current one is passed all the way to the `Observer`.

This changes when you introduce an `observeOn()`, and let's say that we put it between Operation A and Operation B. After Operation A hands an emission to the `observeOn()` operator, it will immediately start the next emission and not wait for the downstream to finish the current one, including Operation B and the `Observer`. This means that the source and Operation A can *produce* emissions faster than Operation B and the `Observer` can *consume* them. This is a classic producer/consumer scenario where the producer is producing emissions faster than the consumer can consume them. If this is the case, unprocessed emissions will be queued in `observeOn()` until the downstream is able to process them. But if you have a lot of emissions, you can potentially run into memory issues.

This is why, when you have a flow of 10,000 emissions or more, you have to use a `Flowable` (which supports backpressure) instead of an `Observable`. Backpressure communicates upstream all the way to the source to slow down and only produce so many emissions at a time. It restores the *pull-based* requesting of emissions even when complex concurrency operations are introduced. We will cover this in `Chapter 8`, *Flowable and Backpressure*.

Parallelization

Parallelization, also called **parallelism** or **parallel computing**, is a broad term that can be used for any concurrent activity (including what we covered). But for the purposes of RxJava, let's define it as processing multiple emissions at a time for a given `Observable`. If we have 1,000 emissions to process in a given `Observable` chain, we might be able to get work done faster if we process eight emissions at a time instead of one. If you recall, the `Observable` contract dictates that emissions must be pushed *serially* down an `Observable` chain and never race each other due to concurrency. As a matter of fact, pushing eight emissions down an `Observable` chain at a time would be downright catastrophic and wreak havoc.

This seems to put us at odds with what we want to accomplish, but thankfully, RxJava gives you enough operators and tools to be clever. While you cannot push items concurrently on the same `Observable`, you are allowed to have multiple observables running at once, each having its own single thread pushing items through. As we have done throughout this chapter, we created several observables running on different threads/schedulers and *even combined them*. You actually have the tools already, and the secret to achieving parallelization is in the `flatMap()` operator, which is, in fact, a powerful concurrency operator.

Here, we have an `Observable` emitting 10 integers, and we are performing `intenseCalculation()` on each one. This process can take a while due to the artificial processing we emulated with `sleep()`. Let's print each one with the time in the `Observer` so that we can measure the performance, as shown in the following code:

```
import io.reactivex.rxjava3.core.Observable;
import java.util.concurrent.ThreadLocalRandom;

public class Ch6_17 {
    public static void main(String[] args) {
        Observable.range(1, 10)
                .map(i -> intenseCalculation(i))
                .subscribe(i -> System.out.println("Received " + i +
                                          " " + LocalTime.now()));
    }
    public static <T> T intenseCalculation(T value) {
        sleep(ThreadLocalRandom.current().nextInt(3000));
        return value;
    }
}
```

The output is as follows (yours will be different):

```
Received 1 19:11:41.812
Received 2 19:11:44.174
Received 3 19:11:45.588
Received 4 19:11:46.034
Received 5 19:11:47.059
Received 6 19:11:49.569
Received 7 19:11:51.259
Received 8 19:11:54.192
Received 9 19:11:56.196
Received 10 19:11:58.926
```

The randomness causes some variability, of course, but in this instance, it took roughly 17 seconds to complete (although your time will likely vary). We will probably get better performance if we process emissions in parallel, so how do we do that?

Remember, emitting items one at a time happens on the same `Observable`. The `flatMap()` operator then merges multiple observables derived off each emission even if they are *concurrent*. If a light bulb has not gone off yet, read on.

Inside `flatMap()`, let's wrap each emission into `Observable.just()`, use `subscribeOn()` to emit it on `Schedulers.computation()`, and then `map` it to `intenseCalculation()`. For good measure, let's print the current thread in the `Observer` as well, as shown in the following code:

```
import io.reactivex.rxjava3.core.Observable;
import io.reactivex.rxjava3.schedulers.Schedulers;

public class Ch6_18 {
    public static void main(String[] args) {
        Observable.range(1, 10)
                .flatMap(i -> Observable.just(i)
                        .subscribeOn(Schedulers.computation())
                        .map(i2 -> intenseCalculation(i2)))
                .subscribe(i -> System.out.println("Received " + i +
                        " " + LocalTime.now() + " on thread " +
                            Thread.currentThread().getName()));
        sleep(20000);
    }
}
```

The output is as follows (yours will be different):

```
Received 1 19:28:11.163 on thread RxComputationThreadPool-1
Received 7 19:28:11.381 on thread RxComputationThreadPool-7
Received 9 19:28:11.534 on thread RxComputationThreadPool-1
Received 6 19:28:11.603 on thread RxComputationThreadPool-6
Received 8 19:28:11.629 on thread RxComputationThreadPool-8
Received 3 19:28:12.214 on thread RxComputationThreadPool-3
Received 4 19:28:12.961 on thread RxComputationThreadPool-4
Received 5 19:28:13.274 on thread RxComputationThreadPool-5
Received 2 19:28:13.374 on thread RxComputationThreadPool-2
Received 10 19:28:14.335 on thread RxComputationThreadPool-2
```

It took only 3 seconds to process all the emitted items, which is much faster than 17 seconds. Of course, the computer where this code was run had 8 cores, and that was why 8 threads were used. If your computer has fewer cores, this process will take longer and use fewer threads. But it will likely still be faster than the single-threaded implementation we ran earlier.

As you can see, we created an `Observable` from each emission, used `subscribeOn()` to emit it on the computation `Scheduler`, and then performed the `intenseCalculation()` on the computation thread. Each emission is processed on its own thread from the computation `Scheduler`. The `flatMap()` operator then merges all of them safely back into a sequential stream.

`flatMap()` allows only one thread out of it at a time to push emissions downstream, which maintains that the `Observable` contract demanding emissions stays sequential. A neat little behavior with `flatMap()` is that it does not use excessive synchronization or blocking to accomplish this. If a thread is already pushing an emission out of `flatMap()` downstream toward `Observer`, any threads also waiting to push emissions will simply leave their emissions for that occupying thread to take ownership of.

However, the preceding example is not optimal. Creating an `Observable` for each emission might create some unwanted overhead. There is a leaner way to achieve parallelization, although it has a few more moving parts. If we want to avoid creating excessive `Observable` instances, maybe we should split the source `Observable` into a fixed number of observables where emissions are evenly divided and distributed through each one. Then, we can parallelize and merge them using `flatMap()`. Even better, if there are eight cores on the computer, maybe it would be ideal to have eight observables for eight streams of calculations.

We can achieve this using a `groupBy()` trick. If there are eight cores, we can key each emission to a number in the range from 0 through 7. This way, eight instances of `GroupedObservable` are created that cleanly divide the emissions into eight streams. Now, we can cycle through these eight numbers and assign them as a key to each emission. None of the `GroupedObservable` instances is impacted by `subscribeOn()` (it will emit on the source's thread with the exception of the cached emissions), so we need to use `observeOn()` to parallelize them instead. We can use an `io()` or `newThread()` scheduler since we have already constrained the number of workers to the number of cores simply by constraining the number of `GroupedObservable` instances.

In the following example, instead of hardcoding for eight cores, we dynamically query the number of cores available:

```
import io.reactivex.rxjava3.core.Observable;
import io.reactivex.rxjava3.schedulers.Schedulers;

public class Ch6_19 {
    public static void main(String[] args) {
        int coreCount = Runtime.getRuntime().availableProcessors();
        AtomicInteger assigner = new AtomicInteger(0);
        Observable.range(1, 10)
                .groupBy(i -> assigner.incrementAndGet() % coreCount)
                .flatMap(grp -> grp.observeOn(Schedulers.io())
                                .map(i2 -> intenseCalculation(i2)))
                .subscribe(i -> System.out.println("Received " + i +
                        " " + LocalTime.now() + " on thread " +
```

```
                                       Thread.currentThread().getName()));
            sleep(20000);
        }
    }
```

Here is the output (yours will be different):

```
Received 8 20:27:03.291 on thread RxCachedThreadScheduler-8
Received 6 20:27:03.446 on thread RxCachedThreadScheduler-6
Received 5 20:27:03.495 on thread RxCachedThreadScheduler-5
Received 4 20:27:03.681 on thread RxCachedThreadScheduler-4
Received 7 20:27:03.989 on thread RxCachedThreadScheduler-7
Received 2 20:27:04.797 on thread RxCachedThreadScheduler-2
Received 1 20:27:05.172 on thread RxCachedThreadScheduler-1
Received 9 20:27:05.327 on thread RxCachedThreadScheduler-1
Received 10 20:27:05.913 on thread RxCachedThreadScheduler-2
Received 3 20:27:05.957 on thread RxCachedThreadScheduler-3
```

For each emission, we had to increment the number it groups on, and after it reaches 7, it will start over at 0. This ensures that the emissions are distributed as evenly as possible. We achieve this using AtomicInteger with a modulus operation. If we keep incrementing AtomicInteger for each emission, we can divide that result by the numbers of cores, but return the remainder, which will always be a number between 0 and 7.

 An AtomicInteger instance is just an integer, protected inside a thread-safe container that has convenient thread-safe methods, such as incrementAndGet(). Typically, when you have an object or state existing outside an Observable chain, but which is modified by the Observable chain's operations (this is known as creating side effects), that object should be made thread-safe, especially when concurrency is involved. You can learn more about AtomicInteger and other utilities in Brian Goetz's *Java Concurrency in Practice*.

You do not have to use the cores count to control how many GroupedObservable instances are created. You can specify any number if you, for some reason, deem that more workers would result in better performance. If your concurrent operations are a mix between I/O and computation, and you find that there is more I/O, you might benefit from increasing the number of threads.

Understanding unsubscribeOn()

One last concurrency operator that we need to cover is unsubscribeOn(). Disposing of an Observable can be an expensive (in terms of the time it takes) operation, depending on the nature of the source. For instance, if the Observable emits the results of a database query using RxJava-JDBC, (https://github.com/davidmoten/rxjava-jdbc), it can be expensive to dispose of because it needs to shut down the JDBC resources it is using. This can cause the thread that calls dispose() to become busy. If this is a UI thread in JavaFX or Android (for instance, because a **CANCEL PROCESSING** button was clicked), this can cause undesirable UI freezing.

Here is a simple Observable that is emitting every second. We stop the main thread for 3 seconds and then call dispose() to shut the operation down. Let's use doOnDispose() (which will be executed by the disposing thread) to see that the main thread is indeed disposing of the operation in the following code:

```java
import io.reactivex.rxjava3.core.Observable;
import io.reactivex.rxjava3.schedulers.Schedulers;

public class Ch6_20 {
    public static void main(String[] args) {
        Disposable d = Observable.interval(1, TimeUnit.SECONDS)
            .doOnDispose(() -> System.out.println("Disposing on thread "
                                + Thread.currentThread().getName()))
                .subscribe(i -> System.out.println("Received " + i));
        sleep(3000);
        d.dispose();
        sleep(3000);
    }}
}
```

The output is as follows:

```
Received 0
Received 1
Received 2
Disposing on thread main
```

Let's add `unsubscribeOn()` and set it to be executed on the `Schedulers.io()` scheduler. You can put `unsubscribeOn()` wherever you want all the operations upstream to be affected:

```
import io.reactivex.rxjava3.core.Observable;
import io.reactivex.rxjava3.disposables.Disposable;
import io.reactivex.rxjava3.schedulers.Schedulers;

public class Ch6_21 {
    public static void main(String[] args) {
        Disposable d = Observable.interval(1, TimeUnit.SECONDS)
            .doOnDispose(() -> System.out.println("Disposing on thread "
                                    + Thread.currentThread().getName()))
            .unsubscribeOn(Schedulers.io())
            .subscribe(i -> System.out.println("Received " + i));
        sleep(3000);
        d.dispose();
        sleep(3000);
    }
}
```

The output is as follows:

```
Received 0
Received 1
Received 2
Disposing on thread RxCachedThreadScheduler-1
```

Now, you will see that disposal is being done by the I/O `Scheduler`, whose thread is identified by the name `RxCachedThreadScheduler-1`. This allows the main thread to kick off disposal and continue without waiting for it to complete.

Like any concurrency operators, you really should not need to use `unsubscribeOn()` for lightweight operations such as this example, as it adds unnecessary overhead. But if you have `Observable` operations that are heavy with resources that are slow to dispose of, `unsubscribeOn()` can be a crucial tool if threads calling `dispose()` are sensitive to high workloads.

You can use multiple `unsubscribeOn()` calls if you want to target specific parts of the `Observable` chain to be disposed of with different schedulers. Everything downstream (after) of an `unsubscribeOn()` will be disposed of until another `unsubscribeOn()` is encountered, which will own the next upstream segment.

Summary

This was probably our most intense chapter yet, but it provides a turning point in your proficiency as an RxJava developer as well as a master of concurrency! We covered the different schedulers available in RxJava, as well as ones available in other libraries such as RxJavaFX and RxAndroid. The `subscribeOn()` operator is used to suggest to the upstream in an `Observable` chain which `Scheduler` to push emissions on. `observeOn()` switches emissions to a different `Scheduler` *at that point* in the `Observable` chain and uses that `Scheduler` downstream. You can use these two operators in conjunction with `flatMap()` to create powerful parallelization patterns so that you can fully utilize your multi-CPU power. We finally covered `unsubscribeOn()`, which helps us to specify a different `Scheduler` to dispose of operations on, preventing subtle hang-ups on threads we want to keep free and available even if they call the `dispose()` method.

It is important to note that when you start working with concurrency, you need to become wary of how much data you are juggling between threads now. A lot of data can queue up in your `Observable` chain, and some threads produce work faster than other threads can consume them. When you are dealing with 10,000+ elements, you need to use a `Flowable` to prevent memory issues, and we will cover this in `Chapter 8`, *Flowable and Backpressure*.

Meanwhile, the next chapter will explain how to deal with an observable that produces emissions too quickly. There are some operators that can help with this without backpressure and we will discuss how to use them.

7
Switching, Throttling, Windowing, and Buffering

It is not uncommon to run into a situation when an Observable is producing emissions faster than an Observer can consume them. This happens particularly during concurrent processing, when the Observable chain has different operators running on different schedulers. Whether it is one operator struggling to keep up with the elements coming from upstream, or the final Observer, a bottleneck can occur in an operator where emissions start to queue up.

Of course, the ideal way to handle a bottleneck is to leverage backpressure using Flowable instead of Observable. The Flowable class is not much different to the Observable class. It differs only in its ability to tell the source to slow down when the Observer requests emissions at its own pace, as we will learn about in Chapter 8, *Flowable and Backpressure*. But not every source of emissions can respond to backpressure and adjust the rate of the emission. For example, you cannot instruct Observable.interval() (or even Flowable.interval()) to slow down because their emissions are time-sensitive. Asking it to slow down would make those time-based emissions inaccurate. Another example is user input events, such as button clicks. Such a source cannot be backpressured either because you cannot programmatically control the user's actions.

Thankfully, there are operators that help cope with rapidly firing sources without using backpressure and are especially appropriate for situations where backpressure cannot be utilized. Some of these operators batch up emissions into chunks that are more easily consumed downstream. Others simply sample emissions while ignoring the rest. There is even a powerful switchMap() operator that functions similarly to flatMap(), but will only subscribe to the Observable derived from the latest emission and dispose of any previous ones.

In this chapter, we will cover the following topics:

- Buffering
- Windowing
- Throttling
- Switching

We will end the chapter with an exercise that groups up the keystrokes to emit strings of user inputs.

Buffering

The `buffer()` operator gathers emissions within a certain scope and emits each batch as a list or another collection type. The scope can be defined by a fixed buffer sizing or a timing window that cuts off at intervals or even slices by the emissions of another `Observable`.

Fixed-size buffering

The simplest overload for `buffer()` accepts a `count` argument as the buffer size and groups emissions in the batches of the specified size. If we wanted to batch up emissions into lists of eight elements, we can do that as follows:

```
import io.reactivex.rxjava3.core.Observable;

public class Ch7_01 {
    public static void main(String[] args) {
        Observable.range(1, 50)
                .buffer(8)
                .subscribe(System.out::println);
    }
}
```

The output is as follows:

```
[1, 2, 3, 4, 5, 6, 7, 8]
[9, 10, 11, 12, 13, 14, 15, 16]
[17, 18, 19, 20, 21, 22, 23, 24]
[25, 26, 27, 28, 29, 30, 31, 32]
[33, 34, 35, 36, 37, 38, 39, 40]
[41, 42, 43, 44, 45, 46, 47, 48]
[49, 50]
```

As you can see, if the buffer size does not cleanly divide the total number of emissions, the remaining elements will be emitted in a final list even if its size is smaller than the specified buffer size. This is why the last emission in the preceding code has a list of two elements (not eight), containing only 49 and 50.

You can also supply another argument in the `buffer()` overload, which is a `bufferSupplier` lambda expression that puts emissions in another collection, such as `HashSet`, as demonstrated here:

```
import io.reactivex.rxjava3.core.Observable;
import java.util.HashSet;

public class Ch7_01a {
    public static void main(String[] args) {
        Observable.range(1,50)
                .buffer(8, HashSet::new)
                .subscribe(System.out::println);
    }
}
```

This code yields the same output as the previous example.

To make things more interesting, you can also provide a `skip` argument that specifies how many items should be skipped before starting a new buffer. If `skip` is equal to `count`, the `skip` has no effect. But if they are different, you can get some interesting behavior. For instance, you can buffer 2 emissions but skip 3 before the next buffer starts, as shown here. This will essentially cause every third element to not be buffered:

```
import io.reactivex.rxjava3.core.Observable;
public class Ch7_02 {
    public static void main(String[] args) {
        Observable.range(1, 10)
                .buffer(2, 3)
                .subscribe(System.out::println);
    }
}
```

The output is as follows:

```
[1, 2]
[4, 5]
[7, 8]
[10]
```

If the `skip` value is smaller than `count`, you can get some interesting rolling buffers. In the following code, for instance, the buffer size is 3 and `skip` is 1:

```
import io.reactivex.rxjava3.core.Observable;

public class Ch7_03 {
    public static void main(String[] args) {
        Observable.range(1, 10)
                .buffer(3, 1)
                .subscribe(System.out::println);
    }
}
```

The source `Observable` emits the numbers 1 through 10, but the `buffer()` operator creates buffers `[1, 2, 3]`, then `[2, 3, 4]`, then `[3, 4, 5]`, and so on, as follows:

```
[1, 2, 3]
[2, 3, 4]
[3, 4, 5]
[4, 5, 6]
[5, 6, 7]
[6, 7, 8]
[7, 8, 9]
[8, 9, 10]
[9, 10]
[10]
```

Definitely play with the `skip` argument for `buffer()` and you may find surprising use cases for it. For example, try to use `buffer(2,1)` to emit the *previous* emission and the next emission together, as shown here (we also use `filter()` to omit the last list, which only contains 10):

```
import io.reactivex.rxjava3.core.Observable;

public class Ch7_04 {
    public static void main(String[] args) {
        Observable.range(1, 10)
                .buffer(2, 1)
                .filter(c -> c.size() == 2)
                .subscribe(System.out::println);
    }
}
```

The output is as follows:

```
[1, 2]
[2, 3]
[3, 4]
[4, 5]
[5, 6]
[6, 7]
[7, 8]
[8, 9]
[9, 10]
```

Time-based buffering

You can use the `buffer(long timespan, TimeUnit unit)` operator at fixed time intervals by providing `timespan` and `unit` values. To buffer emissions into a list at 1-second intervals, you can run the following code:

```
import io.reactivex.rxjava3.core.Observable;
import java.util.concurrent.TimeUnit;

public class Ch7_05 {
    public static void main(String[] args) {
        Observable.interval(300, TimeUnit.MILLISECONDS)
                .map(i -> (i + 1) * 300)
                .buffer(1, TimeUnit.SECONDS)
                .subscribe(System.out::println);
        sleep(4000);
    }
}
```

Note that we are making the source emit every 300 milliseconds, and each resulting buffered list will likely contain three or four emissions due to the 1-second interval cutoff. The output will be as follows:

```
[300, 600, 900]
[1200, 1500, 1800]
[2100, 2400, 2700]
[3000, 3300, 3600, 3900]
```

There is an option to also specify a `timeskip` argument, which is the timer-based counterpart to `skip`. It controls the timing for when each buffer starts.

You can also leverage a third `count` argument to provide a maximum buffer size. This will result in a buffer emission at each time interval or when `count` is reached, whichever happens first. If the `count` is reached right before the time window closes, it will result in an empty buffer being emitted.

In the following example, we buffer emissions every 1 second, but we limit the buffer size to `2`:

```
import io.reactivex.rxjava3.core.Observable;
import java.util.concurrent.TimeUnit;
public class Ch7_06 {
    public static void main(String[] args) {
        Observable.interval(300, TimeUnit.MILLISECONDS)
                .map(i -> (i + 1) * 300)
                .buffer(1, TimeUnit.SECONDS, 2)
                .subscribe(System.out::println);
        sleep(5000);
    }
}
```

The output is as follows:

```
[300, 600]
[900]
[1200, 1500]
[1800]
[2100, 2400]
[2700]
[3000, 3300]
[3600, 3900]
[]
[4200, 4500]
[4800]
```

Note that time-based `buffer()` operators will operate on the computation `Scheduler`. This makes sense since a separate thread needs to run on a timer to execute the cutoffs.

Boundary-based buffering

The most powerful overload of the `buffer()` operator is the one that accepts another `Observable` as a `boundary` argument: `buffer(Observable<B> boundary)`. It does not matter what type this other `Observable` emits. All that matters is that every time it emits something, it will use the timing of that emission as the buffer cutoff. In other words, the arbitrary occurrence of emissions of another `Observable` will determine when to *slice* each buffer.

For example, we can perform our previous example with 300-millisecond emissions buffered every 1 second using this technique. We can have an `Observable.interval()` of 1 second serve as the boundary for our `Observable.interval()`, emitting every 300 milliseconds, as shown in the following code example:

```
import io.reactivex.rxjava3.core.Observable;
import java.util.concurrent.TimeUnit;
public class Ch7_07 {
    public static void main(String[] args) {
        Observable<Long> cutOffs =
                        Observable.interval(1, TimeUnit.SECONDS);
        Observable.interval(300, TimeUnit.MILLISECONDS)
                .map(i -> (i + 1) * 300)
                .buffer(cutOffs)
                .subscribe(System.out::println);
        sleep(5000);
    }
}
```

The output is as follows:

```
[300, 600, 900]
[1200, 1500, 1800]
[2100, 2400, 2700]
[3000, 3300, 3600, 3900]
[4200, 4500, 4800]
```

This is probably the most flexible way to buffer items based on highly variable events. While the timing of each slicing is consistent in the preceding example (which is every 1 second), the `boundary` can be any `Observable` representing any kind of event happening at any time. This idea of an `Observable` serving as a cutoff for another `Observable` is a powerful pattern we will see throughout this chapter.

Windowing

The `window()` operator is almost identical to the `buffer()` operator, except that it buffers into another `Observable` rather than a collection. This results in an `Observable<Observable<T>>` that emits observables. Each `Observable` emission caches emissions for each scope and then flushes them once subscribed (much like the `GroupedObservable` from `groupBy()`, which we worked with in *Chapter 4, Combining Observables*). This allows emissions to be worked with immediately as they become available, rather than waiting for each list or collection to be finalized and emitted. The `window()` operator is also convenient to work with if you want to use operators to transform each batch.

Just like `buffer()`, you can limit each batch using fixed sizing, a time interval, or a boundary from another `Observable`.

Fixed-size windowing

Let's modify our earlier example, where we buffered 50 integers into lists of size 8. This time, we will use the `window()` operator to buffer elements of each list as an `Observable`. We can reactively transform each batch into something else besides a collection. For example, we can concatenate emissions into strings using a pipe (|), as a separator, as shown in the following code:

```
import io.reactivex.rxjava3.core.Observable;
public class Ch7_08 {
    public static void main(String[] args) {
        Observable.range(1, 50)
                .window(8)
                .flatMapSingle(obs -> obs.reduce("", (total, next) ->
                        total + (total.equals("") ? "" : "|") + next))
                .subscribe(System.out::println);
    }
}
```

The output is as follows:

```
1|2|3|4|5|6|7|8
9|10|11|12|13|14|15|16
17|18|19|20|21|22|23|24
25|26|27|28|29|30|31|32
33|34|35|36|37|38|39|40
41|42|43|44|45|46|47|48
49|50
```

Just like for the `buffer()` operator, you can also provide a `skip` argument. This is how many emissions need to be skipped before starting a new window. In the following example, our window size is 2, but we skip three items. We then take each windowed `Observable` and reduce it to a `String` concatenation, as shown in the following code:

```java
import io.reactivex.rxjava3.core.Observable;
public class Ch7_09 {
    public static void main(String[] args) {
        Observable.range(1, 50)
                .window(2, 3)
                .flatMapSingle(obs -> obs.reduce("", (total, next) ->
                        total + (total.equals("") ? "" : "|") + next))
                .subscribe(System.out::println);
    }
}
```

The output is as follows:

```
1|2
4|5
7|8
10|11
13|14
16|17
19|20
22|23
25|26
28|29
31|32
34|35
37|38
40|41
43|44
46|47
49|50
```

Time-based windowing

As you might be able to guess, you can cut off a windowed `Observable` at a time interval just like we did with the `buffer()` operator. For example, let's create an `Observable` that emits every 300 milliseconds and then slice it into separate observables every 1 second. We will then use `flatMapSingle()` on each `Observable` to build up a `String` concatenation of the emissions, as the following code demonstrates:

```
import io.reactivex.rxjava3.core.Observable;
import java.util.concurrent.TimeUnit;

public class Ch7_10 {
    public static void main(String[] args) {
        Observable.interval(300, TimeUnit.MILLISECONDS)
                .map(i -> (i + 1) * 300)
                .window(1, TimeUnit.SECONDS)
                .flatMapSingle(obs -> obs.reduce("", (total, next) ->
                        total + (total.equals("") ? "" : "|") + next))
                .subscribe(System.out::println);
        sleep(5000);
    }
}
```

The output is as follows:

```
300|600|900
1200|1500|1800
2100|2400|2700
3000|3300|3600|3900
4200|4500|4800
```

The emitted observables can be transformed in many ways besides `String` concatenations. You can use all the operators we learned up to this point to perform different operations on each windowed `Observable`, and you will likely do that work in `flatMap()`, `concatMap()`, or `switchMap()`.

With time-based `window()` operators, you can also specify `count` or `timeshift` arguments, just like its `buffer()` counterpart.

Boundary-based windowing

As we have mentioned already, the `window()` operator is similar to `buffer()`, so it should not come as a surprise that it is possible to use another `Observable` as a boundary value in the `window()` operator.

For example, we can use an `Observable.interval()` emitting every 1 second to serve as the boundary on an `Observable` emitting every 300 milliseconds. We leverage each emitted `Observable` to concatenate emissions into strings as follows:

```java
import io.reactivex.rxjava3.core.Observable;
import java.util.concurrent.TimeUnit;

public class Ch7_11 {
  public static void main(String[] args) {
    Observable<Long> cutOffs =
                        Observable.interval(1, TimeUnit.SECONDS);
    Observable.interval(300, TimeUnit.MILLISECONDS)
            .map(i -> (i + 1) * 300)
            .window(cutOffs)
            .flatMapSingle(obs -> obs.reduce("", (total, next) ->
                    total + (total.equals("") ? "" : "|") + next))
            .subscribe(System.out::println);
    sleep(5000);
  }
}
```

The output is as follows:

```
300|600|900
1200|1500|1800
2100|2400|2700
3000|3300|3600|3900
4200|4500|4800
```

Again, the benefit of using another `Observable` as a boundary is that it allows you to use the arbitrary timing of emissions from any `Observable` to cut off each window, whether it is a button click, a web request, or any other event. This makes it the most flexible way to slice `window()` or `buffer()` operations when variability is involved.

Throttling

The buffer() and window() operators batch up emissions into collections or observables based on a defined scope, which regularly consolidates rather than omits emissions. The throttle() operator, however, omits emissions when they occur rapidly. This is helpful when rapid emissions are assumed to be redundant or unwanted, such as a user clicking a button repeatedly. For these situations, you can use the throttleLast(), throttleFirst(), and throttleWithTimeout() operators to only let the first or last element in a rapid sequence of emissions through. How you choose one of the many rapid emissions is determined by your choice of the operator and its parameters.

For the examples in this section, we are going to work with the following case: there are three Observable.interval() sources, the first emitting every 100 milliseconds, the second every 300 milliseconds, and the third every 2,000 milliseconds. We only take ten emissions from the first source, three from the second, and two from the third. We will then use Observable.concat() on all three sources together in order to create a rapid sequence that changes pace at three different intervals, as shown in the following code example:

```
public class Ch7_12 {
    public static void main(String[] args) {
        Observable<String> source1 =
            Observable.interval(100, TimeUnit.MILLISECONDS)
                    .map(i -> (i + 1) * 100) //map to elapsed time
                    .map(i -> "SOURCE 1: " + i)
                    .take(10);

        Observable<String> source2 =
            Observable.interval(300, TimeUnit.MILLISECONDS)
                    .map(i -> (i + 1) * 300) //map to elapsed time
                    .map(i -> "SOURCE 2: " + i)
                    .take(3);

        Observable<String> source3 =
            Observable.interval(2000, TimeUnit.MILLISECONDS)
                    .map(i -> (i + 1) * 2000) //map to elapsed time
                    .map(i -> "SOURCE 3: " + i)
                    .take(2);
        Observable.concat(source1, source2, source3)
                .subscribe(System.out::println);
        sleep(6000);
    }
}
```

The output is as follows:

```
SOURCE 1: 100
SOURCE 1: 200
SOURCE 1: 300
SOURCE 1: 400
SOURCE 1: 500
SOURCE 1: 600
SOURCE 1: 700
SOURCE 1: 800
SOURCE 1: 900
SOURCE 1: 1000
SOURCE 2: 300
SOURCE 2: 600
SOURCE 2: 900
SOURCE 3: 2000
SOURCE 3: 4000
```

The first source rapidly pushes ten emissions within a second, the second pushes three emissions within a second, and the third pushes two emissions within 4 seconds.

Let's use the `throttle()` operators to only choose a few of these emissions and ignore the rest.

throttleLast() or sample()

The `throttleLast()` operator (another name for the same operator is `sample()`) emits only the last item at a fixed time interval. Modify the preceding example by adding `throttleLast()` at 1-second intervals, as shown here:

```
Observable.concat(source1, source2, source3)
        .throttleLast(1, TimeUnit.SECONDS)
        .subscribe(System.out::println);
```

The output will change as follows:

```
SOURCE 1: 900
SOURCE 2: 900
SOURCE 3: 2000
```

As you can see, the last emission at every 1-second interval was all that got through. This effectively samples emissions by dipping into the stream on a timer and pulling out the latest one.

If you throttle more liberally at a larger time interval, you will get fewer emissions as this effectively reduces the sampling frequency. For example, let's use `throttleLast()` every 2 seconds as follows:

```
Observable.concat(source1, source2, source3)
        .throttleLast(2, TimeUnit.SECONDS)
        .subscribe(System.out::println);
```

The output becomes as follows:

```
SOURCE 2: 900
SOURCE 3: 2000
```

If you want to throttle more aggressively at shorter time intervals, you will get more emissions, as this increases the sampling frequency. Let's use `throttleLast()` every 500 milliseconds as shown here:

```
Observable.concat(source1, source2, source3)
        .throttleLast(500, TimeUnit.MILLISECONDS)
        .subscribe(System.out::println);
```

The output is as follows:

```
SOURCE 1: 400
SOURCE 1: 900
SOURCE 2: 300
SOURCE 2: 900
SOURCE 3: 2000
```

Again, `throttleLast()` will push the last emission at every fixed time interval.

Next, we will cover `throttleFirst()`, which emits the first item instead.

throttleFirst()

The `throttleFirst()` operates almost identically to `throttleLast()`, but it emits the *first* item that occurs at every fixed time interval. Let's modify our example to `throttleFirst()` every 1 second as follows:

```
Observable.concat(source1, source2, source3)
        .throttleFirst(1, TimeUnit.SECONDS)
        .subscribe(System.out::println);
```

The output is as follows:

```
SOURCE 1: 100
SOURCE 2: 300
SOURCE 3: 2000
SOURCE 3: 4000
```

Effectively, the first emission found after each interval starts is the emission that gets pushed through. The 100 from `source1` was the first emission found on the first interval. On the next interval, 300 from `source2` was emitted, and then 2,000, followed by 4,000. The 4,000 was emitted right on the cusp of the application quitting, hence, we got four emissions from `throttleFirst()` as opposed to three from `throttleLast()`.

Besides the first item being emitted rather than the last at each interval, all the behaviors from `throttleLast()` also apply to `throttleFirst()`. Specifying shorter intervals will yield more emissions, whereas longer intervals will yield fewer emissions.

Both `throttleFirst()` and `throttleLast()` emit on the computation `Scheduler`, but you can specify your own `Scheduler` as a third argument.

throttleWithTimeout() or debounce()

If you play with `throttleFirst()` and `throttleLast()`, you might be dissatisfied with one aspect of their behavior. They are agnostic to the variability of emission frequency, and they simply *dip in* at fixed intervals and pull the first or last emission they find. There is no notion of waiting for a *period of silence*, where emissions stop for a moment, and that might be an opportune time to push forward the last emission that occurred.

Think of Hollywood action movies where a protagonist is under heavy gunfire. While bullets are flying, they have to take cover and are unable to act. But the moment their attackers stop to reload, there is a period of silence where they have time to react. This is essentially what `throttleWithTimeout()` does. When emissions are firing rapidly, it does not emit anything until there is a *period of silence*, and then it pushes the last emission forward.

The `throttleWithTimout()` operator (also called `debounce()`) accepts time-interval arguments that specify how long a period of inactivity (which means no emissions are coming from the source) must be before the last emission can be pushed forward. In our earlier example, our three concatenated `Observable.interval()` sources are rapidly firing at 100 milliseconds and then 300-millisecond spurts for approximately 2 seconds. But after that, the interval increases to 2 seconds.

If we set the timeout to 1 second, no emission will be allowed to go through until the second `Observable.interval()` finishes emitting, and then the following `Observable` starts emitting every 2 seconds, as shown here:

```
public class Ch7_13 {
    public static void main(String[] args) {
        Observable<String> source1 =
            Observable.interval(100, TimeUnit.MILLISECONDS)
                    .map(i -> (i + 1) * 100) // map to elapsed time
                    .map(i -> "SOURCE 1: " + i)
                    .take(10);

        Observable<String> source2 =
            Observable.interval(300, TimeUnit.MILLISECONDS)
                    .map(i -> (i + 1) * 300) // map to elapsed time
                    .map(i -> "SOURCE 2: " + i)
                    .take(3);

        Observable<String> source3 =
            Observable.interval(2000, TimeUnit.MILLISECONDS)
                    .map(i -> (i + 1) * 2000) // map to elapsed time
                    .map(i -> "SOURCE 3: " + i)
                    .take(2);

        Observable.concat(source1, source2, source3)
                    .throttleWithTimeout(1, TimeUnit.SECONDS)
                    .subscribe(System.out::println);

        sleep(6000);
    }
}
```

The output is as follows:

```
SOURCE 2: 900
SOURCE 3: 2000
SOURCE 3: 4000
```

The 900 emission from `source2` was the last emission before `source3` started since `source3` does not push its first emission for 2 seconds, which gave more than the needed 1-second period of silence for the 900 to be fired. The 2,000 emission then emitted next and 1 second later, no further emissions occurred, so it was pushed forward by `throttleWithTimeout()`. Another second later, the 4,000 emission was pushed and the 2-second silence (before the program exited) allowed it to fire as well.

`throttleWithTimeout()` is an effective way to handle excessive inputs (such as a user clicking on a button rapidly) and other noisy, redundant events that sporadically speed up, slow down, or cease. The only disadvantage of `throttleWithTimeout()` is that it delays each winning emission. If an emission does make it through `throttleWithTimeout()`, it is delayed by the specified time interval in order to ensure that no more emissions are coming. This artificial delay may be especially unwelcome for a user interface. For these situations, which are sensitive to delays, a better option might be to leverage `switchMap()`, which we will cover next.

Switching

In RxJava, there is a powerful operator called `switchMap()`. Its usage is similar to `flatMap()`, but it has one important behavioral difference: it emits the latest `Observable` derived from the latest emission and disposes of any previous observables that were processing. In other words, it allows you to cancel an emitting `Observable` and switch to a new one, thereby preventing stale or redundant processing.

If, for example, we have a process that emits nine strings, and it delays each string emission randomly from 0 to 2,000 milliseconds (emulating an intense calculation), this can be demonstrated as follows:

```
import io.reactivex.rxjava3.core.Observable;
import java.util.concurrent.ThreadLocalRandom;
import java.util.concurrent.TimeUnit;

public class Ch7_14 {
    public static void main(String[] args) {
        Observable<String> items = Observable.just("Alpha", "Beta",
          "Gamma", "Delta", "Epsilon", "Zeta", "Eta", "Theta", "Iota");
        //delay each String to emulate an intense calculation
        Observable<String> processStrings =
            items.concatMap(s -> Observable.just(s)
                    .delay(randomSleepTime(), TimeUnit.MILLISECONDS));
        processStrings.subscribe(System.out::println);
        //keep application alive for 20 seconds
        sleep(20000);
    }
    public static int randomSleepTime() {
        //returns random sleep time between 0 to 2000 milliseconds
        return ThreadLocalRandom.current().nextInt(2000);
    }
}
```

The output is as follows:

```
Alpha
Beta
Gamma
Delta
Epsilon
Zeta
Eta
Theta
Iota
```

As you can see, each emission takes between 0-2 seconds to be emitted, and processing all the strings can take up to 20 seconds.

If we want to run this process every 5 seconds, but need to cancel (or, more technically, dispose()) previous instances of the process and only run the latest one, this is easy to do with switchMap(). In the following example, we create another Observable.interval(), emitting every 5 seconds, and then we use switchMap() on it to the Observable we want to process (which, in this case, is processStrings). Every 5 seconds, the emission going into switchMap() will promptly dispose of the currently processing Observable (if there are any) and then emit from the new Observable it maps to. To prove that dispose() is being called, we added the doOnDispose() operator on the Observable inside switchMap() to display a message. Here is the code that does all this:

```java
public class Ch7_15 {
    public static void main(String[] args) {
        Observable<String> items = Observable.just("Alpha", "Beta",
          "Gamma", "Delta", "Epsilon", "Zeta", "Eta", "Theta", "Iota");

        //delay each String to emulate an intense calculation
        Observable<String> processStrings =
            items.concatMap(s -> Observable.just(s)
                    .delay(randomSleepTime(), TimeUnit.MILLISECONDS));

        Observable.interval(5, TimeUnit.SECONDS)
                .switchMap(i -> processStrings.doOnDispose(() ->
                    System.out.println("Disposing! Starting next")))
                .subscribe(System.out::println);

        //keep application alive for 20 seconds
        sleep(20000);
    }
}
```

The output is as follows (yours will be different):

```
Alpha
Beta
Gamma
Delta
Epsilon
Zeta
Eta
Disposing! Starting next
Alpha
Beta
Gamma
Delta
Disposing! Starting next
Alpha
Beta
Gamma
Delta
Disposing! Starting next
```

Again, `switchMap()` is just like `flatMap()` except that it cancels any previous `Observable` that was processing and only takes the emissions from the latest one. This can be helpful in many situations to prevent redundant or stale work and is especially effective in user interfaces where rapid user input creates stale requests. You can use it to cancel database queries, web requests, and other expensive tasks and replace them with a new task.

For `switchMap()` to work effectively, the thread pushing emissions into `switchMap()` cannot be occupied while doing the work inside `switchMap()`. This means that you may have to use `observeOn()` or `subscribeOn()` inside `switchMap()` to do work on a different thread. If the operations inside `switchMap()` are expensive to stop (for instance, a database query using RxJava-JDBC), you might want to use `unsubscribeOn()` as well to keep the triggering thread from becoming occupied with the disposal.

A neat trick you can do to cancel work within `switchMap()` (without providing new work immediately) is to conditionally yield `Observable.empty()`. This can be helpful when canceling a long-running or infinite process. For example, if you bring in RxJavaFX (`https://github.com/ReactiveX/RxJavaFX`) as a dependency, we can quickly create a stopwatch application using `switchMap()`, as shown in the following code snippet:

```
public final class Ch7_16 extends Application {
    public static void main(String... args) { launch(args);}

    @Override
```

```
        public void start(Stage stage) {
            Pane root = new Pane();
            Label counterLabel = new Label("");
            counterLabel.relocate(20, 30);

            ToggleButton startStopButton = new ToggleButton();
            startStopButton.relocate(20, 60);

            root.getChildren().addAll(counterLabel, startStopButton);
            stage.setScene(new Scene(root,100, 100));
            stage.show();

            setObservers(counterLabel, startStopButton);
        }
    }
```

As you can see, it is a typical JavaFX application with a label and a button. Then, the `setObservers()` method adds observers to the label and button. The `setObservers()` method appears as follows:

```
    private void setObservers(Label label, ToggleButton button){
        Observable<Boolean> selectedState =
                JavaFxObservable.valuesOf(button.selectedProperty())
                            .publish()
                            .autoConnect(2);
        selectedState
            .switchMap(selected -> {
               System.out.println(selected);
               if (selected) {
                  return Observable.interval(1, TimeUnit.MILLISECONDS);
               } else {
                  return Observable.empty();
               }
            })
            .observeOn(JavaFxScheduler.platform())  // Run on UI thread
            .map(Object::toString)
            .subscribe(label::setText);

        selectedState.subscribe(selected ->
                        button.setText(selected ? "STOP" : "START"));
    }
```

`Observable<Boolean> selectedState` emits the state of the button – a `Boolean` value. Its `publish()` operator multicasts the emissions, so all subscribers get them.

The first `Observer` uses `switchMap()` on each `Boolean` value. First, it prints the emitted value. Then, if the value is `True`, the `Observable.interval()` starts emitting every millisecond. Since `Observable.interval()` emits on a computation `Scheduler` by default, we use `observeOn()` to put it back on the JavaFX `Scheduler` provided by RxJavaFX. That is how the emitted value can be used to set text on the label (every millisecond). If the source `Observable<Boolean> selectedState` emits `False`, `Observable.interval()` is replaced by `Observable.empty()`. The emissions stop coming, and the label is not updated.

The second `Observer` changes the text of the button to **STOP** or **START** depending on the value emitted by the source `Observable<Boolean> selectedState`.

The preceding code creates a stopwatch application. When it is launched, the button emits `False` by default, and the display shows the following:

The text on the label does not change (set to an empty `String` value initially), and the text of the button is set to **START**, as shown in the following screenshot:

When the button is clicked (its `Observable` emits `True`), the display shows the following:

The text on the label starts changing every millisecond, and the text of the button switches to **STOP**, as depicted in the following screenshot:

The text on the label continues changing.

When the button is clicked again, its `Observable` emits `True`, and the display shows the following:

The text on the label stops changing, and the text of the button switches to **START**, as demonstrated in the following screenshot:

If the button is clicked again, `Observable.interval()` replaces `Observable.empty()` and provides emissions again, starting with `1`.

As a result, the application acts as a stopwatch that displays in milliseconds.

Grouping keystrokes

We will wrap up this chapter by integrating most of what we learned and achieve a complex task: grouping keystrokes that happen in rapid succession to form strings without any delay. It can be helpful in user interfaces to immediately *jump* to items in a list based on what is being typed or perform autocompletion in some way. This can be a challenging task, but as we will see, it is not that difficult with RxJava.

This exercise will use JavaFX again with RxJavaFX. Our user interface will simply have a `Label` that receives rolling concatenations of keys we are typing. But after 1 second, it will reset and receive an empty `""` to clear it. Here is the code that achieves this:

```
public final class Ch7_17 extends Application {
    public static void main(String... args) { launch(args); }

    @Override
    public void start(Stage stage) {
        Pane root = new Pane();
        Label typedTextLabel = new Label("");
        typedTextLabel.relocate(20, 30);
        root.getChildren().addAll(typedTextLabel);

        Scene scene = new Scene(root, 100, 100);
```

```
        stage.setScene(scene);
        stage.show();

        setObservers(scene, typedTextLabel);
    }
}
```

As in our previous example, this code snippet includes the creation of a **graphical user interface (GUI)** and call to the `setObservers()` method that sets `Scene` `scene` as the source `Observable` that emits keystrokes:

```
private void setObservers(Scene scene, Label label){
    Observable<String> typedLetters =
            JavaFxObservable.eventsOf(scene, KeyEvent.KEY_TYPED)
                    .map(KeyEvent::getCharacter);

    // Signal 1 sec of inactivity
    typedLetters.throttleWithTimeout(1000, TimeUnit.MILLISECONDS)
            .startWith("") //trigger initial
            .switchMap(s -> typedLetters.scan("",
                            (rolling, next) -> rolling + next))
            .observeOn(JavaFxScheduler.platform())
            .subscribe(s -> {
                label.setText(s);
                System.out.println(s);
            });

}
```

As you can see, there is also an `Observer` added that observes the emitted keystrokes and emits an empty `String` value at the very beginning (using the `startWith()` operator). This empty `String` value triggers the switch to another `Observable` returned by the `scan()` operator. Well, this new `Observable` takes the values currently emitted by the source `Observable` and concatenates them as a rolling `String` value. Every time a new value is added, the resulting string is passed to the `observeOn()` operator, which switches to the UI thread and passes the value to the `subscribe()` operator, where it is set on the label and printed out on the console.

After 1 second of inactivity, the `throttleWithTimeout()` operator resets and emits the last typed value. We ignore this value in the `switchMap()` operator and let the `scan()` operator do its job again by creating a new `Observable` and adding every newly typed value to the rolling string. Note that the old `Observable` created by the `scan()` operator previously is disposed of, so the new concatenated value contains only newly typed characters (the keystrokes emitted after the pause).

This can be enormously helpful to instantly send search requests or autocomplete suggestions while the user is typing.

Let's see how it works. After the previous example code is run, there is nothing to see on the created GUI because it displays an empty string only. We start typing **Hello** and it appears on the GUI as shown in the following screenshot:

Hello

During the process, as we are typing, the console is printing the following lines:

```
H
He
Hel
Hell
Hello
```

Then we pause for 1 second, and the GUI clears again. The `throttleWithTimeout()` operator resets and forces the `scan()` operator (inside the `switchMap()` operator) to create a new `Observable` that emits nothing until we type another character.

Let's say we type **World!** without a pause. The GUI will show the following:

World!

Meanwhile, the console will display all the concatenated values that look like this:

```
W
Wo
Wor
Worl
World!
```

If we again pause for 1 second, the GUI will clear and the cycle will be ready to start anew.

To help you understand how it works, you also print the value emitted by the `throttleWithTimeout()` operator as follows:

```
private void setObservers1(Scene scene, Label label){
    Observable<String> typedLetters =
            JavaFxObservable.eventsOf(scene, KeyEvent.KEY_TYPED)
                    .map(KeyEvent::getCharacter);

    // Signal 1 sec of inactivity
```

```
typedLetters.throttleWithTimeout(1000, TimeUnit.MILLISECONDS)
        .startWith("") //trigger initial
        .switchMap(s -> {
            System.out.println("The last emitted: " + s);
            return typedLetters.scan("",
                            (rolling, next) -> rolling + next);
        })
        .observeOn(JavaFxScheduler.platform())
        .subscribe(s -> {
            label.setText(s);
            System.out.println(s);
        });
}
```

The console output will then change to the following:

```
The last emitted:

H
He
Hel
Hell
Hello
The last emitted: o
```

As you can guess, the line `The last emitted:` appears only after 1 second of inactivity.

If you find this example dizzying, take your time and keep studying it. It will click ultimately and, once it does, you will have truly mastered the ideas of this chapter!

Summary

In this chapter, you learned how to leverage buffering, windowing, throttling, and switching to cope with a rapidly emitting `Observable`. Ideally, we should leverage `Flowable` and backpressure when we see that an `Observable` is emitting faster than an `Observer` can keep up with, which we will learn about in the next chapter. But for situations where backpressure cannot work, such as user inputs or timer events, you can leverage one of the four categories of operations—buffering, windowing, throttling, or switching—to limit how many emissions are passed downstream.

In the next chapter, we will learn about handling backpressure using `Flowable`, which provides a more proactive way to cope with a common case of rapid emissions that overwhelm an `Observer`.

Flowable and Backpressure

8

In the previous chapter, we learned about different operators that intercept rapidly firing emissions and either consolidate or omit them to decrease the number of emissions passed downstream. Another – arguably better – way to address the issue of when a source is producing emissions faster than the downstream can process them is to proactively make the source slow down and emit at a pace that agrees with the downstream operations. This last technique is especially important when we do not want to miss any of the emissions but do not want to consolidate them or cannot provide a large enough buffer to keep all the excess emissions in the queue.

Sending the request to slow down to the source is known as a backpressure, or flow control, and it can be enabled by using a `Flowable` instead of an `Observable`. This will be the main focus of this chapter. You will learn when, under which circumstances, and how to leverage backpressure in your application.

In this chapter, we will cover the following topics:

- Understanding backpressure
- Understanding `Flowable` and `Subscriber`
- Creating `Flowable`
- Turning `Observable` into `Flowable` and vice versa
- Using `onBackpressureXXX()` operators
- Using `Flowable.generate()`

Understanding backpressure

Throughout this book, we emphasized the *push-based* nature of an `Observable`. Pushing items synchronously and one at a time from the source all the way to the `Observer` is indeed how an `Observable` chain of operators works by default without any concurrency.

For instance, the following demonstrates an `Observable` that emits the numbers from 1 through 999,999,999:

```
import io.reactivex.rxjava3.core.Observable;

public class Ch8_01 {
  public static void main(String[] args) {
      Observable.range(1, 999_999_999)
                .map(MyItem::new)
                .subscribe(myItem -> {
                   sleep(50);
                   System.out.println("Received MyItem " + myItem.id);
                });
    }
  }
}
```

It maps each integer to a `MyItem` instance, which simply holds it as a property:

```
        static final class MyItem {
            final int id;
            MyItem(int id) {
                this.id = id;
                System.out.println("Constructing MyItem " + id);
            }
        }
```

The output is as follows:

```
Constructing MyItem 1
Received MyItem 1
Constructing MyItem 2
Received MyItem 2
Constructing MyItem 3
Received MyItem 3
Constructing MyItem 4
Received MyItem 4
Constructing MyItem 5
Received MyItem 5
Constructing MyItem 6
Received MyItem 6
Constructing MyItem 7
Received MyItem 7

...
```

The outputted alternation between `Constructing MyItem` and `Received MyItem` shows that each emission is processed one at a time from the source all the way to the terminal `Observer`. This is because one thread is doing all the work for this entire operation, making everything synchronous. The consumers and producers are passing emissions in a serialized, consistent flow.

You may have noticed that we slowed down the processing of each emission by 50 milliseconds in the `Observer`. We could set this value to 500 or 500,000 milliseconds. The output would progress slower, but the sequence does not change: the messages **Constructing MyItem** and **Received MyItem** always alternate. That is because all processing in all operators is performed on the same thread.

This shows that, with single-thread processing, even if the downstream is slowly processing each emission, the upstream synchronously keeps pace with it.

An example that needs backpressure

When processing each item takes a long time, adding other threads for concurrent processing of the emissions is the way to address the issue. This can be done by adding concurrent operations to an `Observable` chain using `observeOn()`, parallelization, and operators such as `delay()`. With that, the processing becomes *asynchronous*. This means that multiple parts of the `Observable` chain can process different emissions at the same time, and the producer can outpace the downstream consumer as they are now operating on different threads.

In asynchronous processing, an emission is no longer, strictly speaking, being handed downstream one at a time from the source all the way to the `Observer` before starting the next one. This is because once an emission is pushed to a different `Scheduler` through `observeOn()` (or another concurrent operator), the source is no longer in charge of guiding that emission to the `Observer`. Therefore, the source pushes the next emission even though the previous emission may not have reached the `Observer` yet.

Let's modify our previous example and add `observeOn(Shedulers.io())` right before `subscribe()`, as shown in the following code:

```
import io.reactivex.rxjava3.core.Observable;
import io.reactivex.rxjava3.schedulers.Schedulers;

public class Ch8_02 {
    public static void main(String[] args) {
        Observable.range(1, 999_999_999)
                .map(MyItem::new)
```

```
                        .observeOn(Schedulers.io())
                    .subscribe(myItem -> {
                        sleep(50);
                        System.out.println("Received MyItem " + myItem.id);
                    });
        }
    }
```

The output is as follows:

```
    . . .
    Constructing MyItem 1001899
    Constructing MyItem 1001900
    Constructing MyItem 1001901
    Constructing MyItem 1001902
    Received MyItem 38
    Constructing MyItem 1001903
    Constructing MyItem 1001904
    Constructing MyItem 1001905
    Constructing MyItem 1001906
    Constructing MyItem 1001907
    . .
```

This is just a section of the actual console output. Note that when `MyItem 1001902` is created, the `Observer` is still only processing `MyItem 38`. The emissions are being pushed much faster than the `Observer` can process them. Having two processing threads helps, but, because backlogged emissions get queued by `observeOn()` in an unbounded manner, this could lead to many other problems, including `OutOfMemoryError` exceptions.

So how do we mitigate this? You could try and use native Java concurrency tools such as semaphores but, thankfully, RxJava has a streamlined solution to this problem: the `Flowable` class.

Introducing the Flowable

The `Flowable` class is a variant of the `Observable` that can tell the source to emit at a pace specified by the downstream operations. In other words, it can exert **backpressure** on the source.

In the following code, replace `Observable.range()` with `Flowable.range()`, and this will make this entire chain work with `Flowable` objects instead of `Observable` ones. Run the code and you will see a very different behavior with the output:

```
import io.reactivex.rxjava3.core.Observable;
import io.reactivex.rxjava3.schedulers.Schedulers;

public class Ch8_03 {
    public static void main(String[] args) {
        Flowable.range(1, 999_999_999)
                .map(MyItem::new)
                .observeOn(Schedulers.io())
                .subscribe(myItem -> {
                    sleep(50);
                    System.out.println("Received MyItem " + myItem.id);
                });
        sleep(Long.MAX_VALUE);
    }
}
```

The output is as follows:

```
Constructing MyItem 1
Constructing MyItem 2
Constructing MyItem 3
. . .
Constructing MyItem 127
Constructing MyItem 128
Received MyItem 1
Received MyItem 2
Received MyItem 3
. . .
Received MyItem 95
Received MyItem 96
Constructing MyItem 129
Constructing MyItem 130
Constructing MyItem 131
. . .
Constructing MyItem 223
Constructing MyItem 224
Received MyItem 97
Received MyItem 98
Received MyItem 99
. . .
```

Note that a `Flowable` is not subscribed by an `Observer` but by
an `org.reactivestreams.Subscriber`: the `subscribe()` method of a
`Flowable` accepts `Subscriber`. We will talk about this later.

You can see something very different in the output with `Flowable`. We omitted some parts
of the output, using . . . to highlight the key events. As you can see, 128 emissions were
pushed from `Flowable.range()` first and 128 `MyItem` instances were constructed. After
that, `observeOn()` pushed 96 of the constructed items downstream to `Subscriber`. After
these 96 emissions were processed by `Subscriber`, another 96 were pushed from the
source. Then, another 96 were passed to `Subscriber`.

Do you see a pattern yet? The source started by pushing 128 emissions, and after that, a
steady flow of 96 emissions at a time was processed by the `Flowable` chain. It is almost like
the entire `Flowable` chain strives to have no more than 96 emissions in its pipeline at any
given time. Effectively, that is exactly what is happening! This is what we call
backpressure, and it effectively introduces a pull dynamic to the push-based operation to
limit how frequently the source emits.

But why did `Flowable.range()` start with 128 emissions, and why did `observeOn()`
only send 96 downstream before requesting another 96, leaving 32 unprocessed emissions?
The initial batch of emissions is a bit larger, so some extra work is queued if there is any
idle time. If (in theory) our `Flowable` operation started by requesting 96 emissions and
continued to emit steadily at 96 emissions at a time, there would be moments where
operations might wait idly for the next 96. Therefore, an extra rolling cache of 32 emissions
is maintained to provide work during these idle moments, which can yield greater
throughput. This is much like a warehouse holding a little extra inventory to supply orders
while it waits for more from the factory.

Note the line `sleep(Long.MAX_VALUE)`. We had to add it in order to let the processing
chain work through all the emissions. Otherwise, due to the asynchronous nature of the
processing, the application exits before any significant number of the emissions is
processed. We did not need to do this when we used `Observable.range()` because the
main thread was always busy feeding the emissions to the `Scheduler.io()` thread. With
`Flowable`, the main thread emitted only 128 emissions before switching to listening from
the `Subscriber`, so without `sleep(Long.MAX_VALUE)`, it just exits. That's why we paused
it to give the `Scheduler.io()` thread a chance to finish the processing, so it can signal
back to the main thread to continue with pushing the emissions.

What is great about `Flowable` and its operators is that they usually do all the work for you. You do not have to specify any backpressure policies or parameters unless you need to create your own `Flowable` from scratch or deal with sources (such as `Observable`) that do not implement backpressure. We will cover these cases in the rest of the chapter, and hopefully, you will not run into them often.

Otherwise, `Flowable` is just like an `Observable` with nearly all the operators we learned so far. You can convert an `Observable` to a `Flowable` and vice versa, which we will cover later in the *Turning Observable into Flowable and vice versa* section. But first, let's cover when we should use `Flowable` instead of `Observable`.

When to use Flowable and backpressure

It is critical to know when to use `Flowable` as opposed to `Observable`. Overall, the benefits offered by `Flowable` are leaner usage of memory (preventing `OutOfMemoryError` exceptions) as well as prevention of `MissingBackpressureException`. The latter can occur if operations backpressure against a source, but the source has no backpressure protocol in its implementation. However, the disadvantage of `Flowable` is that it adds overhead and may not perform as quickly as an `Observable`.

Here are a few guidelines to help you choose between an `Observable` and a `Flowable`:

- **Use an Observable if...**
    - You expect few emissions over the life of the `Observable` subscription (fewer than 1,000) or the emissions are intermittent and far apart. If you expect only a trickle of emissions coming from a source, an `Observable` will do the job just fine and have less overhead. But when you are dealing with large amounts of data and performing complex operations on them, you will likely want to use a `Flowable`.
    - Your data processing is strictly synchronous and has limited usage of concurrency. This includes simple usage of `subscribeOn()` at the start of an `Observable` chain because the process is still operating on a single thread and emitting items synchronously downstream. However, when you start zipping and combining different streams on different threads, parallelize, or use operators such as `observeOn()`, `interval()`, and `delay()`, your application is no longer synchronous and you might be better off using a `Flowable`.

- You want to emit user interface events such as button clicks, `ListView` selections, or other user inputs on Android, JavaFX, or Swing. Since users cannot programmatically be told to slow down, there is rarely any opportunity to use a `Flowable`. To cope with rapid user inputs, you are likely better off using the operators discussed in `Chapter 7`, *Switching, Throttling, Windowing, and Buffering*.

- **Use a Flowable if...**
  - You are dealing with over 10,000 elements and there is an opportunity for the source to generate emissions in a regulated manner. This is especially true when the source is asynchronous and pushes large amounts of data.
  - You want to emit from IO operations that support blocking while returning results, which is how many IO sources work. Data sources that iterate records, such as lines from files or a `ResultSet` in JDBC, are especially easy to control because iteration can pause and resume as needed. Network and streaming APIs that can request a certain amount of returned results can easily be backpressured as well.

Note that in RxJava 1.0, the `Observable` was backpressured and was essentially what the `Flowable` is in RxJava 2.0. The reason the `Flowable` and `Observable` became separate types is due to the merits of both for different situations, as was just described.

You will find that you can easily convert `Observable` and `Flowable` and vice versa. Refer to the *Turning Observable into Flowable and vice versa* section for how to do it. But you need to be careful and aware of the context they are being used in and where an undesired bottleneck can occur.

Understanding Flowable and Subscriber

Pretty much all the `Observable` factories and operators you learned up to this point also apply to `Flowable`. On the factory side, there are `Flowable.range()`, `Flowable.just()`, `Flowable.fromIterable()`, and `Flowable.interval()`. Most of these sources support backpressure. Their usage is generally the same as the `Observable` equivalent.

However, consider `Flowable.interval()`, which pushes time-based emissions at fixed time intervals. Can this be backpressured? Contemplate the fact that each emission is tied to the time it emits. If we slowed down `Flowable.interval()`, our emissions would no longer reflect the specified time interval and become misleading. Therefore, `Flowable.interval()` is one of those few cases in the standard API that can throw `MissingBackpressureException` the moment the downstream starts backpressuring. In the following example, if we emit every millisecond against a slow `intenseCalculation()` that occurs after `observeOn()`, we will get an error:

```
import io.reactivex.rxjava3.core.Observable;
import io.reactivex.rxjava3.schedulers.Schedulers;

public class Ch8_04 {
    public static void main(String[] args) {
        Flowable.interval(1, TimeUnit.MILLISECONDS)
                .observeOn(Schedulers.io())
                .map(i -> intenseCalculation(i))
                .subscribe(System.out::println,
                            Throwable::printStackTrace);
        sleep(Long.MAX_VALUE);
    }
    public static <T> T intenseCalculation(T value) {
        sleep(ThreadLocalRandom.current().nextInt(3000));
        return value;
    }
}
```

The output is as follows:

```
0
io.reactivex.exceptions.MissingBackpressureException:
Cant deliver value 128 due to lack of requests
    at io.reactivex.internal.operators.flowable.FlowableInterval
    ...
```

To overcome this issue, you can use operators such as `onBackpresureDrop()` or `onBackPressureBuffer()`, which we will learn about later in this chapter in the *Using onBackpressureXXX() operators* section. `Flowable.interval()` is one of those factories that logically cannot be backpressured at the source, so you can add to the processing chain the operators to handle backpressure for you. Otherwise, most of the other `Flowable` factories support backpressure.

Later in this chapter, we will discuss how to create our own `Flowable` source that supports backpressure. But first, let's explore the `Subscriber` interface a bit deeper.

Interface Subscriber

Instead of an Observer, Flowable uses a Subscriber to consume emissions and events at the end of a Flowable chain. If you pass only lambda event arguments (and not an entire Subscriber object), subscribe() does not return a Disposable, but rather an org.reactivestreams.Subscription, which can be disposed of by calling cancel() instead of dispose(). Subscription can also serve another purpose; it communicates upstream how many items are wanted using its request() method. Subscription can also be leveraged in the onSubscribe() method of Subscriber, which can call the request() method (and pass in the number of the requested elements) the moment it is ready to receive emissions.

Just like an Observer, the quickest way to create a Subscriber is to pass lambda arguments to subscribe(), as we have been doing earlier (and show again in the following code). This default implementation of Subscriber requests an unbounded number of emissions, but any operators preceding it still automatically handle the backpressure:

```
import io.reactivex.rxjava3.core.Observable;
import io.reactivex.rxjava3.schedulers.Schedulers;

public class Ch8_5 {
    public static void main(String[] args) {
        Flowable.range(1, 1000)
                .doOnNext(s -> System.out.println("Source pushed " + s))
                .observeOn(Schedulers.io())
                .map(i -> intenseCalculation(i))
                .subscribe(s ->
                        System.out.println("Subscriber received " + s),
                        Throwable::printStackTrace,
                        () -> System.out.println("Done!")
                );
        sleep(20000);
    }
    public static <T> T intenseCalculation(T value) {
        //sleep up to 200 milliseconds
        sleep(ThreadLocalRandom.current().nextInt(200));
        return value;
    }
}
```

The output is as follows:

```
Source pushed 1
Source pushed 2
. . .
Source pushed 128
Subscriber received 1
. . .
Subscriber received 96
Source pushed 129
. . .
Source pushed 224
Subscriber received 97
. . .
```

Of course, you can implement your own Subscriber as well, which would have the onNext(), onError(), and onComplete() methods as well as onSubscribe(). However, this is not as straightforward as implementing an Observer because you need to call request() on Subscription to request emissions at the right moment.

The quickest and easiest way to implement a Subscriber is to have the onSubscribe() method call request(Long.MAX_VALUE) on Subscription, which essentially tells the upstream *give me everything now*. Even though the operators preceding Subscriber will request emissions at their own backpressured pace, no backpressure will exist between the last operator and the Subscriber. This is usually fine since the upstream operators constrain the flow anyway.

Here, we reimplement our previous example, but implement our own Subscriber:

```java
import io.reactivex.rxjava3.core.Flowable;
import io.reactivex.rxjava3.schedulers.Schedulers;
import org.reactivestreams.Subscriber;
import org.reactivestreams.Subscription;

public class Ch8_06 {
    public static void main(String[] args) {
        Flowable.range(1, 1000)
                .doOnNext(s -> System.out.println("Source pushed " + s))
                .observeOn(Schedulers.io())
                .map(i -> intenseCalculation(i))
                .subscribe(new Subscriber<Integer>() {
                    @Override
                    public void onSubscribe(Subscription subscription) {
                        subscription.request(Long.MAX_VALUE);
                    }
                    @Override
```

```
                    public void onNext(Integer s) {
                        sleep(50);
                        System.out.println("Subscriber received " + s);
                    }
                    @Override
                    public void onError(Throwable e) {
                        e.printStackTrace();
                    }
                    @Override
                    public void onComplete() {
                        System.out.println("Done!");
                    }
                });
        sleep(20000);
    }
}
```

If you want your `Subscriber` to establish an explicit backpressured relationship with the operator preceding it, you will need to micromanage the `request()` calls. Say, for some extreme situation, you decide that you want `Subscriber` to request 40 emissions initially and then 20 emissions at a time after that. This is what you would need to do:

```
import io.reactivex.rxjava3.core.Flowable;
import io.reactivex.rxjava3.schedulers.Schedulers;
import org.reactivestreams.Subscriber;
import org.reactivestreams.Subscription;

public class Ch8_07 {
    public static void main(String[] args) {
        Flowable.range(1, 1000)
                .doOnNext(s -> System.out.println("Source pushed " + s))
                .observeOn(Schedulers.io())
                .map(i -> intenseCalculation(i))
                .subscribe(new Subscriber<Integer>() {
                    Subscription subscription;
                    AtomicInteger count = new AtomicInteger(0);

                    @Override
                    public void onSubscribe(Subscription subscription) {
                        this.subscription = subscription;
                        System.out.println("Requesting 40 items!");
                        subscription.request(40);
                    }
                    @Override
                    public void onNext(Integer s) {
                        sleep(50);
                        System.out.println("Subscriber received " + s);
                        if (count.incrementAndGet() % 20 == 0 &&
```

```
                                    count.get() >= 40) {
                    System.out.println("Requesting 20 more !");
                    subscription.request(20);
                }
            }
            @Override
            public void onError(Throwable e) {
                e.printStackTrace();
            }
            @Override
            public void onComplete() {
                System.out.println("Done!");
            }
        });
        sleep(20000);
    }
}
```

The output is as follows:

```
Requesting 40 items!
Source pushed 1
Source pushed 2
...
Source pushed 127
Source pushed 128
Subscriber received 1
Subscriber received 2
...
Subscriber received 39
Subscriber received 40
Requesting 20 more!
Subscriber received 41
Subscriber received 42
...
Subscriber received 59
Subscriber received 60
Requesting 20 more!
Subscriber received 61
Subscriber received 62
...
Subscriber received 79
Subscriber received 80
Requesting 20 more!
Subscriber received 81
Subscriber received 82
...
```

Note that the source is still emitting 128 emissions initially and then still pushes 96 emissions at a time. But our `Subscriber` receives only 40 emissions, as specified, and then consistently calls for 20 more. The `request()` call in our `Subscriber` only communicates to the immediate operator upstream, which is `map()`. The `map()` operator likely relays that request to `observeOn()`, which caches items and only flushes out 40 and then 20, as requested by the `Subscriber`. When its cache gets low or clears out, it requests another 96 from the upstream.

 This is a warning: you should not rely on these exact numbers of requested emissions, such as 128 and 96. These are an internal implementation we happen to observe, and these numbers may be changed to aid further implementation optimizations in the future.

This custom implementation may actually reduce the throughput, but it demonstrates how to manage custom backpressure with custom `Subscriber` implementation. Just keep in mind that the `request()` calls do not go all the way upstream. They only go to the preceding operator, which decides how to relay that request upstream.

Creating Flowable

Earlier in this book, we used `Observable.create()` to create our own `Observable` from scratch, which describes how to emit items when it is subscribed to, as shown in the following code snippet:

```java
import io.reactivex.rxjava3.core.Observable;
import io.reactivex.rxjava3.schedulers.Schedulers;

public class Ch8_09 {
    public static void main(String[] args) {
        Observable<Integer> source = Observable.create(emitter -> {
            for (int i = 0; i <= 1000; i++) {
                if (emitter.isDisposed()) {
                    return;
                }
                emitter.onNext(i);
            }
            emitter.onComplete();
        });
        source.observeOn(Schedulers.io())
                .subscribe(System.out::println);
        sleep(1000);
    }
}
```

The output is as follows:

```
0
1
2
3
4
. . .
```

This `Observable.create()` emits the integers from 0 through 1000 and then calls `onComplete()`. It can be stopped abruptly if `dispose()` is called on the `Disposable` returned from `subscribe()`. The `for` loop checks for this.

However, think for a moment how something like this can be backpressured if we execute `Flowable.create()`, the `Flowable` equivalent of `Observable.create()`. Using a simple `for` loop like the preceding one, there is no notion of emissions *stopping* and *resuming* based on the requests of a downstream `Subscriber`. Supporting backpressure properly adds some complexity.

However, there are simpler ways to support backpressure. They often involve compromising strategies such as buffering and dropping, which we will cover first. There are also a few utilities to implement backpressure at the source, which we will cover afterward.

Using Flowable.create() and BackpressureStrategy

Leveraging `Flowable.create()` to create a `Flowable` feels much like `Observable.create()`, but there is one critical difference: you must specify a `BackpressureStrategy` as a second argument. It indicates which of the canned backpressure supporting algorithms to use. The choice is to cache or to drop emissions or not implement backpressure at all.

Here, we use `Flowable.create()` to create a `Flowable`. As a backpressure supporting strategy, we provide a second `BackpressureStrategy.BUFFER` argument to buffer the emissions before they are backpressured, as shown in the following code example:

```
import io.reactivex.rxjava3.core.BackpressureStrategy;
import io.reactivex.rxjava3.core.Flowable;
import io.reactivex.rxjava3.schedulers.Schedulers;

public class Ch8_10 {
```

```
public static void main(String[] args) {
    Flowable<Integer> source = Flowable.create(emitter -> {
        for (int i = 0; i <= 1000; i++) {
            if (emitter.isCancelled()) {
                return;
            }
            emitter.onNext(i);
        }
        emitter.onComplete();
    }, BackpressureStrategy.BUFFER);
    source.observeOn(Schedulers.io())
            .subscribe(System.out::println);
    sleep(1000);
}
}
```

The output is as follows:

```
0
1
2
3
4
. . .
```

This is not optimal because the emissions will be held in an unbounded queue, and it is possible that when `Flowable.create()` pushes too many emissions, you will get an `OutOfMemoryError`.

But at least it prevents `MissingBackpressureException` and can make your custom `Flowable` workable to a certain degree. We will learn about a more robust way to implement backpressure later in this chapter in the *Using Flowable.generate()* section.

There are currently five `BackpressureStrategy` options you can choose from.

BackpressureStrategy	Description
MISSING	Essentially results in no backpressure implementation at all. The downstream must deal with backpressure overflow, which can be helpful when used with `onBackpressureXXX()` operators, which we will cover later in this chapter in the *Using onBackpressureXXX() operators* section.
ERROR	Generates `MissingBackpressureException` the moment the downstream cannot keep up with the source.
BUFFER	Queues up emissions in an unbounded queue until the downstream is able to consume them, but can cause an `OutOfMemoryError` if the queue gets too large.

DROP	If the downstream cannot keep up, this ignores upstream emissions and does not queue them while the downstream is busy.
LATEST	This keeps only the latest emission until the downstream is ready to receive it.

Next, we will see some of these strategies used as operators, particularly converting `Observable` into `Flowable`.

Turning Observable into Flowable and vice versa

There is another way to implement `BackpressureStrategy` against a source that has no notion of backpressure. You can turn an `Observable` into `Flowable` by calling its `toFlowable()` operator, which accepts a `BackpressureStrategy` as an argument. In the following code, we turn `Observable.range()` into `Flowable` using `BackpressureStrategy.BUFFER`. An `Observable` has no notion of backpressure, so it is going to push items as quickly as it can, regardless of whether the downstream can keep up. But `toFlowable()`, with a buffering strategy, will act as a proxy to backlog the emissions when the downstream cannot keep up:

```
import io.reactivex.rxjava3.core.BackpressureStrategy;
import io.reactivex.rxjava3.core.Observable;
import io.reactivex.rxjava3.schedulers.Schedulers;

public class Ch8_11 {
    public static void main(String[] args) {
        Observable<Integer> source = Observable.range(1, 1000);
        source.toFlowable(BackpressureStrategy.BUFFER)
            .observeOn(Schedulers.io())
            .subscribe(System.out::println);
        sleep(10000);
    }
}
```

 Again, note that `toFlowable()`, with a buffering strategy, is going to have an unbounded queue, which can cause an `OutOfMemoryError`. In the real world, it would be better to use `Flowable.range()` in the first place, but sometimes, you may only be provided with an `Observable`.

Flowable also has a toObservable() operator, which will turn a Flowable<T> into an Observable<T>. This can be helpful in making a Flowable usable in an Observable chain, especially with operators such as flatMap(), as shown in the following code:

```
import io.reactivex.rxjava3.core.Flowable;
import io.reactivex.rxjava3.core.Observable;
import io.reactivex.rxjava3.schedulers.Schedulers;

public class Ch8_12 {
    public static void main(String[] args) {
        Flowable<Integer> integers =
                Flowable.range(1, 1000)
                        .subscribeOn(Schedulers.computation());
        Observable.just("Alpha", "Beta", "Gamma", "Delta", "Epsilon")
                .flatMap(s -> integers.map(i -> i + "-" + s)
                                    .toObservable())
                .subscribe(System.out::println);
        sleep(5000);
    }
}
```

If Observable<String> had many more than five emissions (for example, 1,000 or 10,000 emissions), then it would probably be better to turn it into a Flowable instead of turning the flat-mapped Flowable into an Observable.

Even if you call toObservable(), the Flowable still leverages backpressure, but at the point it becomes an Observable, the downstream will no longer be backpressured and will request a Long.MAX_VALUE number of emissions. This may be fine as long as no more intensive operations or concurrency changes happen downstream and the Flowable operations upstream constrain the number of emissions.

But typically, when you commit to using a Flowable, you should strive to make your operations remain Flowable.

Using onBackpressureXXX() operators

If you have a Flowable that has no backpressure implementation (including ones derived from Observable), but you need to support backpressure, you can apply BackpressureStrategy using onBackpressureXXX() operators. They have a few configuration options.

For example, a `Flowable.interval()` may emit faster than consumers can keep up. `Flowable.interval()` cannot be slowed down at the source because it is time-driven, but we can use an `onBackpressureXXX()` operator to proxy between it and the downstream. We will use `Flowable.interval()` for these examples, but the same approach works for any `Flowable` that does not have backpressure support.

Sometimes, for instance, `Flowable` may simply be configured with `BackpressureStrategy.MISSING` so that these `onBackpressureXXX()` operators can specify the strategy later.

onBackPressureBuffer()

The `onBackPressureBuffer()` takes an existing `Flowable` that is assumed to not have backpressure implemented and applies `BackpressureStrategy.BUFFER` at that point to the downstream.

Since `Flowable.interval()` cannot be backpressured at the source, putting `onBackPressureBuffer()` after it will proxy a backpressured queue to the downstream, as demonstrated by the following code:

```
import io.reactivex.rxjava3.core.Flowable;
import io.reactivex.rxjava3.schedulers.Schedulers;

public class Ch8_13 {
    public static void main(String[] args) {
        Flowable.interval(1, TimeUnit.MILLISECONDS)
                .onBackpressureBuffer()
                .observeOn(Schedulers.io())
                .subscribe(i -> {
                    sleep(5);
                    System.out.println(i);
                });
        sleep(5000);
    }
}
```

The output is as follows:

```
0
1
2
3
4
5
```

```
        6
        7
        . . .
```

There are quite a few overload versions of the `onBackPressureBuffer()` operator that take different arguments. We will not get into all of them, and you can refer to the JavaDoc for more information, but we will highlight the common ones.

The `capacity` argument creates a maximum threshold for the buffer rather than allowing it to be unbounded. An `Action onOverflow` function can be specified to fire an action when an overflow exceeds the capacity. You can also specify a `BackpressureOverflowStrategy` enum to instruct how to handle an overflow that exceeds capacity.

Here are the three `BackpressureOverflowStrategy` enum items that you can choose from:

BackpressureOverflowStrategy	Description
ERROR	Simply throws an error the moment the specified capacity is exceeded
DROP_OLDEST	Drops the oldest value from the buffer to make way for a new one
DROP_LATEST	Drops the latest value from the buffer to prioritize older, unconsumed values

In the following code, we hold a maximum capacity of 10 and specify the `BackpressureOverflowStrategy.DROP_LATEST` strategy for an overflow:

```
import io.reactivex.rxjava3.core.BackpressureOverflowStrategy;
import io.reactivex.rxjava3.core.Flowable;
import io.reactivex.rxjava3.schedulers.Schedulers;

public class Ch8_14 {
    public static void main(String[] args) {
        Flowable.interval(1, TimeUnit.MILLISECONDS)
                .onBackpressureBuffer(10,
                        () -> System.out.println("overflow!"),
                        BackpressureOverflowStrategy.DROP_LATEST)
                .observeOn(Schedulers.io())
                .subscribe(i -> {
                    sleep(5);
                    System.out.println(i);
                });
        sleep(5000);
    }
}
```

As you can see, we also print a notification in the event of an overflow. The output is as follows:

```
...
overflow!
overflow!
135
overflow!
overflow!
overflow!
overflow!
overflow!
136
overflow!
overflow!
overflow!
overflow!
overflow!
492
overflow!
overflow!
overflow!
...
```

Note the large range of numbers skipped between `136` and `492`. This is because these emissions were dropped from the queue due to `BackpressureOverflowStrategy.DROP_LATEST`. The queue was already filled with emissions waiting to be consumed, so the new emissions were ignored.

onBackPressureLatest()

A slight variant of `onBackpressureBuffer()` is the `onBackPressureLatest()` operator. This retains the latest value from the source while the downstream is busy. Once the downstream is free to process more, it provides the latest value. Any previous values emitted during this busy period are lost. The following is an example that demonstrates this behavior:

```
import io.reactivex.rxjava3.core.Flowable;
import io.reactivex.rxjava3.schedulers.Schedulers;

public class Ch8_15 {
    public static void main(String[] args) {
        Flowable.interval(1, TimeUnit.MILLISECONDS)
                .onBackpressureLatest()
                .observeOn(Schedulers.io())
```

```
                .subscribe(i -> {
                    sleep(5);
                    System.out.println(i);
                });
        sleep(5000);
    }
}
```

The output is as follows:

```
    . . .
    122
    123
    124
    125
    126
    127
    494
    495
    496
    497
    . . .
```

If you look more closely at the output, you will notice that there is a jump between `127` and `494`. This is because all numbers in between were ultimately beaten by `494` being the latest value and, at that time, the downstream was ready to process more emissions. It started by consuming the cached `494` and the others before it was dropped.

onBackPressureDrop()

The `onBackpressureDrop()` operator simply discards emissions if the downstream is too busy to process them. This is helpful when emissions are considered redundant if the downstream is already busy (such as the same request being sent repeatedly and is currently being executed). You can optionally provide an `onDrop` lambda argument, specifying what to do with each dropped item, as shown in the following code (the dropped items are simply printed):

```
import io.reactivex.rxjava3.core.Flowable;
import io.reactivex.rxjava3.schedulers.Schedulers;

public class Ch8_16 {
    public static void main(String[] args) {
        Flowable.interval(1, TimeUnit.MILLISECONDS)
            .onBackpressureDrop(i ->
                        System.out.println("Dropping " + i))
```

```
                    .observeOn(Schedulers.io())
                    .subscribe(i -> {
                        sleep(5);
                        System.out.println(i);
                    });
            sleep(5000);
        }
    }
```

The output is as follows:

```
. . .
Dropping 653
Dropping 654
Dropping 655
Dropping 656
127
Dropping 657
Dropping 658
Dropping 659
Dropping 660
Dropping 661
493
Dropping 662
Dropping 663
Dropping 664
. . .
```

Note that, in the output, there is a large jump between `127` and `493`. The items were dropped because the downstream was already busy when they were ready to be processed, so they were discarded rather than queued.

Using Flowable.generate()

Despite a lot of the content that has been covered so far in this chapter, we have not yet demonstrated the optimal approach to apply backpressure to a source. Although the standard `Flowable` factories and operators automatically handle the backpressure, the `onBackPressureXXX()` operators, while quick and effective for some cases, just cache or drop emissions, which is not always desirable. It would be better to force the source to slow down as needed in the first place.

Thankfully, `Flowable.generate()` exists to help create backpressure, respecting sources at a nicely abstracted level. It accepts a `Consumer<Emitter<T>>`, much like `Flowable.create()`, but uses a lambda to specify which `onNext()`, `onComplete()`, and `onError()` events to pass each time an item is requested from the upstream.

Before you use `Flowable.generate()`, consider making your source `Iterable<T>` instead and passing it to `Flowable.fromIterable()`.
`Flowable.fromIterable()` respects backpressure and might be easier to use for many cases. Otherwise, `Flowable.generate()` is your next best option if you need something more specific.

The simplest overload for `Flowable.generate()` accepts just `Consumer<Emitter<T>>` and assumes that there is no state maintained between emissions. This can be helpful in creating a backpressure-aware random integer generator, as demonstrated in the following code example:

```java
import io.reactivex.rxjava3.core.Flowable;
import io.reactivex.rxjava3.schedulers.Schedulers;
import java.util.concurrent.ThreadLocalRandom;

public class Ch8_17 {
    public static void main(String[] args) {
        randomGenerator(1, 10000)
                .subscribeOn(Schedulers.computation())
                .doOnNext(i -> System.out.println("Emitting " + i))
                .observeOn(Schedulers.io())
                .subscribe(i -> {
                    sleep(50);
                    System.out.println("Received " + i);
                });
        sleep(10000);
    }
}
```

The `randomGenerator()` method appears as follows:

```java
static Flowable<Integer> randomGenerator(int min, int max) {
    return Flowable.generate(emitter ->
                            emitter.onNext(ThreadLocalRandom.current()
                                    .nextInt(min, max))
        );
}
```

Note that 128 emissions are emitted immediately, but after that, 96 are pushed downstream, then another 96, and so on. The output is as follows:

```
...
Emitting 8014
Emitting 3112
Emitting 5958
Emitting 4834    // 128th emission
Received 9563
Received 4359
Received 9362
...
Received 4880
Received 3192
Received 979     // 96th emission
Emitting 8268
Emitting 3889
Emitting 2595
...
```

Using `Flowable.generate()`, invoking multiple `onNext()` operators within `Consumer<Emitter<T>>` results in `IllegalStateException`. The downstream only needs it to invoke `onNext()` once, so it can make the repeated calls, as required, to maintain flow. It also emits `onError()` in the event that an exception occurs.

You can provide a state as well that acts somewhat like a *seed* in the `reduce()` operator and maintains a state that is passed from one emission to the next.

Suppose we want to create something similar to `Flowable.range()` but instead, we want to emit integers between `upperBound` and `lowerBound` in reverse order. Using `AtomicInteger` as the state holder, we can decrement it and pass its value to the emitter's `onNext()` operator until `lowerBound` is encountered. This can be demonstrated as follows:

```
import io.reactivex.rxjava3.core.Flowable;
import io.reactivex.rxjava3.schedulers.Schedulers;

public class Ch8_18 {
    public static void main(String[] args) {
        rangeReverse(100, -100)
                .subscribeOn(Schedulers.computation())
                .doOnNext(i -> System.out.println("Emitting " + i))
                .observeOn(Schedulers.io())
                .subscribe(i -> {
                    sleep(50);
                    System.out.println("Received " + i);
```

```
                              });
               sleep(50000);
          }
     }
```

The `rangeReverse()` method contains the following code:

```
Flowable<Integer> rangeReverse(int upperBound, int lowerBound) {
     return Flowable.generate(() -> new AtomicInteger(upperBound + 1),
               (state, emitter) -> {
                    int current = state.decrementAndGet();
                    emitter.onNext(current);
                    if (current == lowerBound) {
                         emitter.onComplete();
                    }
               }
     );
}
```

The output is as follows:

```
Emitting 100
Emitting 99
...
Emitting -25
Emitting -26
Emitting -27    // 128th emission
Received 100
Received 99
Received 98
...
Received 7
Received 6
Received 5      // 96th emission
Emitting -28
Emitting -29
Emitting -30
```

`Flowable.generator()` provides a mechanism to create a source that respects backpressure. For this reason, you might want to prefer this over `Flowable.create()` if you do not want to mess with caching or dropping emissions.

With `Flowable.generate()`, you can also provide a third `Consumer<? super S> disposeState` argument to do any disposal operation on termination, which can be helpful for IO sources.

Summary

In this chapter, you learned about `Flowable` and backpressure and the situations in which they should be preferred over an `Observable`. A `Flowable` is especially useful when the application uses concurrency and a lot of data can flow through it, as it regulates how much data comes from the source at a given time. Some `Flowable` objects, such as `Flowable.interval()` or those derived from an `Observable`, do not have backpressure implemented. In these situations, you can use `onBackpressureXXX()` operators to queue or drop emissions for the downstream. If you are creating your own `Flowable` source from scratch, prefer to use the existing `Flowable` factories. If that fails, use `Flowable.generate()` instead of `Flowable.create()`.

If you have reached this point and have understood most of the content in this book so far, congratulations! You have all the core concepts of RxJava in your toolkit, and the rest of the book is all a walk in the park from here. The next chapter will cover how to create your own operators, which can be a somewhat advanced task. As a minimum, you should know how to compose existing operators to create new operators, which will be one of the next topics.

9
Transformers and Custom Operators

In RxJava, there are ways to implement your own custom operators using the `compose()` and `lift()` methods, which exist on both `Observable` and `Flowable`. Most of the time, you will likely want to compose existing RxJava operators to create a new operator. But on occasion, you may find yourself needing an operator that must be built from scratch. The latter is a lot more work, but we will cover how to do both of these tasks in this chapter.

By the end of this chapter, you will be able to create a custom operator either from scratch or by combining the existing ones. Do not feel discouraged if the content of this section seems difficult. Go through it and study all the examples. Creating custom operators is much easier than you may think.

However, before creating your own operator, check a few of the most popular libraries and see whether one of them already has what you need. In the last section of this chapter, we describe two such popular libraries: RxJava2-Extras and RxJava2Extensions.

In this chapter, we will cover the following topics:

- Composing new operators from existing ones using `compose()` and transformers
- Using the `to()` operator for fluent conversion
- Creating new operators from scratch using `lift()`
- Creating a new operator for `Single`, `Maybe`, or `Completable`
- Using RxJava2-Extras and RxJava2Extensions

Composing new operators from existing ones using compose() and transformers

When working with RxJava, you may find yourself wanting to reuse pieces of an `Observable` or `Flowable` chain and somehow consolidate these operators into a new operator. Good developers find opportunities to reuse code, and RxJava provides this ability using `ObservableTransformer` and `FlowableTransformer`, which you can pass to the `compose()` operator.

Using ObservableTransformer

The examples of this section require Google Guava as a dependency. If you removed it, then you need to add it back.

In Chapter 3, *Basic Operators*, we covered the `collect()` operator and used it to turn `Observable<T>` into `Single<ImmutableList<T>>`. Effectively, we want to collect `T` emissions into a Google Guava `ImmutableList<T>`. Suppose we do this operation enough times until it starts to feel redundant. Here, we use this `ImmutableList` operation for two different `Observable` sequences, one created by `Observable.just()` and another created by `Observable.range()`:

```
import com.google.common.collect.ImmutableList;
import io.reactivex.rxjava3.core.Observable;

public class Ch9_01a {
    public static void main(String[] args) {
        Observable.just("Alpha", "Beta", "Gamma", "Delta", "Epsilon")
            .collect(ImmutableList::builder, ImmutableList.Builder::add)
            .map(ImmutableList.Builder::build)
            .subscribe(System.out::println);
        Observable.range(1, 10)
            .collect(ImmutableList::builder, ImmutableList.Builder::add)
            .map(ImmutableList.Builder::build)
            .subscribe(System.out::println);
    }
}
```

The output is as follows:

```
[Alpha, Beta, Gamma, Delta, Epsilon]
[1, 2, 3, 4, 5, 6, 7, 8, 9, 10]
```

Take a look at this part of the `Observable` chain used in two places in the preceding code:

```
collect(ImmutableList::builder, ImmutableList.Builder::add)
.map(ImmutableList.Builder::build)
```

Since this code fragment is used twice, the logical question is: Is it possible to compose a new operator from these two – `collect()` and `map()`? As a matter of fact, yes! It is possible to implement `ObservableTransformer<T,R>` that has an `apply()` method that accepts an `Observable<T>` upstream and returns an `Observable<R>` downstream.

For our example, we will target any generic type, `T`, for a given `Observable<T>`, and `R` will be an `ImmutableList<T>` emitted by an `Observable<ImmutableList<T>>`. We will package all of this up in an `ObservableTransformer<T, ImmutableList<T>>` implementation, as shown in the following code snippet:

```
<T> ObservableTransformer<T, ImmutableList<T>> toImmutableList(){
    return new ObservableTransformer<T, ImmutableList<T>>() {
        @Override
        public ObservableSource<ImmutableList<T>> apply(Observable<T> up){
            return up.collect(ImmutableList::<T> builder,
                                           ImmutableList.Builder::add)
                .map(ImmutableList.Builder::build)
                .toObservable();
        }
    };
}
```

Since `collect()` returns a `Single` object, we use `toObservable()` because `ObservableTransformer` expects an `Observable` type, not `Single`, to be returned. It is not uncommon for a transformer to be delivered through a static factory method, so that is what we do here.

There is only one abstract method in the `ObservableTransformer` interface. That's why we can streamline the code more by using a lambda expression. The following reads a bit easier, as it reads left to right/top to bottom:

```
static <T> ObservableTransformer<T, ImmutableList<T>>
toImmutableList(){
    return up ->
        up.collect(ImmutableList::<T> builder, ImmutableList.Builder::add)
            .map(ImmutableList.Builder::build)
            .toObservable();
}
```

Now, we can invoke the newly created transformer inside an `Observable` chain using the `compose()` operator, as shown in the following code:

```
import com.google.common.collect.ImmutableList;
import io.reactivex.rxjava3.core.Observable;
import io.reactivex.rxjava3.core.ObservableTransformer;

public class Ch9_01b {
    public static void main(String[] args) {
        Observable.just("Alpha", "Beta", "Gamma", "Delta", "Epsilon")
                .compose(toImmutableList())
                .subscribe(System.out::println);
        Observable.range(1, 10)
                .compose(toImmutableList())
                .subscribe(System.out::println);
    }
}
```

When called on an `Observable<T>`, the `compose()` operator accepts an `ObservableTransformer<T,R>` and returns the transformed `Observable<R>`. The output does not change:

```
[Alpha, Beta, Gamma, Delta, Epsilon]
[1, 2, 3, 4, 5, 6, 7, 8, 9, 10]
```

It is common for APIs to organize transformers in a static factory class. In a real-world application, you may store your `toImmutableList()` transformer inside a `GuavaTransformers` class. Then, you can invoke it by calling `compose(GuavaTransformers.toImmutableList())` in your `Observable` operation.

 Note that, for this example, we could actually make the `toImmutableList()` a reusable singleton since it does not take any parameters.

It is also possible to create transformers for a specific emission type and with arguments. As shown in the following example, you can create a `joinToString()` transformer that accepts a separator argument and concatenates `String` emissions using the separator provided:

```
import io.reactivex.rxjava3.core.Observable;
import io.reactivex.rxjava3.core.ObservableTransformer;

public class Ch9_02 {
    public static void main(String[] args) {
        Observable.just("Alpha", "Beta", "Gamma", "Delta", "Epsilon")
```

```
                    .compose(joinToString("/"))
                    .subscribe(System.out::println);
        }
    private static ObservableTransformer<String, String>
                                    joinToString(String separator) {
        return upstream -> upstream
                .collect(StringBuilder::new, (b, s) -> {
                    if (b.length() == 0){
                        b.append(s);
                    }
                    else {
                        b.append(separator).append(s);
                    }
                })
                .map(StringBuilder::toString)
                .toObservable();
        }
    }
```

Note that the emission type has to match, which means that
ObservableTransformer<String, String> will only compile when invoked on an
Observable<String>.

The output is as follows:

Alpha/Beta/Gamma/Delta/Epsilon

Transformers are a great way to wrap a series of operators into one. This way, you can
greatly increase your Rx code reusability. Usually, you will get the most flexibility and
speed by implementing the operator composition through a static factory method, but you
can also extend ObservableTransformer onto your own class implementation.

As we will learn in Chapter 12, *Using RxJava with Kotlin*, the Kotlin language enables
powerful features that streamline RxJava even more. Instead of using transformers, you can
leverage extension functions to add operators to the Observable and Flowable types
without inheritance. We will talk about this in Chapter 12, *Using RxJava with Kotlin*.

Using FlowableTransformer

When you implement your own ObservableTransformer, you might want to create a
FlowableTransformer counterpart as well. This way, you can use your operator on
both—Observable and Flowable.

FlowableTransformer is not much different to ObservableTransformer. Of course, it supports backpressure since it is composed of Flowable operators. Otherwise, it is pretty much the same in its usage except that you obviously pass it to compose() on a Flowable, not an Observable.

Here, we take our toImmutableList() method returning an ObservableTransformer and implement it as a FlowableTransformer instead:

```
import com.google.common.collect.ImmutableList;
import io.reactivex.rxjava3.core.Flowable;
import io.reactivex.rxjava3.core.FlowableTransformer;

public class Ch9_03 {
    public static void main(String[] args) {
        Flowable.just("Alpha", "Beta", "Gamma", "Delta", "Epsilon")
                .compose(toImmutableList())
                .subscribe(System.out::println);
        Flowable.range(1, 10)
                .compose(toImmutableList())
                .subscribe(System.out::println);
    }
    private static <T> FlowableTransformer<T, ImmutableList<T>>
                                               toImmutableList() {
        return upstream ->
                upstream.collect(ImmutableList::<T>builder,
                                          ImmutableList.Builder::add)
                        .map(ImmutableList.Builder::build)
                        .toFlowable();
    }
}
```

The output is as follows:

```
[Alpha, Beta, Gamma, Delta, Epsilon]
[1, 2, 3, 4, 5, 6, 7, 8, 9, 10]
```

You can make a similar conversion to FlowableTransformer in the case of our joinToString() example as well.

In practice, consider creating separate static utility classes to store your `FlowableTransformers` and `ObservableTransformers` separately to prevent name clashes. Our `FlowableTransformer` and `ObservableTransformer` variants of `toImmutableList()` cannot exist in the same static utility class unless they have different method names. But it might be cleaner to put them in separate classes, such as `MyObservableTransformers` and `MyFlowableTransformers`. You could also have them in separate packages with the same class name, `MyTransformers`, one for `Observable` transformers and the other for `Flowable` transformers.

Avoiding a shared state with transformers

When you start creating your own transformers and custom operators, an easy way to shoot yourself in the foot is to share states between more than one subscription. This can quickly create unwanted side effects and buggy applications and is one of the reasons you have to tread carefully as you create your own operators.

Say you want to create an `ObservableTransformer<T, IndexedValue<T>>`, which pairs each emission with its consecutive index starting at `0`. First, you create an `IndexedValue<T>` class to simply pair each `T` value with an `int` index, as shown in the following code example:

```
static final class IndexedValue<T> {
    final int index;
    final T value;

    IndexedValue(int index, T value) {
        this.index = index;
        this.value = value;
    }

    @Override
    public String toString() {
        return  index + " - " + value;
    }
}
```

Then, you create an `ObservableTransformer<T, IndexedValue<T>>` that uses an `AtomicInteger` to increment and attach an integer to each emission. At the first attempt, you may come up with the following implementation:

```
static <T> ObservableTransformer<T,IndexedValue<T>> withIndex() {
    final AtomicInteger indexer = new AtomicInteger(-1);
    return upstream -> upstream
```

```
                    .map(v -> new IndexedValue<T>(indexer.incrementAndGet(), v));
    }
```

See anything wrong yet? Try to run this `Observable` operation in the following code (the examples for the following discussion are named Ch9_04a, Ch9_04b, and Ch9_04c):

```java
import io.reactivex.rxjava3.core.Observable;
import io.reactivex.rxjava3.core.ObservableTransformer;

public class Ch9_04a {
    public static void main(String[] args) {
        Observable<IndexedValue<String>> indexedStrings =
            Observable.just("Alpha", "Beta", "Gamma", "Delta", "Epsilon")
                    .compose(withIndex());
        indexedStrings.subscribe(v ->
                            System.out.println("Subscriber 1: " + v));
        indexedStrings.subscribe(v ->
                            System.out.println("Subscriber 2: " + v));
    }
}
```

The output is as follows:

```
Subscriber 1: 0 - Alpha
Subscriber 1: 1 - Beta
Subscriber 1: 2 - Gamma
Subscriber 1: 3 - Delta
Subscriber 1: 4 - Epsilon
Subscriber 2: 5 - Alpha
Subscriber 2: 6 - Beta
Subscriber 2: 7 - Gamma
Subscriber 2: 8 - Delta
Subscriber 2: 9 - Epsilon
```

Note that a single instance of `AtomicInteger` was shared between both subscriptions, which means its state was shared as well. On the second subscription, instead of starting over at 0, it picks up at the index left by the previous subscription and starts at index 5 since the previous subscription ended at 4.

Unless you need such stateful behavior, this is probably an unwanted side effect that can result in a difficult-to-find bug. Constants are usually fine, but a mutable shared state between subscriptions is often something you want to avoid.

A quick and easy way to create a new resource (such as `AtomicInteger`) for each subscription is to wrap everything in `Observable.defer()`, including the `AtomicInteger` instance. This way, a new `AtomicInteger` object is created each time with the returned indexing operations (refer to the Ch9_04b example):

```
static <T> ObservableTransformer<T,IndexedValue<T>> withIndex() {
    return upstream -> Observable.defer(() -> {
        AtomicInteger indexer = new AtomicInteger(-1);
        return upstream
            .map(v -> new IndexedValue<T>(indexer.incrementAndGet(), v));
    });
}
```

The output changes to the following:

```
Subscriber 1: 0 - Alpha
Subscriber 1: 1 - Beta
Subscriber 1: 2 - Gamma
Subscriber 1: 3 - Delta
Subscriber 1: 4 - Epsilon
Subscriber 2: 0 - Alpha
Subscriber 2: 1 - Beta
Subscriber 2: 2 - Gamma
Subscriber 2: 3 - Delta
Subscriber 2: 4 - Epsilon
```

You can also create an `AtomicInteger` within `Observable.fromCallable()` and use `flatMap()` on it to the `Observable` that uses it.

In this particular example, you can also use `Observable.zip()` or `zipWith()` with `Observable.range()`. Since this is a pure Rx approach as well, no state will be shared between multiple subscribers, and this will also solve the problem, as the following code shows (refer to the Ch9_04c example):

```
static <T> ObservableTransformer<T,IndexedValue<T>> withIndex() {
    return upstream ->
            Observable.zip(upstream,
                        Observable.range(0, Integer.MAX_VALUE),
                        (v, i) -> new IndexedValue<T>(i, v)
            );
}
```

The output is as was expected:

```
Subscriber 1: 0 - Alpha
Subscriber 1: 1 - Beta
Subscriber 1: 2 - Gamma
```

```
Subscriber 1: 3 - Delta
Subscriber 1: 4 - Epsilon
Subscriber 2: 0 - Alpha
Subscriber 2: 1 - Beta
Subscriber 2: 2 - Gamma
Subscriber 2: 3 - Delta
Subscriber 2: 4 - Epsilon
```

Again, an inadvertent shared state and side effects are dangerous in Rx! Whatever implementation you use to create your transformer, it is better to rely on pure Rx factories and operators in your implementation if possible. Avoid creating imperative states and objects that risk being shared across subscriptions unless you are fulfilling some business requirement where a shared state is explicitly wanted.

Using the to() operator for fluent conversion

On rare occasions, you may find yourself having to pass an Observable to another API that converts it into a proprietary type. This can be done simply by passing an Observable as an argument to a factory that does this conversion. However, this does not always feel fluent, and this is where the to() operator comes in.

For example, JavaFX has a Binding<T> type that houses a mutable value of type T and notifies the affected user interface elements to update when it changes. RxJavaFX has JavaFxObserver.toBinding() and JavaFxSubscriber.toBinding() factories, which can turn an Observable<T> or Flowable<T> into a JavaFX Binding<T>.

Here is a simple JavaFX Application:

```
Pane root = new Pane();
Label label = new Label("0");
label.setScaleX(2.00);
label.setScaleY(2.00);
label.relocate(40, 40);
root.getChildren().addAll(label);

Scene scene = new Scene(root, 100, 100);
stage.setScene(scene);
stage.show();
```

It shows **0**.

Now, let's add to the label a binding that will update the text every second. We create an Observable<String> that emits a different String value every second and puts it on the JavaFxScheduler.platform() thread, where it is converted to a Binding<String> used to bind to a textProperty() the emitted value as follows:

```
Observable<String> seconds =
        Observable.interval(1, TimeUnit.SECONDS)
                .map(i -> i.toString())
                .observeOn(JavaFxScheduler.platform());

Binding<String> binding = JavaFxObserver.toBinding(seconds);
label.textProperty().bind(binding);
```

Now, the displayed value is updated every second and shows sequentially **0**, **1**, **2**, **3**, and so on.

But since we have gotten so used to fluent programming with RxJava, would it not be nice to make the conversion of the Observable<String> to a Binding<String> part of the Observable chain too? This way, we do not have to break our fluent style and declare intermediary variables. That can be done with the to() operator, which simply accepts a Function<Observable<T, R> to turn an Observable<T> into any arbitrary R type. In this case, we can turn our Observable<String> into a Binding<String> at the end of our Observable chain using to(), as demonstrated in the following example:

```
Binding<String> binding =
    Observable.interval(1, TimeUnit.SECONDS)
            .map(i -> i.toString())
            .observeOn(JavaFxScheduler.platform())
            .to(JavaFxObserver::toBinding);

label.textProperty().bind(binding);
```

Simple but helpful, right? When you are dealing with proprietary non-Rx types that can be built from Rx Observable or Flowable, this is a handy utility to maintain the fluent Rx style, especially for interoperating with binding frameworks.

Creating new operators from scratch using lift()

Ideally, you will rarely get to the point where you need to build your own operator from scratch by implementing `ObservableOperator` or `FlowableOperator`. `ObservableTransformer` and `FlowableTransformer` will hopefully satisfy most cases where you can use existing operators to compose new ones, and this is usually the safest route.

But on occasion, you may find yourself having to do something that the existing operators cannot do or not do easily. After you exhaust all other options, you may have to create an operator that manipulates each `onNext()`, `onComplete()`, or `onError()` event between the upstream and the downstream.

Before you go out and create your own operator, try to use existing operators first with `compose()` and a transformer. Once that fails, it is recommended that you post a question on StackOverflow and ask the RxJava community whether such an operator exists or can be composed easily. The RxJava community is very active on StackOverflow and they will likely provide a solution and only escalate the complexity of the solution as required.

Note that David Karnok's RxJava2Extensions and Dave Moten's RxJava2-Extras libraries have many useful transformers and operators to augment RxJava as well. We will talk about these libraries in the forthcoming *Using RxJava2-Extras and RxJava2Extensions* section.

If it is determined that there are no existing solutions, then proceed carefully to build your own operator. Again, it is recommended that you solicit help from StackOverflow first. Building a native operator is no easy task, and getting insight and experience from an Rx expert is highly valuable and most likely necessary.

Implementing an ObservableOperator

Implementing your own `ObservableOperator` (as well as `FlowableOperator`) is more involved than creating an `ObservableTransformer` (or `FlowableTransformer`, correspondingly). Instead of composing a series of existing operators, you intercept the `onNext()`, `onComplete()`, `onError()`, and `onSubscribe()` calls from the upstream by implementing your own `Observer` instead. This `Observer` will then logically pass the `onNext()`, `onComplete()`, and `onError()` events to the downstream `Observer` in a way that fulfills the desired operation.

Let's say you want to create your own doOnEmpty() operator that will execute an Action when onComplete() is called and no emissions have occurred. To create your own ObservableOperator<Downstream, Upstream> (where Upstream is the upstream emission type and Downstream is the downstream emission type), you will need to implement its apply() method. This accepts an Observer<Downstream> observer argument and returns an Observer<Upstream>. Here is an example:

```java
private static <T> ObservableOperator<T, T> doOnEmpty(Action action) {
    return new ObservableOperator<T, T>() {
        @Override
        public Observer<? super T> apply(Observer<? super T> observer){
            return new DisposableObserver<T>() {
                boolean isEmpty = true;

                @Override
                public void onNext(T value) {
                    isEmpty = false;
                    observer.onNext(value);
                }

                @Override
                public void onError(Throwable t) {
                    observer.onError(t);
                }

                @Override
                public void onComplete() {
                    if (isEmpty) {
                        try {
                            action.run();
                        } catch (Exception e) {
                            onError(e);
                            return;
                        }
                    }
                    observer.onComplete();
                }
            };
        }
    };
}
```

You can then use this ObservableOperator by calling it in the lift() operator in your Observable chain, as shown here:

```java
import io.reactivex.rxjava3.functions.Action;
import io.reactivex.rxjava3.core.Observable;
```

```
import io.reactivex.rxjava3.core.ObservableOperator;
import io.reactivex.rxjava3.core.Observer;
import io.reactivex.rxjava3.observers.DisposableObserver;

public class Ch9_07 {
  public static void main(String[] args) {
    Observable.range(1, 5)
             .lift(doOnEmpty(() ->
                        System.out.println("Operation 1 Empty!")))
             .subscribe(v -> System.out.println("Operation 1: " + v));
    Observable.<Integer>empty()
             .lift(doOnEmpty(() ->
                        System.out.println("Operation 2 Empty!")))
             .subscribe(v -> System.out.println("Operation 2: " + v));

  }
}
```

The output is as follows:

```
Operation 1: 1
Operation 1: 2
Operation 1: 3
Operation 1: 4
Operation 1: 5
Operation 2 Empty!
```

Inside `apply()`, you take the passed `Observer` that accepts events for the downstream. You create another `Observer` (in this case, we should use a `DisposableObserver` that handles disposal requests for us) to receive emissions and events from the upstream and relay them to the downstream `Observer`. You can manipulate the events to execute the desired logic as well as add any side effects.

In this case, we simply passed the events from the upstream to the downstream untampered, but track whether `onNext()` was called to flag whether emissions were present. When `onComplete()` is called and no emissions are present, it executes the user-specified action within `onComplete()`. It is usually a good idea to wrap any code that could throw runtime errors in `try-catch` and pass those captured errors to `onError()`.

With `ObservableOperator`, it may seem odd that you get the downstream as an input and have to produce an `Observer` for the upstream as the output. With the `map()` operator, for example, the function receives the upstream value and returns the value to be emitted toward the downstream. The reason for this is that code from an `ObservableOperator` gets executed at subscription time where the call travels from the end `Observer` (downstream) toward the source `Observable` (upstream).

Since it is a single abstract method class, you can also implement your
`ObservableOperator` as a lambda expression, as shown here:

```
public static <T> ObservableOperator<T,T> doOnEmpty(Action action) {
    return observer -> new DisposableObserver<T>() {
        boolean isEmpty = true;

        @Override
        public void onNext(T value) {
            isEmpty = false;
            observer.onNext(value);
        }

        @Override
        public void onError(Throwable t) {
            observer.onError(t);
        }

        @Override
        public void onComplete() {
            if (isEmpty) {
                try {
                    action.run();
                } catch (Exception e) {
                    onError(e);
                    return;
                }
            }
            observer.onComplete();
        }
    };
}
```

Just like with transformers, be mindful to not share states between subscriptions unless you
need to.

That was a relatively simple operator because it was a simple reactive building block. In
other cases, operators can be made enormously complex. This is especially the case when
the operators deal with concurrency (for example, `observeOn()` and `subscribeOn()`) or
share states between subscriptions (for example, `replay()`). The implementations of
`groupBy()`, `flatMap()`, and `window()` are complicated and intricate as well.

There are a couple of rules in the Observable contract that you must follow when calling the three events:

1. Never call onComplete() after onError() has occurred (or vice versa).
2. Do not call onNext() after onComplete() or onError() is called and do not call any events after disposal. Breaking these rules can have unintended consequences downstream.

Another thing that needs to be pointed out is that onNext(), onComplete(), and onError() calls can be manipulated and mixed as needed. For example, toList() does not pass an onNext() call downstream for every onNext() it receives from the upstream. It keeps collecting emissions in an internal list. When onComplete() is called from the upstream, it calls onNext() on the downstream to pass that list before it calls onComplete().

In the following code example, we implement our own myToList() operator to understand how toList() could work, even though, under normal circumstances, we should use collect() or toList():

```
private static <T> ObservableOperator<List<T>, T> myToList() {
    return observer -> new DisposableObserver<T>() {
        ArrayList<T> list = new ArrayList<>();

        @Override
        public void onNext(T value) {
            //add to List, but don't pass anything downstream
            list.add(value);
        }

        @Override
        public void onError(Throwable t) {
            observer.onError(t);
        }

        @Override
        public void onComplete() {
            observer.onNext(list); //push List downstream
            observer.onComplete();
        }
    };
}
```

The following processes can use it like this:

```
import io.reactivex.rxjava3.core.Observable;
import io.reactivex.rxjava3.core.ObservableOperator;
import io.reactivex.rxjava3.observers.DisposableObserver;

public class Ch9_08 {
  public static void main(String[] args) {
    Observable.range(1, 5)
              .lift(myToList())
              .subscribe(v -> System.out.println("Operation 1: " + v));
    Observable.<Integer>empty()
              .lift(myToList())
              .subscribe(v -> System.out.println("Operation 2: " + v));
  }
}
```

The output is as follows:

```
Operation 1: [1, 2, 3, 4, 5]
Operation 2: []
```

Before you start getting ambitious in creating your own operators, it might be a good idea to study the source code of RxJava (`https://github.com/ReactiveX/RxJava`) or other libraries, such as RxJava2-Extras (`https://github.com/davidmoten/rxjava2-extras`). Operators can be difficult to implement correctly as you need to have a good understanding of how to build reactive patterns from imperative ones. You will also want to test them well (which we will cover in `Chapter 10`, *Testing and Debugging*) in order to ensure that they behave correctly before putting them into production.

Implementing a FlowableOperator

When you create your own `ObservableOperator`, you will most likely want to create a `FlowableOperator` counterpart as well. This way, your operator can be used for both `Observable` and `Flowable`.

Thankfully, `FlowableOperator` is implemented in a manner similar to how `ObservableOperator` is implemented, as shown here:

```
private static <T> FlowableOperator<T, T> doOnEmpty(Action action) {
    return new FlowableOperator<T, T>() {
        @Override
        public Subscriber<? super T> apply(Subscriber<? super
                T> subscriber) throws Exception {
            return new DisposableSubscriber<T>() {
```

```
                        boolean isEmpty = true;

                        @Override
                        public void onNext(T value) {
                            isEmpty = false;
                            subscriber.onNext(value);
                        }

                        @Override
                        public void onError(Throwable t) {
                            subscriber.onError(t);
                        }

                        @Override
                        public void onComplete() {
                            if (isEmpty) {
                                try {
                                    action.run();
                                } catch (Exception e) {
                                    onError(e);
                                    return;
                                }
                            }
                            subscriber.onComplete();
                        }
                    };
                }
            };
        }
```

Instead of `Observer`, we used `Subscriber`, which hopefully is not surprising at this point. The `Subscriber` passed via `apply()` receives events for the downstream, and the implemented `Subscriber` receives events from the upstream, which it relays to the downstream (just as we used `DisposableObserver`, we use `DisposableSubscriber` to handle disposal/unsubscription). As in the previous example, `onComplete()` verifies that no emissions occurred and runs the specified action if that is the case.

`FlowableOperator` can be used in a similar manner to `ObservableOperator`, as shown here:

```
import io.reactivex.rxjava3.core.Flowable;
import io.reactivex.rxjava3.core.FlowableOperator;
import io.reactivex.rxjava3.functions.Action;
import io.reactivex.rxjava3.subscribers.DisposableSubscriber;
import org.reactivestreams.Subscriber;

public class Ch9_09 {
```

```
public static void main(String[] args) {
    Flowable.range(1, 5)
            .lift(doOnEmpty(() ->
                        System.out.println("Operation 1 Empty!")))
            .subscribe(v -> System.out.println("Operation 1: " + v));
    Flowable.<Integer>empty()
            .lift(doOnEmpty(() ->
                        System.out.println("Operation 2 Empty!")))
            .subscribe(v -> System.out.println("Operation 2: " + v));
    }
}
```

The result is the same as with `ObservableOperator`:

```
Operation 1: 1
Operation 1: 2
Operation 1: 3
Operation 1: 4
Operation 1: 5
Operation 2 Empty!
```

And, of course, you can express your `FlowableOperator` as a lambda, too:

```
public static <T> FlowableOperator<T,T> doOnEmpty(Action action) {
    return subscriber -> new DisposableSubscriber<T>() {
        boolean isEmpty = true;

        @Override
        public void onNext(T value) {
            isEmpty = false;
            subscriber.onNext(value);
        }

        @Override
        public void onError(Throwable t) {
            subscriber.onError(t);
        }

        @Override
        public void onComplete() {
            if (isEmpty) {
                try {
                    action.run();
                } catch (Exception e) {
                    onError(e);
                    return;
                }
            }
        }
```

```
                    subscriber.onComplete();
            }
        };
    }
```

Again, be studious and thorough when you start implementing your own operators, especially as they pass a threshold of complexity. Strive to use existing operators to compose a transformer, and ask StackOverflow or the RxJava community to see whether others can point out an obvious solution first. Implementing operators is something you should be conservative about and only pursue when all other options have been exhausted.

Creating a new operator for Single, Maybe, or Completable

There are transformer and operator counterparts for `Single`, `Maybe`, and `Completable`. When you want to create an `Observable` or `Flowable` operator that yields `Single`, you might find it easier to convert it back into an `Observable`/`Flowable` by calling its `toObservable()` or `toFlowable()` operators. This also applies to `Maybe`.

If, on some rare occasion, you need to create a transformer or operator specifically to take a `Single` and transform it into another `Single`, you want to use `SingleTransformer` or `SingleOperator`. The `Maybe` and `Completable` have counterparts with `MaybeTransformer`/`MaybeOperator` and `CompletableTransformer`/`CompletableOperator`, respectively.

The implementation of `apply()` for all of these should largely be the same experience, and you will use `SingleObserver`, `MaybeObserver`, and `CompletableObserver` to proxy the upstream and downstream.

Here is an example of a `SingleTransformer` that takes `Single<Collection<T>>` and maps the emitted `Collection` to an unmodifiable collection:

```
import io.reactivex.rxjava3.core.Observable;
import io.reactivex.rxjava3.core.SingleTransformer;
import java.util.Collection;
import java.util.Collections;

public class Ch9_10 {
    public static void main(String[] args) {
        Observable.just("Alpha", "Beta", "Gamma", "Delta", "Epsilon")
                .toList()
                .compose(toUnmodifiable())
```

```
                    .subscribe(System.out::println);
    }

    private static <T> SingleTransformer<Collection<T>,
                                  Collection<T>> toUnmodifiable() {
        return singleObserver ->
              singleObserver.map(Collections::unmodifiableCollection);
    }
  }
```

The output is as follows:

[Alpha, Beta, Gamma, Delta, Epsilon]

As you can see, instead of repeating the same lambda expression in several places, we can just create a transformer that can be passed into the `compose()` operator and do the job. This makes the code easier to read and less prone to have defects because of the higher level of code reuse. Our example was intentionally very simple for demonstration purposes. In real life, though, the transformer implementation can be quite complex, so you don't want to write it or copy and paste every time.

But before creating your own transformer, it would be a good idea to check the existing libraries and see whether they already contain what you need. In the following section, we describe two popular libraries.

Using RxJava2-Extras and RxJava2Extensions

If you are interested in learning about additional operators beyond what RxJava provides, it may be worthwhile exploring the RxJava2-Extras and RxJava2Extensions libraries. While neither of these libraries is at a 1.0 version, useful operators, transformers, and `Observable`/`Flowable` factories are continually added as an ongoing project. Here is the configuration for Maven:

```
<dependency>
    <groupId>com.github.davidmoten</groupId>
    <artifactId>rxjava2-extras</artifactId>
    <version>0.1.33</version>
</dependency>
```

Two useful operators are `toListWhile()` and `collectWhile()`. These will buffer emissions into a collection while they meet a certain condition. Because a `BiPredicate` passes both the collection and the next `T` item as a lambda expression, you can use this to buffer items but cut off the moment something changes regarding the emissions.

In the following example (not yet migrated to RxJava 3.0), we keep collecting strings in a list but push that list forward when the length changes (kind of like `distinctUntilChanged()`):

```
import com.github.davidmoten.rx2.flowable.Transformers;
import io.reactivex.Flowable;

public class Ch9_11 {
  public static void main(String[] args) {
    Flowable.just("Alpha","Beta","Zeta","Gamma",
                                "Delta","Theta","Epsilon")
          .compose(Transformers.toListWhile((list, next) ->
            list.size() == 0 || list.get(0).length() == next.length()
          ))
          .subscribe(System.out::println);
    }
}
```

Please note that we also qualify a list being empty, as that is the start of the next buffer, as well as sample an item from the list to compare lengths with the next emission. The output is as follows:

```
[Alpha]
[Beta, Zeta]
[Gamma, Delta, Theta]
[Epsilon]
```

Spend some quality time with RxJava2-Extras and RxJava2Extensions to learn about their custom operators. This way, you will not have to reinvent something that may already have been invented, including many powerful factories and operators. One of the most popular is a resettable `cache()` operator, which works like the cache we studied in Chapter 5, *Multicasting, Replaying, and Caching,* but it can be cleared and then resubscribed to the source at any time. It can also clear the cache at fixed time intervals or periods of no activity, thereby preventing stale caches from persisting.

Summary

In this chapter, we got our feet wet by creating custom operators. It is preferable to use `ObservableTransformer` and `FlowableTransformer` to compose a new operator from the existing ones, and even with that, you need to be cautious when introducing stateful resources that cause undesirable side effects.

When all else fails, you can create your own `ObservableOperator` or `FlowableOperator` and create an operator at a low level that intercepts and relays each emission and event. This can be tricky and you should exhaust all other options, but with careful study and testing, creating operators can be a valuable advanced skill to have. Just be careful to not reinvent the wheel and seek guidance from the Rx community as you start dabbling in custom operators.

If you truly are interested in implementing your own operators (at a low level, not with transformers), definitely study existing operators in RxJava and other reputable RxJava extension libraries. It is easy to hack an operator together and believe nothing will go wrong when, in fact, there are a lot of complications you can overlook. Your operator needs to be serializable, cancelable, concurrent, and handle re-entrancy (which occurs when an emission invokes a request on the same thread). Of course, some operators are simpler than others, but you should never assume it without a committed study first.

In the next chapter, we will learn about the different strategies of unit testing of RxJava APIs. Whether you create your own custom operators or you have an Rx project at work, automated testing is something you need to be proficient in. We will also learn how to debug RxJava applications, which is not always easy but can be done effectively.

Section 3: Integration of RxJava applications

This final module of the book deals with more practical matters of RxJava programming. It includes discussions on testing and debugging RxJava applications, along with programming for Android using Android Studio, and brings the reader up to speed on the basics of the Kotlin language.

The following chapters are included in this module:

- Chapter 10, *Testing and Debugging*
- Chapter 11, *RxJava on Android*
- Chapter 12, *Using RxJava for Kotlin*

Testing and Debugging

10

While unit testing is not a silver bullet to ensure that your code works properly, it is a good practice to strive for. This is especially true if your logic is highly deterministic and modular enough to isolate.

Testing with RxJava at first glance may not seem straightforward. After all, RxJava declares behaviors rather than states. So how do we test whether behaviors are working correctly, especially when most testing frameworks expect a stateful result? Fortunately, RxJava comes with several tools that aid testing, and you can use these tools with your favorite testing frameworks. There are many testing tools available on the market that can work with RxJava, but in this chapter, we will use JUnit.

We will also cover a few tips to effectively debug RxJava programs. One of the downsides of RxJava is that when a bug occurs, a traditional approach to debugging is not always effective, particularly because the stack trace is not always helpful and breakpoints do not apply easily. But there is a benefit RxJava offers in debugging: with the right approach, you can walk through your entire reactive chain and find the operator that causes things to go wrong. The problem becomes very linear and a matter of isolating the bad link. This can simplify the debugging process significantly.

This chapter has a number of testing features to cover, so we will start with simpler naive approaches to cover basic blocking operators. Then, we will escalate to the more robust tools, such as `TestObserver`, `TestSubscriber`, and `TestScheduler`, which you will likely use in your applications.

In this chapter, we will cover the following topics:

- Configuring JUnit
- Blocking subscribers
- Blocking operators
- Using `TestObserver` and `TestSubscriber`
- Manipulating time with `TestScheduler`
- Debugging RxJava code

Configuring JUnit

In this section, we will be using JUnit as our testing framework. Add the following dependency to your Maven or Gradle project.

Here is the configuration for Maven:

```
<dependency>
    <groupId>junit</groupId>
    <artifactId>junit</artifactId>
    <version>4.13</version>
    <scope>test</scope>
</dependency>
```

Here is the configuration for Gradle:

```
dependencies {
    compile 'junit:junit:4.12'
}
```

To save yourself the hassle, organize your code project to conform to the Maven standard directory layout. You might want to place your test classes in a `src/test/java/` folder so that Maven and Gradle will automatically recognize it as the test code folder. You should also put your production code in a `src/main/java/` folder in your project. You can read more about the Maven standard directory layout at `https://maven.apache.org/guides/introduction/introduction-to-the-standard-directory-layout.html`.

If you use the source code from GitHub provided with this book, make sure that the `Chapter10/src/test/java/` folder is listed as a source folder in the project configuration.

Blocking subscribers

Remember how sometimes, we have to stop the main thread from racing past an `Observable` or `Flowable` that operates on a different thread and keep it from exiting the application before it has a chance to fire? We often prevented this using `Thread.sleep()`, especially when we used `Observable.interval()`, `subscribeOn()`, or `observeOn()`. The following code shows how we did this typically and kept an `Observable.interval()` application alive for 6 seconds (just a second longer than the number of emitted intervals):

```
import io.reactivex.rxjava3.core.Observable;
import org.junit.Test;
```

```
import java.util.concurrent.TimeUnit;

public class Ch10_01 {
    @Test
    public void demoCode() {
        Observable.interval(1, TimeUnit.SECONDS)
                .take(5)
                .subscribe(System.out::println);
        sleep(6000);
    }
    public static void sleep(int millis) {
        try {
            Thread.sleep(millis);
        } catch (InterruptedException e) {
            e.printStackTrace();
        }
    }
}
```

The preceding code produces the following output:

```
0
1
2
3
4
```

When it comes to unit testing, the test usually has to complete before it starts the next one. This can become quite messy when we have an Observable or Flowable operation that happens on a different thread. When a test method declares an asynchronous Observable or Flowable chain operation, we need to block and wait for that operation to complete.

Here, we create a test to ensure that five emissions are emitted from Observable.interval(), and we increment AtomicInteger before validating that it was incremented five times:

```
import io.reactivex.rxjava3.core.Observable;
import org.junit.Test;
import java.util.concurrent.TimeUnit;
import java.util.concurrent.atomic.AtomicInteger;
import static org.junit.Assert.assertTrue;

public class Ch10_02 {
    @Test
    public void testSubscribe() {
        AtomicInteger hitCount = new AtomicInteger();
```

```
Observable<Long> source =
        Observable.interval(1, TimeUnit.SECONDS)
                .take(5);
source.subscribe(i -> hitCount.incrementAndGet());
assertTrue("actual count = " + hitCount.get(),
                                hitCount.get() == 5);
    }
}
```

We use the `@Test` annotation to tell `JUnit` that this is a test method. You can run it in IntelliJ IDEA by clicking on its green triangular play button in the gutter or by running the test task in Gradle or Maven.

There is a problem, though. When you run this test, the assertion fails with the following message:

```
java.lang.AssertionError: actual count = 0
<2 internal calls>
    at Ch10_2.testSubscribe(Ch10_2.java:20) <22 internal calls>
```

`Observable.interval()` is running on a computation thread and the main thread rushes past it. The main thread performs `assertTrue()` before the five emissions are fired and therefore finds `hitCount` to be less than 5. We need to stop the main thread until `subscribe()` finishes and calls `onComplete()`.

Thankfully, we do not have to get creative using synchronizers and other native Java concurrency tools. Instead, we can use `blockingSubscribe()`, which will block the main thread until `onComplete()` (or `onError()`) is called. Once those five emissions are gathered, the main thread can proceed and perform the assertion successfully, as demonstrated here in the following code:

```
import io.reactivex.rxjava3.core.Observable;
import org.junit.Test;
import java.util.concurrent.TimeUnit;
import java.util.concurrent.atomic.AtomicInteger;
import static org.junit.Assert.assertTrue;

public class Ch10_03 {
    @Test
    public void testBlockingSubscribe() {
        AtomicInteger hitCount = new AtomicInteger();
        Observable<Long> source =
                Observable.interval(1, TimeUnit.SECONDS)
                        .take(5);
```

```
source.blockingSubscribe(i -> hitCount.incrementAndGet());
assertTrue(hitCount.get() == 5);
        }
    }
```

The preceding test succeeds and asserts that the `hitCount` value equals 5.

As we will see in this chapter, there are better ways to test other than `blockingSubscribe()`. But `blockingSubscribe()` is a quick and effective way to stop the declaring thread and wait for the `Observable` or `Flowable` to finish before proceeding, even if it is on a different thread. Just make sure that the source terminates at some point, or the test will never finish.

 Be judicious in how you use `blockingSubscribe()` outside the context of testing and using it in production. There are definitely times when it is a legitimate solution to interface with a non-reactive API. For example, it can be valid to use it in production to keep an application alive indefinitely and is an effective alternative to using `Thread.sleep()`. Just be careful to ensure that the asynchronous benefits of RxJava are not undermined.

Blocking operators

In RxJava, there is a set of operators we have not covered yet, called **blocking operators**. Such an operator serves as an immediate proxy between the reactive world and the stateful one, blocking and waiting for results to be emitted, and then returns in a non-reactive way. Even if the reactive operations are working on different threads, the blocking operator stops the declaring thread and makes it wait for the result in a synchronized manner, much like `blockingSubscribe()`.

A blocking operator is especially helpful in making the results of `Observable` or `Flowable` chain processing available for evaluation. However, you should avoid using it in production because it encourages anti-patterns and undermines the benefits of reactive programming. For testing, you still want to prefer `TestObserver` and `TestSubscriber`, which we will cover later. In this section, however, we discuss blocking operators, should you ever have a need for them.

blockingFirst()

The `blockingFirst()` operator will stop the calling thread and make it wait for the first value to be emitted, and then return even if the chain is operating on a different thread with `observeOn()` and `subscribeOn()`. Let's say that we want to test an `Observable` chain that filters a sequence of the `String` type emissions for only ones that have a length of four. If we want to assert that the first emission to make it through this operation is `Beta`, we can test for it like this:

```
import io.reactivex.rxjava3.core.Observable;
import org.junit.Test;
import static org.junit.Assert.assertTrue;

public class Ch10_04 {
    @Test
    public void testFirst() {
        Observable<String> source =
            Observable.just("Alpha", "Beta", "Gamma",
                "Delta", "Zeta");
        String firstWithLengthFour = source.filter(s -> s.length()
      == 4)
                                        .blockingFirst();
        assertTrue(firstWithLengthFour.equals("Beta"));
    }
}
```

Here, our unit test is called `testFirst()`, and it asserts that the first `String` value emitted with a length of four is `Beta`. Note that instead of using `subscribe()` or `blockingSubscribe()` to receive the emissions, we use `blockingFirst()`, which returns the first emission in a non-reactive way. In other words, it returns a `String` value and not an `Observable` emitting strings.

This blocks the declaring thread until the value is returned and assigned to `firstWithLengthFour`. We then use that saved value to assert that it is, in fact, `Beta`.

 Looking at `blockingFirst()`, you may be tempted to use it in production code to save a result statefully and refer to it later. Try not to do that! While there are certain cases where you might be able to justify it (such as saving emissions into a `HashMap` for expensive computations and lookups), blocking operators can easily be abused. If you need to persist values, try to use `replay()` and other reactive caching strategies so that you can easily change their behavior and concurrency policies down the road. Blocking often makes your code less flexible and undermines the benefits of Rx.

Note that the `blockingFirst()` operator throws an error and fails the test if no emissions come through. However, you can provide a default value as an overload to `blockingFirst()`, so that it always has a value to fall back on.

A similar blocking operator to `blockingFirst()` is `blockingSingle()`, which expects only a single item to be emitted, but throws an error if there are more.

blockingGet()

The `Maybe` and `Single` interfaces do not have `blockingFirst()` since there can only be one element at most. Logically, for `Single` and `Maybe`, it is not exactly the **first** element, but rather the **only** element, so the equivalent operator is `blockingGet()`.

Here, we assert that all items of length four include only `Beta` and `Zeta`, and we collect them with `toList()`, which yields a `Single<List<String>>`. We can use `blockingGet()` to wait for this list and assert that it contains the expected values as follows:

```
import io.reactivex.rxjava3.core.Observable;
import org.junit.Test;
import java.util.Arrays;
import java.util.List;
import static org.junit.Assert.assertTrue;

public class Ch10_05 {
    @Test
    public void testSingle() {
        Observable<String> source =
            Observable.just("Alpha", "Beta", "Gamma",
                "Delta", "Zeta");
        List<String> allLengthFour =
            source.filter(s -> s.length() == 4)
                .toList()
                .blockingGet();
        assertTrue(allLengthFour.equals(Arrays.asList("Beta","Zeta")));
    }
}
```

blockingLast()

If there is `blockingFirst()`, it only makes sense to have `blockingLast()`. This will block and return the last value emitted from an `Observable` or `Flowable` source. Of course, it will not return anything until `onComplete()` is called, so this is something you will want to avoid using with infinite sources.

In the following example, we assert that the last four-character `String` value emitted from our operation is `Zeta`:

```
import io.reactivex.rxjava3.core.Observable;
import org.junit.Test;
import static org.junit.Assert.assertTrue;

public class Ch10_06 {
    @Test
    public void testLast() {
        Observable<String> source =
            Observable.just("Alpha", "Beta", "Gamma",
                "Delta", "Zeta");
        String lastLengthFour = source.filter(s -> s.length() == 4)
                                    .blockingLast();
        assertTrue(lastLengthFour.equals("Zeta"));
    }
}
```

Just like `blockingFirst()`, `blockingLast()` will throw an error if no emissions occur, but you can use an overloaded version to specify a default value.

blockingIterable()

One of the most interesting blocking operators is `blockingIterable()`. Rather than returning a single emission like our previous examples, it provides the emissions as they become available through `iterable<T>`. The `Iterator<T>` provided by the `Iterable<T>` keeps blocking the iterating thread until the next emission is available, and the iteration ends when `onComplete()` is called. In the following code, we iterate through each returned `String` value to ensure that its length is actually 5:

```
import io.reactivex.rxjava3.core.Observable;
import org.junit.Test;
import static org.junit.Assert.assertTrue;

public class Ch10_07 {
    @Test
```

```
public void testIterable() {
    Observable<String> source =
        Observable.just("Alpha", "Beta", "Gamma",
            "Delta", "Zeta");
    Iterable<String> allLengthFive =
        source.filter(s -> s.length() == 5)
            .blockingIterable();
    for (String s: allLengthFive) {
        assertTrue(s.length() == 5);
    }
}
}
```

The `blockingIterable()` queues up unconsumed values until the `Iterator` is able to process them. This can be problematic without backpressure as you may run into `OutOfMemoryException` errors.

Unlike C#, note that Java's `for-each` construct does not handle cancellation, breaking, or disposal. You can work around this by iterating the `Iterator` from the iterable inside `try-finally`. In the `finally` block, cast the `Iterator` to a `disposable` so that you can call its `dispose()` method.

The `blockingIterable()` can be helpful in quickly turning an `Observable` or `Flowable` into pull-driven functional sequence types such as a Java 8 Stream or Kotlin sequence, which can be built from an `Iterable`. However, for Java 8 streams, you are likely better off using David Karnok's RxJava2Jdk8Interop library (`https://github.com/akarnokd/RxJava2Jdk8Interop`), so that termination is handled more safely.

blockingForEach()

A more fluent way in which we can execute a blocking for each task is to use the `blockingForEach()` operator instead of `blockingIterable()`. This blocks the declaring thread and waits for each emission to be processed before allowing the thread to continue. We can streamline our earlier example, where we iterated over each emitted value and ensured that its length was five and specify the assertion as a lambda expression in the `forEach()` operator instead as follows:

```
import io.reactivex.rxjava3.core.Observable;
import org.junit.Test;
import static org.junit.Assert.assertTrue;

public class Ch10_08 {
    @Test
```

```
        public void testBlockingForEach() {
            Observable<String> source =
                Observable.just("Alpha", "Beta", "Gamma", "Delta", "Zeta");
            source.filter(s -> s.length() == 5)
                .blockingForEach(s -> assertTrue(s.length() == 5));
        }
    }
```

A variant of `blockingForEach()` is `blockingForEachWhile()`, which accepts a predicate that gracefully terminates the sequence if the predicate evaluates to `false` against an emission. This can be desirable if not all emissions are going to be consumed and you want to terminate gracefully.

blockingNext()

`blockingNext()` will return an iterable and block each iterator's `next()` request until the next value is provided. Emissions that occur after the last fulfilled `next()` request and before the current `next()` are ignored. In the following code example, we have a source that emits every microsecond (1/1,000th of a millisecond). Note that the iterable returned from `blockingNext()` ignores previous values that it missed:

```
import io.reactivex.rxjava3.core.Observable;
import org.junit.Test;
import java.util.concurrent.TimeUnit;

public class Ch10_09 {
    @Test
    public void testBlockingNext() {
        Observable<Long> source =
                Observable.interval(1, TimeUnit.MICROSECONDS)
                        .take(1000);
        Iterable<Long> iterable = source.blockingNext();
        for (Long i: iterable) {
            System.out.println(i);
        }
    }
}
```

The output obtained is as follows (you may get different results):

```
0
6
9
11
17
23
26
```

blockingLatest()

The iterable from `blockingLatest()`, on the other hand, does not wait for the next value. Instead, it requests the last emitted value. Any previous values that were not captured are forgotten. It does not reconsume the latest value if the iterator's `next()` consumed it previously and blocks until the next one comes. The following code demonstrates this behavior:

```
import io.reactivex.rxjava3.core.Observable;
import org.junit.Test;
import java.util.concurrent.TimeUnit;

public class Ch10_10 {
    @Test
    public void testBlockingLatest() {
        Observable<Long> source =
                Observable.interval(1, TimeUnit.MICROSECONDS)
                        .take(1000);
        Iterable<Long> iterable = source.blockingLatest();
        for (Long i: iterable) {
            System.out.println(i);
        }
    }
}
```

The output obtained is as follows (you may get different results):

```
0
49
51
53
55
56
58
...
```

blockingMostRecent()

`blockingMostRecent()` is similar to `blockingLatest()`, but it reconsumes the latest value repeatedly for every `next()` call from the iterator, even if already consumed. It also requires a `defaultValue` argument so that it has something to return if no value is emitted yet. In the following example, we use `blockingMostRecent()` against an `Observable` emitting every `10` milliseconds, and the default value is `-1`:

```
import io.reactivex.rxjava3.core.Observable;
import org.junit.Test;
import java.util.concurrent.TimeUnit;

public class Ch10_11 {
    @Test
    public void testBlockingMostRecent() {
        Observable<Long> source =
                Observable.interval(10, TimeUnit.MILLISECONDS)
                        .take(5);
        Iterable<Long> iterable = source.blockingMostRecent(-1L);
        for (Long i: iterable) {
            System.out.println(i);
        }
    }
}
```

The `blockingMostRecent()` operator consumes each value repeatedly until the next value is provided. The output is as follows:

```
-1
-1
-1
...
0
0
0
...
1
1
1
...
```

As we finish covering blocking operators, it should be emphasized again that they can be an effective way to do simple assertions and provide a means to block results so that they can be consumed easily by a testing framework. However, you should avoid using blocking operators for production as much as possible. Try not to give in to the sirens of convenience, as you will find that they can quickly undermine the flexibility and benefits of reactive programming.

Using TestObserver and TestSubscriber

We've so far covered `blockingSubscribe()` and several blocking operators in this chapter. While you can use these blocking tools to do simple assertions, there is a much more comprehensive way to test reactive code than simply blocking for one or more values. After all, we should do more than test `onNext()` calls. We also have `onComplete()` and `onError()` events to account for! It would also be great to streamline testing other RxJava events, such as subscription, disposal, and cancellation.

So let's introduce the `TestObserver` and `TestSubscriber`, your two best friends in testing RxJava applications.

`TestObserver` and `TestSubscriber` are a treasure trove of convenient methods to aid testing, many of which assert that certain events have occurred or specific values were received. There are also blocking methods, such as `awaitTerminalEvent()`, which stops the calling thread until the reactive operation terminates.

`TestObserver` is used for `Observable`, `Single`, `Maybe`, and `Completable` sources, while `TestSubscriber` is used for `Flowable` sources. Here is a unit test showcasing several `TestObserver` methods, which also exist on `TestSubscriber` if you are working with `Flowable`. These methods perform tasks such as asserting that certain events have (or have not) occurred, awaiting terminations or asserting that certain values were received, as follows:

```
import io.reactivex.rxjava3.core.Observable;
import io.reactivex.rxjava3.observers.TestObserver;
import org.junit.Test;
import static org.junit.Assert.assertFalse;
import static org.junit.Assert.assertTrue;

import java.util.concurrent.TimeUnit;

public class Ch10_12 {
    @Test
    public void usingTestObserver() {
```

```
//An Observable with 5 one-second emissions
Observable<Long> source =
        Observable.interval(1, TimeUnit.SECONDS)
                .take(3);

//Declare TestObserver
TestObserver<Long> testObserver = new TestObserver<>();

//Assert no subscription has occurred yet
//testObserver.assertNotSubscribed();        //RxJava 2.x
assertFalse(testObserver.hasSubscription());
    }
}
```

After `TestObserver` is subscribed, it can be asserted, too, as follows:

```
//Subscribe TestObserver to source
source.subscribe(testObserver);

//Assert TestObserver is subscribed
//testObserver.assertSubscribed();        //RxJava 2.x
assertTrue(testObserver.hasSubscription());
```

Other assertions can be made, too; for example:

```
//Block and wait for Observable to terminate
//testObserver.awaitTerminalEvent();        //RxJava 2.x

try {
    testObserver.await(4L, TimeUnit.SECONDS);
} catch (InterruptedException e) {
    e.printStackTrace();
}

//Assert TestObserver called onComplete()
testObserver.assertComplete();
```

It is also possible to assert the values and errors received by the `TestObserver` as follows:

```
//Assert there were no errors
testObserver.assertNoErrors();

//Assert 5 values were received
testObserver.assertValueCount(3);

//Assert the received emissions were 0, 1, 2, 3, 4
testObserver.assertValues(0L, 1L, 2L);
```

This is just a handful of the many testing methods available, and they will make your unit tests much more comprehensive and streamlined. Most of the `TestObserver` methods return `TestObserver` so you can actually chain these assertions fluently (it also applies to `TestSubscriber`).

Spend some time going through all these testing methods so that you are aware of the different assertions you make. Prefer `TestObserver` and `TestSubscriber` over blocking operators as much as possible. This way, you can spend less time maintaining your tests and ensure that you cover the full spectrum of events in the life cycle of an `Observable` or `Flowable` operation.

`TestObserver` implements `Observer`, `MaybeObserver`, `SingleObserver`, and `CompetableObserver` to support all these reactive types. It also implements `Disposable`.

Manipulating time with TestScheduler

In our previous examples, did you notice that testing a time-driven `Observable` or `Flowable` requires that time to elapse before the test completes? In the last example, we took five emissions from an `Observable.interval()` emitting every 1 second, so that test took 5 seconds to complete. If we have a lot of unit tests that deal with time-driven sources, it can take a long time for testing to complete. Would it not be nice if we could simulate time elapses rather than experiencing them?

`TestScheduler` does exactly this. It is a scheduler implementation that allows us to **fast-forward** by a specific amount of elapsed time, and we can do any assertions after each fast-forward to see what events have occurred.

In the following example, we create a test against `Observable.interval()` that emits every minute:

```
import io.reactivex.rxjava3.core.Observable;
import io.reactivex.rxjava3.observers.TestObserver;
import io.reactivex.rxjava3.schedulers.TestScheduler;
import org.junit.Test;
import java.util.concurrent.TimeUnit;

public class Ch10_13 {
    @Test
    public void usingTestScheduler() {
        TestScheduler testScheduler = new TestScheduler();
        TestObserver<Long> testObserver = new TestObserver<>();
```

```
Observable<Long> minuteTicker =
        Observable.interval(1, TimeUnit.MINUTES,
            testScheduler);
minuteTicker.subscribe(testObserver);
    }
}
```

Now, we would like to assert that no emissions happened after 30 seconds (after subscription), one emission happened after 70 seconds and, finally, that 90 emissions have occurred after 90 minutes. The following is the code that does this:

```
//Fast forward by 30 seconds
testScheduler.advanceTimeBy(30, TimeUnit.SECONDS);
testObserver.assertValueCount(0);

//Fast forward to 70 seconds after subscription
testScheduler.advanceTimeTo(70, TimeUnit.SECONDS);
testObserver.assertValueCount(1);

//Fast Forward to 90 minutes after subscription
testScheduler.advanceTimeTo(90, TimeUnit.MINUTES);
testObserver.assertValueCount(90);
```

Rather than having to wait the entire 90 minutes in real time, we use `TestObserver` to artificially elapse these 90 minutes. This allows the test to run instantly. Cool, right? It is almost like time travel! We put `Observable.interval()` on our `TestScheduler`. This way, `TestScheduler` controls how the `Observable` interprets time and pushes emissions. We fast-forward 30 seconds using `advanceTimeBy()` and then assert that no emissions have happened yet. We then use `advanceTimeTo()` to jump 70 seconds after subscription occurred and assert that one emission did happen. Finally, we advance 90 minutes after subscription, and we assert that 90 emissions did, in fact, occur.

The test runs instantly comparing to 90 minutes, showing that it is indeed possible to test time-driven `Observable`/`Flowable` operations without having to actually elapse that time. Carefully note that `advanceTimeBy()` will fast-forward the specified time interval relative to the *current* time, whereas `advanceTimeTo()` will jump to the exact time elapsed since the subscription occurred.

In summary, use `TestScheduler` when you need to represent time elapsing virtually, but note that this is not a thread-safe `Scheduler` and should not be used with actual concurrency. A common pitfall is that a complicated flow that uses many operators and schedulers is not easily configurable for using `TestScheduler`. In this case, you can use `RxJavaPlugins.setComputationScheduler()` and similar methods that override the standard `Scheduler` and inject `TestScheduler` in its place.

There are two other methods to note: `TestScheduler.now()` will return how much time has elapsed virtually in the unit you specify, while the `triggerActions()` method kicks-off any action that was scheduled to be triggered, but that has not elapsed virtually yet.

Debugging RxJava code

RxJava is not easy to debug at first glance, primarily due to the lack of debugging tools and the large stack traces it can produce. Attempts are underway to create effective debugging tools for RxJava, most notably the Frodo library for Android (`https://github.com/android10/frodo`). We will not cover any debugging tools for RxJava as nothing has been standardized quite yet, but we will learn about an effective approach that you can take to debug reactive code.

A common theme in debugging RxJava operations is finding the bad link or the operator in the `Observable`/`Flowable` chain that is causing the problem. Whether an error is being emitted, `onComplete()` is never being called, or an `Observable` is unexpectedly empty, you often have to start at the beginning of the chain at the source and then validate each step downstream until you find the one not working correctly.

Let's say we have an `Observable` pushing five `String` values containing numbers and alphabetic words separated by slashes, `"/"`. We want to break each value on the slashes as follows:

```
import io.reactivex.rxjava3.core.Observable;
import io.reactivex.rxjava3.observers.TestObserver;
import org.junit.Test;

public class Ch10_14 {
    @Test
    public void debugWalkthrough() {
        TestObserver<String> testObserver = new TestObserver<>();

        //Source pushing three strings
        Observable<String> items =
                Observable.just("521934/2342/Foxtrot",
                                "Bravo/12112/78886/Tango",
                                "283242/4542/Whiskey/2348562");

        //Split and concatMap() on "/"
        items.concatMap(s -> Observable.fromArray(s.split("/")))
    }
}
```

After the split, we would like to filter only the alphabetic words, and capture them in `TestObserver`, as shown in the following code:

```
.filter(s -> s.matches("[A-Z]+"))
.subscribe(testObserver);
```

Then, we try to print the captured values and assert them as follows:

```
System.out.println(testObserver.values());
testObserver.assertValues("Foxtrot","Bravo","Tango","Whiskey");
```

However, if you run the preceding example, the test fails with the following output:

```
[]

java.lang.AssertionError: Value count differs; expected: 4 [Foxtrot, Bravo, Tango, Whiskey] but was: 0 [] (latch = 0, values = 0, errors = 0, completions = 1)
Expected :4 [Foxtrot, Bravo, Tango, Whiskey]
Actual   :0 [] (latch = 0, values = 0, errors = 0, completions = 1)
<Click to see difference>

    at io.reactivex.observers.BaseTestConsumer.fail(BaseTestConsumer.java:189)
    at io.reactivex.observers.BaseTestConsumer.assertValues(BaseTestConsumer.java:538)
    at Ch10_14.debugWalkthrough(Ch10_14.java:29) <22 internal calls>
```

So what in the world went wrong? How do we debug this failing test? Well, remember that RxJava operations are a pipeline. The correct emissions are supposed to flow through and make it to the `Observer`, but no emissions were received instead. Let's get our plumber gear on and find out where the clog in the pipeline is. We start at the source.

Place `doOnNext()` immediately after the source and before `concatMap()` and print each emission. This gives us visibility into what is coming out of the source `Observable`. As shown here, we should see all the emissions from the source print, which shows that no emissions are being omitted and that the source upstream is working correctly:

```
//Split and concatMap() on "/"
  items.doOnNext(s -> System.out.println("Source pushed: " + s))
        .concatMap(s -> Observable.fromArray(s.split("/")))
```

The output is as follows:

```
Source pushed: 521934/2342/Foxtrot
Source pushed: Bravo/12112/78886/Tango
Source pushed: 283242/4542/Whiskey/2348562
[]

java.lang.AssertionError: Value count differs; Expected ...
```

Let's move downstream and look at `concatMap()` next. Maybe that is omitting emissions, so let's check it. Move `doOnNext()` after `concatMap()` and print each emission to see whether all of them are coming through, as shown in the next code snippet:

```
//Split and concatMap() on "/"
 items.concatMap(s -> Observable.fromArray(s.split("/")))
        .doOnNext(s -> System.out.println("concatMap() pushed: " + s))
```

The output is as follows:

```
concatMap() pushed: 521934
concatMap() pushed: 2342
concatMap() pushed: Foxtrot
concatMap() pushed: Bravo
concatMap() pushed: 12112
concatMap() pushed: 78886
concatMap() pushed: Tango
concatMap() pushed: 283242
concatMap() pushed: 4542
concatMap() pushed: Whiskey
concatMap() pushed: 2348562
[]

java.lang.AssertionError: Value count differs; Expected ...
```

Okay, so `concatMap()` is working fine and all the emissions are going through. So nothing is wrong with the splitting operation inside `concatMap()`. Let's move downstream and put `doOnNext()` after `filter()`. Print each emission to see whether the ones we want are coming out of the `filter()`, as shown in this code snippet:

```
//filter for only alphabetic Strings using regex
 .filter(s -> s.matches("[A-Z]+"))
 .doOnNext(s -> System.out.println("filter() pushed: " + s))
```

The output is as follows:

```
[]

java.lang.AssertionError: Value count differs; Expected ...
```

Aha! No emissions were printed after `filter()`, so `filter()` is the operator causing the problem. We intended to filter out the numeric strings and only emit the alphabetic words, but for some reason, all emissions were filtered out. If you know anything about regular expressions, note that we are only qualifying strings that are entirely uppercase.

We actually need to qualify lowercase letters too, so here is the correction we need:

```
//filter for only alphabetic Strings using regex
 .filter(s -> s.matches("[A-Za-z]+"))
 .doOnNext(s -> System.out.println("filter() pushed: " + s))
```

The output now changes to the following:

```
filter() pushed: Foxtrot
filter() pushed: Bravo
filter() pushed: Tango
filter() pushed: Whiskey
[Foxtrot, Bravo, Tango, Whiskey]
```

Alright, it is fixed! Our unit test passed finally. Now that the problem is solved and we are finished debugging, we can remove doOnNext() and any print calls, so the corrected version of the code example appears as follows:

```
import io.reactivex.rxjava3.core.Observable;
import io.reactivex.rxjava3.observers.TestObserver;
import org.junit.Test;

public class Ch10_15 {
    @Test
    public void debugWalkthrough() {
        TestObserver<String> testObserver = new TestObserver<>();
        Observable<String> items =
                Observable.just("521934/2342/Foxtrot",
                                "Bravo/12112/78886/Tango",
                                "283242/4542/Whiskey/2348562");
        items.concatMap(s -> Observable.fromArray(s.split("/")))
                .filter(s -> s.matches("[A-Za-z]+"))
                .subscribe(testObserver);
        System.out.println(testObserver.values());
        testObserver.assertValues("Foxtrot","Bravo","Tango","Whiskey");
    }
}
```

The test now completes without an error and the output is as follows:

```
[Foxtrot, Bravo, Tango, Whiskey]
```

In summary, when you have an `Observable` or `Flowable` operation that emits an error, the wrong items, or no items at all, start at the source and work your way downstream until you find the operator causing the problem. You can also put `TestObserver` at each step to get a more comprehensive report of what happened in that operation, but using an operator such as `doOnNext()`, `doOnError()`, `doOnComplete()`, or `doOnSubscribe()` is a quick and easy way to get an insight into what is happening in that part of the pipeline.

It may not be optimal that you have to modify the code with `doXXX()` operators to debug it. If you are using IntelliJ IDEA, you can try to use breakpoints within lambdas (although, in practice, this approach is not always easier). You can also research RxJava debugging libraries to get detailed logs without modifying your code. Hopefully, as RxJava continues to gain traction, more useful debugging tools will pop up and become standardized.

Summary

In this chapter, you learned how to test and debug RxJava code. When you create an application or an API that is built on RxJava, you may want to build unit tests around it in order to ensure that sanity checks are always enforced. You can use blocking operators to help perform assertions, but `TestObserver` and `TestSubscriber` will give you a much more comprehensive and streamlined testing experience.

You can also use `TestScheduler` to simulate time elapses so that a time-based `Observable` can be tested instantly. Finally, we covered a debugging strategy in RxJava, which often involves finding the operator that causes the problem, starting at the source, and moving downstream until it is found.

This chapter closes our journey covering the RxJava library, so congratulations if you got here! You now have a solid foundation of building reactive Java applications. In the final two chapters, we will cover RxJava in two specific domains: Android and Kotlin.

11
RxJava on Android

As discussed throughout this book, ReactiveX is very useful for many domains. If there is one domain where reactive programming is thriving, it is definitely the mobile domain, where apps are becoming increasingly complex, and users have a short tolerance for unresponsive, slow, or buggy apps. Therefore, mobile app developers were early adopters of ReactiveX to solve these problems. RxSwift has quickly become popular on iOS after RxJava got a foothold on Android. There are also RxAndroid and RxBinding libraries to integrate RxJava easily with the Android environment, which we will cover in this chapter.

One of the pain points for Android developers was being stuck with Java 6. The widely used versions of Android (KitKat, Lollipop, and Marshmallow) do not support Java 8 lambdas (although this changed in Android Nougat, which finally uses OpenJDK 8). At first glance, this means you are stuck using boilerplate-riddled anonymous classes to express your RxJava operators (refer to `Appendix A`, *Introducing Lambda Expressions*, for examples). However, by using Retrolambda, you can, in fact, use earlier versions of Android while using lambdas, which we will go through in this chapter.

Another option you have is using the Kotlin language, which has become an increasingly popular platform for Android development. Kotlin is an arguably more modern and expressive language than Java and can compile to Java 6 bytecode. We will cover Kotlin with RxJava in the next `Chapter 12`, *Using RxJava for Kotlin*.

If you have no interest in Android development, feel free to skip this chapter. But the rest of you reading this book are most likely Android developers, so it is assumed that you have done some Android development already.

 If you have little or no experience with Android and would like to learn, a great book to get started is *Android Programming: The Big Nerd Ranch Guide*, by Bill Phillips, Chris Stewart, and Kristin Marsicano (`https://www.bignerdranch.com/books/android-programming/`). This is an excellent book that will enable you to become thoroughly proficient in Android development quickly.

In this chapter, we will cover the following topics:

- Creating an Android project
- Configuring Retrolambda
- Configuring RxJava and friends
- Using RxJava and RxAndroid
- Using RxBinding
- Other RxAndroid bindings libraries
- Life cycles and cautions using RxJava with Android

Creating an Android project

We are going to use Android Studio for the examples in this chapter, with Android 5.1 Lollipop as our platform target. You can download the latest version of the studio at `https://developer.android.com/studio/index.html`. If you use the source code provided with this book and create an IntelliJ IDEA project that includes all the source code downloaded from GitHub, make sure that the `Chapter11` folder is excluded from the project configuration.

After installation, launch Android Studio and observe the steps described as follows:

1. Click on the **Start a new Android Studio project**, as shown in the following screenshot:

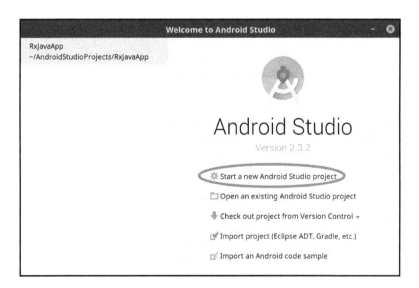

2. On the next screen, choose **Empty Activity** as your template, as shown in the following screenshot:

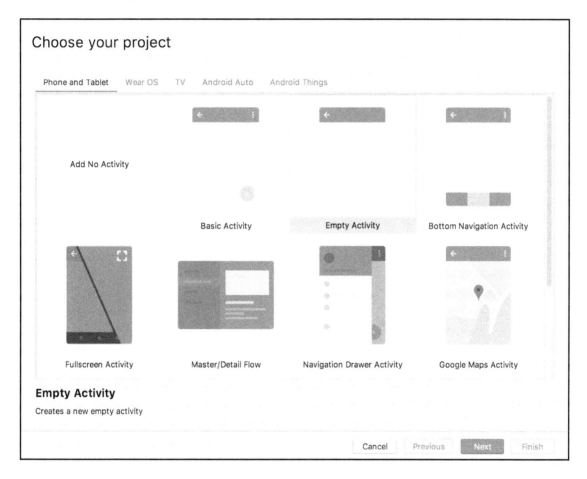

As you probably know, an activity is an interactive screen that includes controls.

3. Click on **Next**.

4. In the next screen (shown in the following screenshot), name your project `RxJavaApp` with a **Package name** of `com.packtpub.rxjavaapp` or whatever you prefer. Select a location for your project (wherever you would like your project top level to reside), **Language** as `Java`, and **Minimum API level** as shown in the following screenshot:

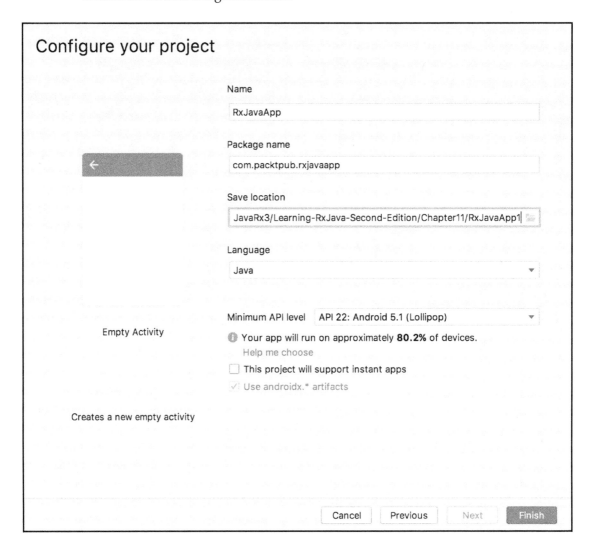

5. Click on **Finish**.
6. The next screen will look similar to the one shown in the following screenshot:

Feel free to leave **Activity Name** as `MainActivity`. We will populate this activity later.

The entire Android project should already be configured with Gradle. Open `build.gradle (Module: app)` so that we can configure our required dependencies next, as shown in the following screenshot:

You will need to make a few changes to the `build.gradle` script targeting the app module so that we can use RxJava and Retrolambda, as described in the following sections.

Configuring Retrolambda

First, let's get Retrolambda set up. We will also leverage a quick unit test to see whether it works correctly.

Open the `ExampleUnitTest.java` file that was created with the project template under
`app/java/com/packtpub/rxjavaapp`, as shown in the following screenshot:

```
rxjavaapp    C  ExampleUnitTest                        ▶  ↖    ▨ app  ▼   ▶  ↯  ☼  ↻  ⌀  ⇶  ▨    Git:

  RxJavaApp1 ×      activity_main.xml ×    C  MainActivity.java ×    app ×    C  ExampleUnitTest.java ×

1          package com.packtpub.rxjavaapp;
2
3          import ...
6
7          /**
8           * Example local unit test, which will execute on the development machine (host).
9           *
10          * @see <a href="http://d.android.com/tools/testing">Testing documentation</a>
11          */
12  ▷      public class ExampleUnitTest {
13              @Test
14  ▷          public void addition_isCorrect() { assertEquals( expected: 4,   actual: 2 + 2); }
17          }
```

Remove the sample unit test method inside it and declare a new one called
`lambdaTest()` as follows:

```
rxjavaapp    C  ExampleUnitTest                        ▶  ↖    ▨ app  ▼   ▶  ↯  ☼  ↻  ⌀  ⇶  ▨    Git:

  RxJavaApp1 ×      activity_main.xml ×    C  MainActivity.java ×    app ×    C  ExampleUnitTest.java ×

1          package com.packtpub.rxjavaapp;
2
3          import org.junit.Test;
4
5          import java.util.concurrent.Callable;
6          |
7          /**
8           * Example local unit test, which will execute on the development machine (host).
9           *
10          * @see <a href="http://d.android.com/tools/testing">Testing documentation</a>
11          */
12  ▷      public class ExampleUnitTest {
13              @Test
14  ▷          public void lambdaTest() throws Exception {
15  ↖↑              Callable<Integer> callable = () -> 4;
16                  System.out.println(callable.call());
17              }
18          }
```

Note that it throws a compiler error because we are not using Java 8 to support lambdas. If you navigate to the lambda expression, you will see the error message as shown in the following screenshot:

```
rxjavaapp    ExampleUnitTest                    app                                          Git:
RxJavaApp1    activity_main.xml    MainActivity.java    app    ExampleUnitTest.java

1        package com.packtpub.rxjavaapp;
2
3        import org.junit.Test;
4
5        import java.util.concurrent.Callable;
6
7        /**
8         * Example local unit test, which will execute on the development machine (host).
9         *
10        * @see <a href="http://d.android.com/tools/testing">Testing documentation</a>
11        */
12       public class ExampleUnitTest {
13           @Test
14           public void lambdaTest() throws Exception {
15               Callable<Integer> callable = () -> 4;
16               Sys
17           }        Lambda expressions are not supported at language level '7'
18       }
```

We cannot use Java 8 if we are targeting Android Lollipop, so we need Retrolambda to save us from creating boilerplate-riddled anonymous inner classes. This will compile our lambda expressions to anonymous classes at the bytecode level, so it supports Java 6.

To get Retrolambda set up, we are going to use the gradle-retrolambda plugin to make the configuration process as seamless as possible. Go back to your `build.gradle (Module: app)` script and modify it to the following. Set the dependency to Retrolambda in a `buildscript` block as follows:

```
buildscript {
    repositories {
        mavenCentral()
    }
    dependencies {
        classpath 'me.tatarka:gradle-retrolambda:3.6.1'
    }
}
```

We can then apply the Retrolambda plugin and add a `compileOptions { }` block inside the `android` one, `{ }`, and set the source and target to be compatible with Java 8 as follows:

```
apply plugin: 'com.android.application'
android {
    compileSdkVersion 28
    defaultConfig {
        applicationId "com.packtpub.rxjavaapp"
        minSdkVersion 22
        targetSdkVersion 28
        versionCode 1
        versionName "1.0"
        testInstrumentationRunner
                    "android.support.test.runner.AndroidJUnitRunner"
    }
    buildTypes {
        release {
            minifyEnabled false
            proguardFiles getDefaultProguardFile('proguard-android.txt'),
                                            'proguard-rules.pro'
        }
    }
    compileOptions {
        sourceCompatibility = '1.8'
        targetCompatibility = '1.8'
    }
}
```

Finally, we can set the `dependencies` we need for this project as follows:

```
dependencies {
    implementation fileTree(dir: 'libs', include: ['*.jar'])
    androidTestImplementation('com.android.support.test
                                    .espresso:espresso-core:2.2.2', {
        exclude group: 'com.android.support',
                                    module: 'support-annotations'
    })
    implementation 'com.android.support:appcompat-v7:28.0.0'
    implementation
                'com.android.support.constraint:constraint-layout:1.0.2'
    testImplementation 'junit:junit:4.12'
}
```

You can read more about the `build.gradle` syntax at `https://developer.android.com/studio/build`.

Click on the **Sync Now** prompt after you save the script to rebuild the project. You may get the following error:

```
ERROR: Failed to install the following Android SDK packages as some licences have not
    build-tools;28.0.3 Android SDK Build-Tools 28.0.3
    platforms;android-25 Android SDK Platform 25
To build this project, accept the SDK license agreements and install the missing compo
Alternatively, to transfer the license agreements from one workstation to another, see

Using Android SDK: /Users/ab54696/Library/Android/sdk
Install missing SDK package(s)
```

If that is the case, click on the link provided. The following screen will tell you about the progress of the installation:

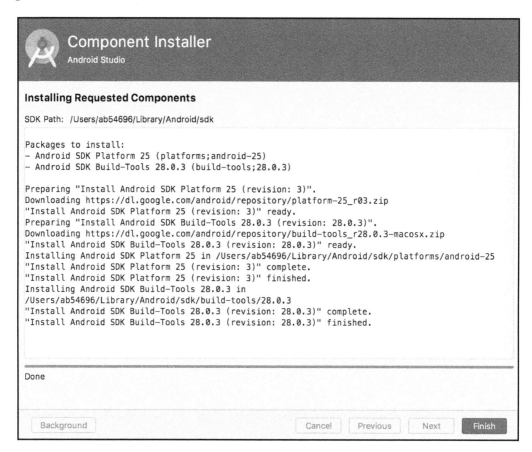

Click **Finish** when the button is available and click the **Try Again** link that should appear as the replacement for the **Sync Now** link. If there are no more errors, run our unit test containing the lambda expression now. The result should be as shown in the following screenshot:

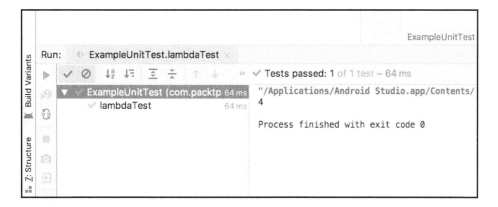

Everything compiles and runs successfully, and we are now running lambdas on Java 6!

Retrolambda is a brilliant tool for Android developers constrained to using Java 6. It cleverly compiles lambdas as traditional anonymous classes, and you can save yourself some terrible boilerplate work when using RxJava.

 To learn more about Retrolambda and the additional tweaks and configurations you can make, check out its GitHub page at `https://github.com/evant/gradle-retrolambda`. At the time of writing, there are also upcoming lambda tools on Android Studio (`https://developer.android.com/studio/preview/features/java8-support.html`). These features may serve as an alternative to Retrolambda.

Configuring RxJava and friends

Now that the hard part is over and you have Retrolambda set up, all that is left for the configuration is to bring in RxJava and RxAndroid. Another set of libraries to add to your stack is Jake Wharton's RxBinding (`https://github.com/JakeWharton/RxBinding`), which streamlines RxJava usage for Android UI controls.

Add these three libraries to your `dependencies` block, { }, for your module (not the one inside the buildscript block, { }!):

```
implementation 'io.reactivex.rxjava2:rxjava:2.2.2'
implementation 'io.reactivex.rxjava2:rxandroid:2.0.1'
implementation 'com.jakewharton.rxbinding2:rxbinding:2.0.0'
```

So the following should now be your full `dependencies` block content:

```
dependencies {
    implementation fileTree(dir: 'libs', include: ['*.jar'])
    androidTestImplementation('com.android.support.test
                                    .espresso:espresso-core:2.2.2', {
        exclude group: 'com.android.support',
                                    module: 'support-annotations'
    })
    implementation 'com.android.support:appcompat-v7:28.0.0'
    implementation
            'com.android.support.constraint:constraint-layout:1.0.2'
    testImplementation 'junit:junit:4.12'

    implementation 'io.reactivex.rxjava2:rxjava:2.2.2'
    implementation 'io.reactivex.rxjava2:rxandroid:2.0.1'
    implementation 'com.jakewharton.rxbinding2:rxbinding:2.0.0'
}
```

Ensure that you click on the **Sync Now** prompt to rebuild the project with these dependencies in place. For the remainder of the chapter, we will touch on a few ways in which you can use RxJava, RxAndroid, and RxBinding together in your Android application. You could easily write a small book about different reactive features, bindings, and patterns that you can use with Android, but in this chapter, we will take a minimalistic approach to focus on the core Rx features. We will touch on other libraries and resources you can research at the end of this chapter.

Using RxJava and RxAndroid

The primary feature of the RxAndroid library (`https://github.com/ReactiveX/RxAndroid`) is that it has Android schedulers to help your concurrency goals for your Android app. It has a `Scheduler` class for the Android main thread as well as an implementation that can target any message `Looper` class. Striving to be a core library, RxAndroid does not have many other features. You will need specialized reactive bindings libraries for Android to do more than that, which we will explore later.

Let's start simple. Let's execute the Android application that comes out of the box:

1. Select **Run** or **Run 'MainActivity'** from the **Run** menu:

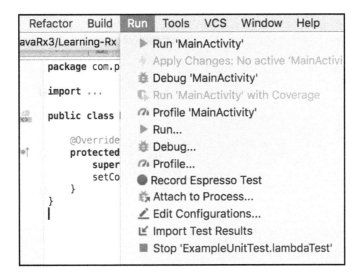

2. If you have not created a virtual device to execute an Android application yet, the following screen will prompt you to create a virtual device:

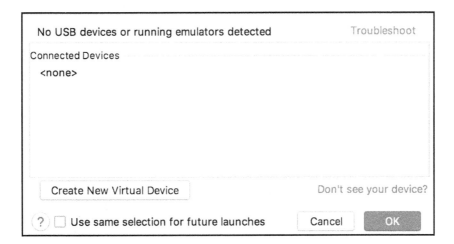

3. Check **Use same selection for future launches**, if you are not going to change the devices, and click **Create New Virtual Device**.

4. Select the target device on the following screen (for this demo, we selected **Pixel 3**):

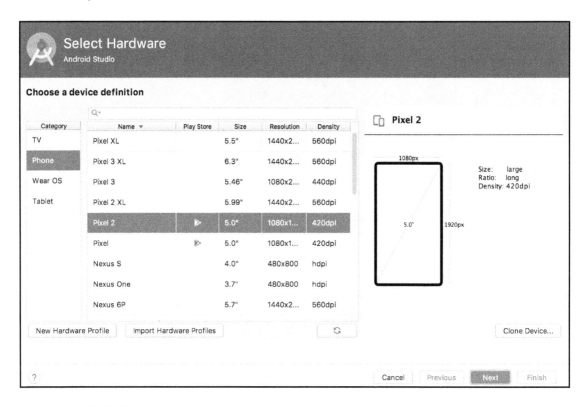

5. Click **Next**.

6. Select (click the **Download** link) the image you prefer (we have chosen **Q Download**) on the following screen:

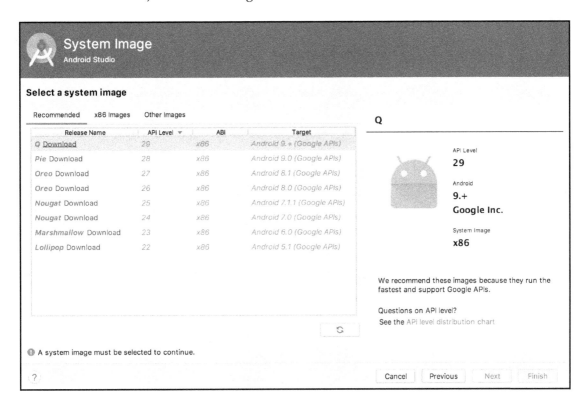

7. Click **Next** and make a choice **Decline/Accept** on the following screen:

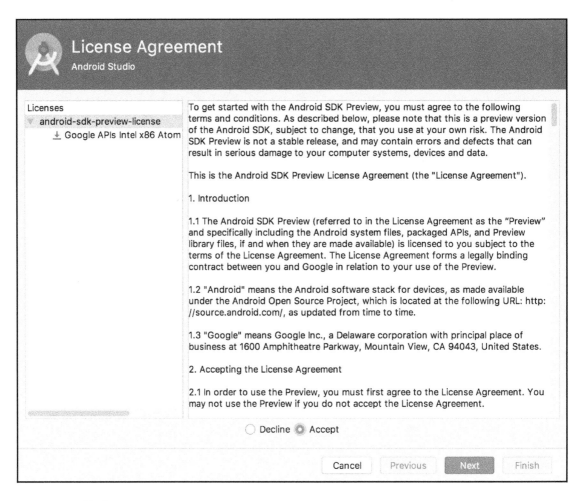

8. Click **Next**.

9. If you have accepted the license agreement on the previous screen, the following screen will appear:

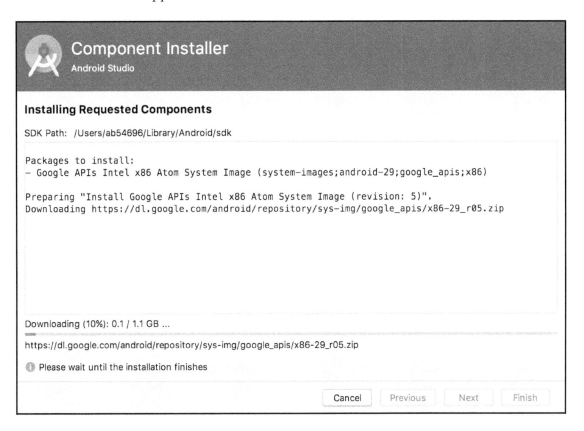

10. Wait until the installation is complete and then click the **Finish** button.

11. Click the **Next** button on the following screen, too:

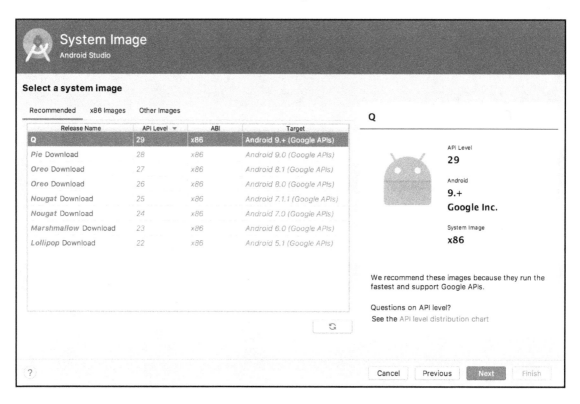

12. Click the **Finish** button on the next screen. The image of the device you have chosen should now appear and the default `MainActivity` application should have the **Hello World!** message on it, as shown in the following screenshot:

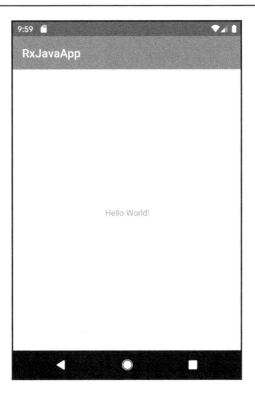

Let's now change the default application by switching to `Goodbye World!` after 3 seconds. In order to do that, we modify `TextView` in the middle of the `MainActivity` screen. The `res/layout/activity_main.xml` file already contains the text **Hello World!** as follows:

```
<?xml version="1.0" encoding="utf-8"?>
<androidx.constraintlayout.widget.ConstraintLayout
xmlns:android="http://schemas.android.com/apk/res/android"
    xmlns:app="http://schemas.android.com/apk/res-auto"
    xmlns:tools="http://schemas.android.com/tools"
    android:layout_width="match_parent"
    android:layout_height="match_parent"
    tools:context=".MainActivity">

    <TextView
        android:layout_width="wrap_content"
        android:layout_height="wrap_content"
        android:text="Hello World!"
        app:layout_constraintBottom_toBottomOf="parent"
        app:layout_constraintLeft_toLeftOf="parent"
        app:layout_constraintRight_toRightOf="parent"
```

```
                app:layout_constraintTop_toTopOf="parent" />

    </androidx.constraintlayout.widget.ConstraintLayout>
```

We would like to change it to `Goodbye World!` after 3 seconds and we will do this reactively using `Observable.delay()`.

Because this emits on a computational `Scheduler`, we need to leverage `observeOn()` to safely switch the emission to the Android main thread. First, in the `res/layout/activity_main.xml` file, we modify the `TextView` block to have an ID property called `my_text_view`, as shown in the following code block:

```
<?xml version="1.0" encoding="utf-8"?>
<androidx.constraintlayout.widget.ConstraintLayout
xmlns:android="http://schemas.android.com/apk/res/android"
    xmlns:app="http://schemas.android.com/apk/res-auto"
    xmlns:tools="http://schemas.android.com/tools"
    android:layout_width="match_parent"
    android:layout_height="match_parent"
    tools:context=".MainActivity">

    <TextView
        android:id="@+id/my_text_view"
        android:layout_width="wrap_content"
        android:layout_height="wrap_content"
        android:text="Hello World!"
        app:layout_constraintBottom_toBottomOf="parent"
        app:layout_constraintLeft_toLeftOf="parent"
        app:layout_constraintRight_toRightOf="parent"
        app:layout_constraintTop_toTopOf="parent" />

    </androidx.constraintlayout.widget.ConstraintLayout>
```

Rebuild your project and go to the `MainActivity.java` file. In the `onCreate()` method implementation, we are going to look up our component by ID, `my_text_view`, and save it to a variable called `myTextView` (and cast it to `TextView`).

Then, immediately afterward, we are going to create an `Observable`, emitting just the string `Goodbye World!` and delay it for 3 seconds. Because `delay()` will put it on a computational `Scheduler`, we will use `observeOn()` to put that emission back in `AndroidSchedulers.mainThread()` once it is received. Implement all of this as shown in the following code block:

```
package com.packtpub.rxjavaapp;

import androidx.appcompat.app.AppCompatActivity;
```

```
import android.os.Bundle;
import android.widget.TextView;
import java.util.concurrent.TimeUnit;
import io.reactivex.Observable;
import io.reactivex.android.schedulers.AndroidSchedulers;

public class MainActivity extends AppCompatActivity {

    @Override
    protected void onCreate(Bundle savedInstanceState) {
        super.onCreate(savedInstanceState);
        setContentView(R.layout.activity_main);

        TextView myTextView = (TextView) findViewById(R.id.my_text_view);

        Observable.just("Goodbye World!")
                .delay(3, TimeUnit.SECONDS)
                .observeOn(AndroidSchedulers.mainThread())
                .subscribe(s -> myTextView.setText(s));
    }
}
```

Run this application either on an emulated virtual device or an actual connected device. Sure enough, you will get an app that shows **Hello World!** for 3 seconds as before, and then changes to `Goodbye World!` as follows:

If you do not use this `observeOn()` operation to switch back to the Android `mainThread()`, the app will likely crash. Therefore, it is important to make sure any emissions that modify the Android UI happen on the `mainThread()`. Thankfully, RxJava makes this easy to do compared with traditional concurrency tools.

Pretty much everything you learned earlier in this book can be applied to Android development, and you can mix RxJava and RxAndroid with your favorite Android utilities, libraries, and design patterns. However, if you want to create an `Observable` from the Android widget, you will need to use RxBinding and other libraries to augment your Rx capabilities on Android.

There is also an `AndroidSchedulers.from()` factory that accepts an event `Looper` and returns a `Scheduler` that executes emissions on any Android `Looper`. It executes the `Observable/Flowable` on a new thread and emits results through `onNext()` on the thread running a background operation.

Using RxBinding

RxAndroid does not have any tool to create an `Observable` from an Android event, but there are many libraries that provide the means to do this. The most popular library is RxBinding, which allows you to create an `Observable` from UI widgets and events.

There are many factories available in RxBinding. One static factory class you may use frequently is `RxView`, which allows you to create an `Observable` from controls that extend `View` and broadcast different events as emissions. For instance, create a new project by following the steps in the previous section and make sure that the `build.gradle` file has the same content. If not, copy its content from the previous project. Then, change your `activity_main.xml` file by adding `Button` and `TextView` classes inside `LinearLayout` as follows:

```
<Button
    android:id="@+id/increment_button"
    android:text="Increment"
    android:layout_width="wrap_content"
    android:layout_height="wrap_content" />
<TextView
    android:id="@+id/my_text_view"
    android:layout_width="wrap_content"
    android:layout_height="wrap_content"
    android:text="0"
    android:textStyle="bold"/>
```

Notice how we have added the `bold` text style for the text that is going to be displayed.

Save `Button` and `TextView` to `increment_button` and `my_text_view` IDs, respectively, by adding these two lines to the `MainActivity` class:

```
TextView myTextView = (TextView) findViewById(R.id.my_text_view);
Button incrementButton = (Button) findViewById(R.id.increment_button);
```

Now, let's have the `Button` broadcast the number of times it was pressed to `TextView`. Use the `RxView.clicks()` factory to emit each `Button` click as an `Object` and map it to a `1`. As we did in `Chapter 3`, *Basic Operators*, we can use the `scan()` operator to emit a rolling count of emissions, as shown in the following code block:

```
package com.packtpub.rxjavaapp;

import androidx.appcompat.app.AppCompatActivity;
import android.os.Bundle;
import android.widget.Button;
import android.widget.TextView;
import com.jakewharton.rxbinding2.view.RxView;
public class MainActivity extends AppCompatActivity {
    @Override
    protected void onCreate(Bundle savedInstanceState) {
        super.onCreate(savedInstanceState);
        setContentView(R.layout.activity_main);

        TextView myTextView = (TextView) findViewById(R.id.my_text_view);
        myTextView.setPadding(100, 0, 0, 0);
        Button incrementButton =
                        (Button) findViewById(R.id.increment_button);
        RxView.clicks(incrementButton)
              .map(o -> 1)
              .scan(0, (total, next) -> total + next)
              .subscribe(i -> myTextView.setText(i.toString()));

    }
}
```

We have added padding to the text so that it will show 100 pixels away from the left border.

Now, run this app and press the button a few times. Each press will result in the number incrementing in `TextView`, as shown in the following screenshot:

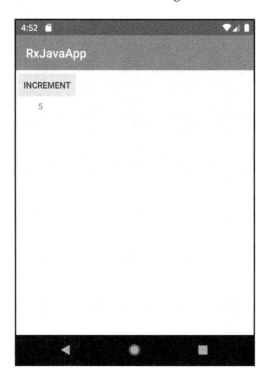

Just in the RxView alone, there are dozens of factories to emit the states and events of a variety of properties on a `View` widget. To name just a few, some of these other factories include `hover()`, `drag()`, and `visibility()`. There are also a large number of specialized factories for different widgets, such as `RxTextView`, `RxSearchView`, and `RxToolbar`.

There is so much functionality in RxBinding that it is difficult to cover all of it in one chapter. The most effective way to see what is available is to explore the RxBinding project source code on GitHub, which you can find at `https://github.com/JakeWharton/RxBinding/`.

 Note that RxBinding has several *support* modules you can optionally bring in, including design bindings, RecyclerView bindings, and even Kotlin extensions. You can read more about these modules in the project's GitHub README.

Other RxAndroid bindings libraries

If you are fully embracing the reactive approach in your Android apps, there are many other specialized reactive binding libraries that you can leverage. These often deal with specific domains of Android, but can be helpful if you work with these domains. Outside of RxBinding, here are some notable bindings libraries you can use reactively with Android:

- SqlBrite (`https://github.com/square/sqlbrite`): A SQLite wrapper that brings reactive semantics to SQL queries
- RxLocation (`https://github.com/patloew/RxLocation`): A reactive location API
- rx-preferences (`https://github.com/f2prateek/rx-preferences`): A reactive SharedPreferences API
- RxFit (`https://github.com/patloew/RxFit`): A reactive fitness API for Android
- RxWear (`https://github.com/patloew/RxWear`): A reactive API for the Wearable library
- ReactiveNetwork (`https://github.com/pwittchen/ReactiveNetwork`): Reactively listens for the network connectivity state
- ReactiveBeacons (`https://github.com/pwittchen/ReactiveBeacons`): Reactively scans for **BLE** (**Bluetooth Low Energy**) beacons in proximity

As you can see, there is quite an RxJava ecosystem for Android. You can view a bigger list on the RxAndroid wiki (`https://github.com/ReactiveX/RxAndroid/wiki`). Definitely leverage Google to see whether other libraries exist for your specific needs. If you cannot find a library, there might be an opportunity to start one!

Life cycles and cautions using RxJava with Android

As always, be deliberate and careful about how you manage the life cycle of your subscriptions. Make sure that you do not rely on weak references in your Android app and do not assume that reactive streams will dispose of themselves because they will not! So always call `dispose()` on a `Disposable` instance when a piece of your Android application is no longer being used.

For example, let's say you create a simple app that displays the number of seconds since it was launched. For this exercise, create a new project and set up your layout as shown in the following code snippet in order to have `timer_field` in the `TextView` class:

```xml
<?xml version="1.0" encoding="utf-8"?>
<android.support.constraint.ConstraintLayout
    xmlns:android="http://schemas.android.com/apk/res/android"
    xmlns:app="http://schemas.android.com/apk/res-auto"
    xmlns:tools="http://schemas.android.com/tools"
    android:layout_width="match_parent"
    android:layout_height="match_parent"
    tools:context=".MainActivity">

<TextView
    android:id="@+id/timer_field"
    android:layout_width="wrap_content"
    android:layout_height="wrap_content"
    android:text="0"
    android:textStyle="bold"
    app:layout_constraintBottom_toBottomOf="parent"
    app:layout_constraintLeft_toLeftOf="parent"
    app:layout_constraintRight_toRightOf="parent"
    app:layout_constraintTop_toTopOf="parent" />

</android.support.constraint.ConstraintLayout>
```

We can use an `Observable.interval()` to emit every second to a `TextField`. If we run this application, it will display the number of seconds since it was launched, as shown in the following screenshot:

But we need to decide carefully how and whether this counter persists when the app is no longer active. When `onPause()` is called, we might want to dispose of this timer operation. When `onResume()` is called, we can subscribe again and create a new disposable, effectively restarting the timer. For good measure, we should dispose of it when `onDestroy()` is called as well. Here is a simple implementation that manages these life cycle rules:

```
public class MainActivity extends AppCompatActivity {
    private final Observable<String> timer;
    private Disposable disposable;
    MainActivity() {
        timer = Observable.interval(1, TimeUnit.SECONDS)
                .map(i -> Long.toString(i))
                .observeOn(AndroidSchedulers.mainThread());
    }
}
```

The following are the necessary overrides:

```
@Override
protected void onCreate(Bundle savedInstanceState) {
```

```
        super.onCreate(savedInstanceState);
        setContentView(R.layout.activity_main);
    }
    @Override
    protected void onPause() {
        super.onPause();
        disposable.dispose();
    }
    @Override
    protected void onResume() {
        super.onResume();
        TextView tv = (TextView) findViewById(R.id.timer_field);
        disposable = timer.subscribe(s -> tv.setText(s));
    }
    @Override
    protected void onDestroy() {
        super.onDestroy();
        if (disposable != null)
            disposable.dispose();
    }
```

And here are the import statements for your reference:

```
import androidx.appcompat.app.AppCompatActivity;
import android.os.Bundle;
import android.widget.TextView;
import java.util.concurrent.TimeUnit;
import io.reactivex.Observable;
import io.reactivex.android.schedulers.AndroidSchedulers;
import io.reactivex.disposables.Disposable;
```

If you want to persist or save the state of your app, you may have to get creative and find a way to dispose of your reactive operations when `onPause()` is called while allowing it to pick up where it left off when `onResume()` happens. In the following code, the last value emitted from the timer is held in `AtomicInteger` and used as the starting value in the event that a pause/resume occurs with a new subscription:

```
public class MainActivity extends AppCompatActivity {
    private final Observable<String> timer;
    private final AtomicInteger lastValue = new AtomicInteger(0);
    private Disposable disposable;
    MainActivity() {
        timer = Observable.interval(1, TimeUnit.SECONDS)
                .map(i -> 1)
                .startWith(Observable.fromCallable(lastValue::get))
                .scan((current,next) -> current + next)
                .doOnNext(lastValue::set)
                .map(i -> Integer.toString(i))
```

```
                        .observeOn(AndroidSchedulers.mainThread());
        }
    }
```

The following overrides have to be added, too:

```
    @Override
    protected void onCreate(Bundle savedInstanceState) {
        super.onCreate(savedInstanceState);
        setContentView(R.layout.activity_main);
    }
    @Override
    protected void onPause() {
        super.onPause();
        disposable.dispose();
    }
    @Override
    protected void onResume() {
        super.onResume();
        TextView tv = (TextView) findViewById(R.id.timer_field);
        disposable = timer.subscribe(s -> tv.setText(s));
    }
    @Override
    protected void onDestroy() {
        super.onDestroy();
        if (disposable != null)
            disposable.dispose();
    }
```

And here are the import statements to support the preceding code example:

```
import androidx.appcompat.app.AppCompatActivity;
import android.os.Bundle;
import android.widget.TextView;
import java.util.concurrent.TimeUnit;
import java.util.concurrent.atomic.AtomicInteger;
import io.reactivex.Observable;
import io.reactivex.android.schedulers.AndroidSchedulers;
import io.reactivex.disposables.Disposable;
```

So again, make sure that you manage your reactive operations carefully and dispose of them deliberately as part of the life cycle of your app.

Also, make sure that you leverage multicasting for UI events when multiple observers/subscribers are listening. This prevents multiple listeners from being attached to widgets, which may not always be efficient. On the other hand, do not add the overhead of multicasting when there is only one Observer/Subscriber to a widget's events.

Summary

In this chapter, we touched on various parts of the rich RxAndroid ecosystem to build reactive Android applications. We covered Retrolambda so that we can leverage lambdas with earlier versions of Android that only support Java 6. This way, we do not have to resort to anonymous inner classes to express our RxJava operators. We also touched on RxAndroid, which is the core of the reactive Android ecosystem, and it only contains Android schedulers. To plug in your various Android widgets, controls, and domain-specific events, you will need to rely on other libraries, such as RxBinding.

In the next chapter, you will learn how to use RxJava with Kotlin—an exciting new language that has essentially become the Swift of Android. You will learn the basics of Kotlin and why it works so well with RxJava.

Using RxJava for Kotlin 12

In our final chapter, we will apply RxJava to an exciting new frontier of the JVM: the Kotlin language.

Kotlin was developed by JetBrains, the company behind IntelliJ IDEA, PyCharm, and several other major IDEs and developer tools. For some time, JetBrains used Java to build its products, but after 2010, JetBrains began to question whether it was the best language to meet their needs and modern demands. After investigating existing languages, they decided to build an open source language of their own. In 2016 (5 years later), Kotlin 1.0 was released. In 2017, Kotlin 1.1 was released to a growing community of users. Shortly afterward, Google announced Kotlin as an officially supported language for Android.

Kotlin is a language that can quickly be picked up by Java developers within a few days. If you want to learn Kotlin in detail, there is an excellent online reference (`https://kotlinlang.org/docs/reference/`) provided by JetBrains. In this chapter, we will quickly go through some basic features of Kotlin to sell its pertinence in expressing RxJava more quickly. We will also discuss how to configure a Kotlin project and how to set it using RxJava and RxKotlin, define and demonstrate related operations and functions, how Kotlin supports data classes, and other powerful Kotlin features.

In this chapter, we will cover the following topics:

- Why Kotlin?
- Configuring Kotlin
- Kotlin basics
- Extension operators
- Using RxKotlin
- Dealing with SAM ambiguity
- Using `let()` and `apply()`
- Tuple and data classes
- The future of ReactiveX and Kotlin

Why Kotlin?

Kotlin strives to be a pragmatic and industry-focused language, seeking a minimal (but legible) syntax that expresses business logic rather than boilerplate. However, it does not cut corners like many concise languages. It is statically typed and performs robustly in production, and yet is speedy enough for prototyping. It also works 100% with Java libraries and source code, making it feasible for a gradual transition.

Android developers, who were stuck on Java 6 until recently, were quick to adopt Kotlin and effectively make it the *Swift of Android*. Funnily enough, Swift and Kotlin have similar feel and syntax, but Kotlin came into existence first. On top of that, the Kotlin community and ecosystem of libraries continued to grow quickly. Due to JetBrains' and Google's commitment, it is clear that Kotlin has a bright future in the JVM.

But what does Kotlin have to do with RxJava? Kotlin has many useful language features that Java does not, and they can greatly improve the expressibility of RxJava. Also, more Android developers are using Kotlin as well as RxJava, so it makes sense to show how these two platforms can work together.

Configuring Kotlin

You can use either Gradle or Maven to build your Kotlin project. You can create a new Kotlin project in IntelliJ IDEA without any build automation, but here is how to set up a Kotlin project for Gradle and Maven and how to set it to use RxJava and RxKotlin.

Configuring Kotlin with Gradle

To use the Kotlin language with Gradle, first, add the following `buildscript {}` block to your `build.gradle` file:

```
buildscript {
    ext.kotlin_version = '<version to use>'
    repositories {
        mavenCentral()
    }
    dependencies {
        classpath "org.jetbrains.kotlin:kotlin-gradle-
        plugin:$kotlin_version"
    }
}
```

Then, you will need to apply the plugin, as shown in the following code, as well as the directories that will hold the source code:

```
apply plugin: "kotlin"
sourceSets {
    main.kotlin.srcDirs += 'src/main/kotlin'
}
```

Note that src/main/kotlin is already specified by default, but you could use the sourceSets { } block to specify a different directory if needed.

 You can learn more about the Kotlin Gradle configuration in detail on the Kotlin website at https://kotlinlang.org/docs/reference/using-gradle.html.

Configuring Kotlin with Maven

For Maven, define a kotlin.version property and Kotlin-stdlib as a dependency in the pom.xml file, as shown in the following code:

```
<properties>
    <kotlin.version>1.3.61</kotlin.version>
</properties>

<dependencies>
    <dependency>
        <groupId>org.jetbrains.kotlin</groupId>
        <artifactId>kotlin-stdlib</artifactId>
        <version>${kotlin.version}</version>
    </dependency>
</dependencies>
```

The source code directory has to be specified inside the build tag as follows:

```
<build>
    <sourceDirectory>
        ${project.basedir}/src/main/kotlin
    </sourceDirectory>
    <testSourceDirectory>
        ${project.basedir}/src/test/kotlin
    </testSourceDirectory>
</build>
```

The `kotlin-maven-plugin` has to be set inside the `build` tag as well, as demonstrated in the following code:

```
<plugins>
    <plugin>
        <artifactId>kotlin-maven-plugin</artifactId>
        <groupId>org.jetbrains.kotlin</groupId>
        <version>${kotlin.version}</version>
        <executions>
            <execution>
                <id>compile</id>
                <goals><goal>compile</goal></goals>
            </execution>
            <execution>
                <id>test-compile</id>
                <goals><goal>test-compile</goal></goals>
            </execution>
        </executions>
    </plugin>
</plugins>
```

Now we can build the project.

 You can learn more about the Kotlin Maven configuration in detail on the Kotlin website at `https://kotlinlang.org/docs/reference/using-maven.html`.

Configuring RxJava and RxKotlin

In this chapter, we will also be using RxJava as well as an extension library called RxKotlin. For Gradle, add these two libraries as your dependencies as follows:

```
implementation 'io.reactivex.rxjava3:rxjava:3.0.0'
implementation 'io.reactivex.rxjava3:rxkotlin:3.0.0-RC1'
```

For Maven, set them up like this:

```
<dependency>
    <groupId>io.reactivex.rxjava3</groupId>
    <artifactId>rxjava</artifactId>
    <version>3.0.0</version>
</dependency>
<dependency>
    <groupId>io.reactivex.rxjava3</groupId>
    <artifactId>rxkotlin</artifactId>
```

```
      <version>3.0.0-RC1</version>
  </dependency>
```

With the configuration completed, we can now start coding using the Kotlin language. But first, let's review the basics of Kotlin.

Kotlin basics

Although Kotlin has a standalone compiler and can work with Eclipse, we are going to use IntelliJ IDEA.

A Kotlin project is structured much like a Java project. Following a standard Maven convention, you typically put your Kotlin source code in an `src/main/kotlin/` folder instead of an `src/main/java/` folder. The Kotlin source code is stored in text files with a `.kt` extension instead of `.java`. However, Kotlin files do not have to contain a class sharing the same name as the file.

Creating a Kotlin file

In IntelliJ IDEA, import your Kotlin project, if you haven't done so already. Right-click on the `/src/main/kotlin/` folder and navigate to **New** | **Kotlin File/Class**, as shown in the following screenshot:

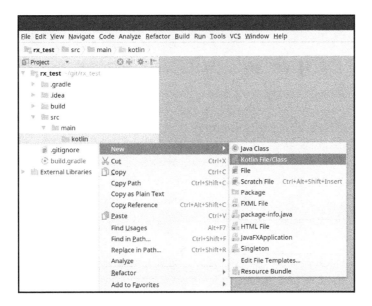

In the following dialog, name the file `Launcher` and then click on **OK**. You should now see the `Launcher.kt` file in the **Project** pane. Double-click on it to open the editor. Write the following `"Hello World"` Kotlin code, as shown here, and then run it by clicking on the **K** icon in the gutter:

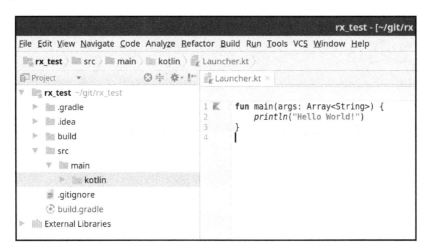

This is our first Kotlin application. Kotlin uses *functions* instead of methods, but it has a `main()` function just like Java has a `main()` method. Note that we do not have to house our `main()` function in a Java class. This is one benefit of Kotlin. Although it does compile to Java bytecode, you are not restricted to only object-oriented conventions and can use procedural or functional as well.

Assigning properties and variables

To declare a variable or property, you must decide whether to make it mutable. Preceding a variable declaration with a `val` will make it only assignable once, whereas `var` is mutable and can be reassigned a value multiple times. The name of the variable then follows, with a colon separating it from the type. Then, you can assign a value if you have it on hand. In the following code (the `ch12_01.kt` example), we assign a variable for an `Int` and a `String` and print them in an interpolated string:

```
fun main(args: Array<String>) {
    val myInt: Int = 5
    val myString: String = "Alpha"

    println("myInt=$myInt and myString=$myString")
}
```

The output is as follows:

```
myInt=5 and myString=Alpha
```

Kotlin's compiler is pretty smart and does not always have to have the type explicitly declared for variables and properties. If you assign it a value immediately, it will infer the type from that value. Therefore, we can remove the type declarations as follows (the ch12_02.kt example):

```kotlin
fun main(args: Array<String>) {
    val myInt = 5 //infers type as `Int`
    val myString = "Alpha" //infers type as `String`

    println("myInt=$myInt and myString=$myString")
}
```

Extension functions

When you are doing RxJava work in Kotlin, the creation of extension functions is immensely helpful. We will now show a non-reactive example and cover the reactive case later.

Say we want to add a convenient function to LocalDate in order to quickly compute the number of days to another LocalDate. Rather than invoking verbose helper classes to do this task repeatedly, we can quickly add an extension function to LocalDate called numberOfDaysTo(), as shown here (the ch12_03.kt example):

```kotlin
import java.time.LocalDate
import java.time.temporal.ChronoUnit

fun main(args: Array<String>) {
    val startDate = LocalDate.of(2017,5,1)
    val endDate = LocalDate.of(2017,5,11)
    val daysBetween = startDate.numberOfDaysTo(endDate)
    println(daysBetween)
}
fun LocalDate.numberOfDaysTo(otherLocalDate: LocalDate): Long {
    return ChronoUnit.DAYS.between(this, otherLocalDate)
}
```

This does not extend LocalDate, but rather lets the compiler resolve it as a static method. The output is as follows:

```
10
```

An extension function is just like a normal function in Kotlin, but you immediately declare the type you are adding the function to, followed by a dot, and then the extension function name (for example, `fun LocalDate.numberOfDaysTo()`). In the block that follows, it treats the targeted `LocalDate` as `this`, just as if it was inside the class. But again, it resolves all this as a static method upon compilation. Kotlin magically abstracts this away for you.

This allows a more fluent **Domain-Specific Language** (**DSL**) to be created that is streamlined for the particular business. As an added bonus, IntelliJ IDEA shows this extension function in the autocompletion as you work with `LocalDate`.

Since the body of this extension function is only one line, you can actually use the equals (=) syntax to declare a function more succinctly and omit the return keyword as well as the explicit type declaration, as shown in the following code:

```
fun LocalDate.numberOfDaysTo(otherLocalDate: LocalDate) =
                    ChronoUnit.DAYS.between(this, otherLocalDate)
```

As we will see soon, Kotlin extension functions are a powerful tool to add new operators to an `Observable` or `Flowable`, and they offer much more flexibility and convenience than `compose()` and `lift()`. But first, let's look at Kotlin lambda expressions.

Kotlin lambda expressions

You could spend a lot of time deconstructing lambda expressions in Kotlin, but in the interest of brevity, we will show only how they are expressed in the context of RxJava. You can learn about Kotlin lambda expressions in depth on the Kotlin site (`https://kotlinlang.org/docs/reference/lambdas.html`).

Kotlin offers a few more ways to express lambdas than Java 8. For example, it allows curly brackets { } to be used instead of round brackets ( ) to accept lambda arguments into functions. The following is how we express an `Observable` chain emitting strings, and then map and print their lengths (the `ch12_04.kt` example):

```
import io.reactivex.rxjava3.core.Observable

fun main(args: Array<String>) {
    Observable.just("Alpha", "Beta", "Gama", "Delta", "Epsilon")
            .map { s: String -> s.length }
            .subscribe { i: Int -> println(i) }
}
```

The output is as follows:

```
5
4
4
5
7
```

Note how we express our lambda arguments for `map()` and `subscribe()`. Using the curly brackets `{ }` to accept lambda arguments feels weird at first, but it does not take long before it becomes pretty natural. They help make a distinction between stateful arguments and functional ones. You can put rounded brackets around them if you like, but this is messy and is only needed when multiple lambda arguments have to be passed in (for operators such as `collect()`, for example), as shown in the following code (the `ch12_05.kt` example):

```kotlin
import io.reactivex.rxjava3.core.Observable

fun main(args: Array<String>) {
    Observable.just("Alpha", "Beta", "Gama", "Delta", "Epsilon")
            .map( { s: String -> s.length } )
            .subscribe( { i: Int -> println(i) } )
}
```

As specified earlier, the Kotlin compiler is smart when it comes to type inference. So, most of the time, we do not need to declare the lambda's s or i parameters as `String` and `Int`. The compiler can figure that out for us, as shown in the following code (the `ch12_06.kt` example):

```kotlin
import io.reactivex.rxjava3.core.Observable

fun main(args: Array<String>) {
    Observable.just("Alpha", "Beta", "Gama", "Delta", "Epsilon")
            .map { s -> s.length }
            .subscribe { i -> println(i) }
}
```

Even better, these are simple single-parameter lambda expressions, so we do not even have to name these parameters. We can omit them entirely and refer to them using the `it` keyword, as shown in the following code snippet (the `ch12_07.kt` example):

```kotlin
import io.reactivex.rxjava3.core.Observable

fun main(args: Array<String>) {
    Observable.just("Alpha", "Beta", "Gama", "Delta", "Epsilon")
            .map { it.length }
```

```
                    .subscribe { println(it) }
    }
```

Similar to Java 8, we can also use a function-reference syntax. If we are simply passing our arguments exactly in the same manner and order to a function or a constructor, we can use a double-colon (::) syntax, as follows (the ch12_08.kt example):

```
import io.reactivex.rxjava3.core.Observable

fun main(args: Array<String>) {
    Observable.just("Alpha", "Beta", "Gama", "Delta", "Epsilon")
            .map(String::length)
            .subscribe(::println)
}
```

Note that we *do* use rounded brackets here.

Something else that is interesting about Kotlin lambda arguments is that when you have multiple arguments where the last one is a lambda expression, you can put this lambda expression outside the rounded parentheses. In the following codex, scan() emits the rolling total of string lengths and provides a seed value of 0:

```
import io.reactivex.rxjava3.core.Observable

fun main(args: Array<String>) {
    Observable.just("Alpha", "Beta", "Gama", "Delta", "Epsilon")
            .map { s: String -> s.length }
            .scan(0) { total, next -> total + next }
            .subscribe {
                println("Rolling sum of String lengths is $it")
            }
}
```

As you can see, we were able to put the final lambda argument outside the rounded parentheses ( ), which allows for a more expressive style of Kotlin code writing.

Extension operators

As was stated earlier, Kotlin provides extension functions. These can be an enormously helpful alternative to using just compose() and lift().

For instance, we could not use transformers and `compose()` to turn an `Observable<T>` into a `Single<R>`. But this is more than doable with Kotlin extension functions. In the following code (the `ch12_09.kt` example), we create a `toSet()` operator and add it to `Observable<T>`:

```
import io.reactivex.rxjava3.core.Observable

fun main(args: Array<String>) {
    val source =
        Observable.just("Alpha", "Beta", "Gama", "Delta", "Epsilon")
    val asSet = source.toSet()
    println(asSet.blockingGet())

}
 fun <T> Observable<T>.toSet() =
        collect({ HashSet<T>() }, { set, next -> set.add(next) })
        .map { it as Set<T> }
```

`toSet()` returns a `Single<Set<T>>`, and it was called on an `Observable<T>`. In the extension function, the `collect()` operator is called on the invoked `Observable`, and then it casts `HashSet` to a `Set` so that the implementation is hidden.

If you run the preceding example, it will display something similar to the following (the sequence of elements may be different at each run):

[Delta, Alpha, Epsilon, Beta, Gama]

As you can see, it is easy to create new operators and make them easy to discover.

You can also make extension functions target only certain generic types. For example, you can create a `sum()` extension function that only targets `Observable<Int>` (`Int` is the `Integer`/`int` abstraction type in Kotlin). It will only be valid when used with an `Observable` emitting integers and can only compile or show up in autocomplete for that type (the `ch12_10.kt` example):

```
import io.reactivex.rxjava3.core.Observable

fun main(args: Array<String>) {
    val source = Observable.just(100, 50, 250, 150)
    val total = source.sum()
    println(total.blockingGet())
}
 fun Observable<Int>.sum() = reduce(0) { total, next -> total + next }
```

If you run the preceding example, the result will be as follows:

```
550
```

As you can see, creating a new extension operator in Kotlin is easy. But, before you do it, check the popular libraries. It may well be that the extension you need is already created. One such library is called RxKotlin, and we will describe it in the following section.

Using RxKotlin

There is a small library called RxKotlin (`https://github.com/ReactiveX/RxKotlin/`), which we made a dependency at the beginning of this chapter. At the time of writing, it is hardly a complex library, but rather a small collection of convenient extension functions for common reactive conversions. It also attempts to standardize some conventions when using RxJava with Kotlin.

For instance, there are the `toObservable()` and `toFlowable()` extension functions that can be invoked on iterables, sequences, and a few other sources. In the following code, instead of using `Observable.fromIterable()` to turn a `List` into an `Observable`, we just call its `toObservable()` extension function (the `ch12_11.kt` example):

```
import io.reactivex.rxkotlin3.toObservable

fun main(args: Array<String>) {
    val myList = listOf("Alpha", "Beta", "Gamma", "Delta", "Epsilon")
    myList.toObservable()
        .map(String::length)
        .subscribe(::println)
}
```

The result is as follows:

```
5
4
5
5
7
```

There are some other extensions in RxKotlin worth exploring, and you can view them all on the GitHub page. The library is deliberately small and focused since it is easy to clutter an API with every extension function for every task possible, but it holds the functionality for common tasks such as the one just demonstrated.

RxKotlin also has useful helpers to get around the **Single Abstract Method** (**SAM**) problem that exists between Java and Kotlin (you might have noticed this issue if you have been experimenting already). We will cover this next.

Dealing with SAM ambiguity

In Java, an interface with a single abstract method is called a functional interface. This means a functional interface in Java is SAM in Kotlin.

At the time of writing, when Kotlin invokes Java libraries with functional parameters, a problem may rear its head in RxJava 2.x when several overloads of the method with functional parameters are introduced. Kotlin does not have this issue when invoking Kotlin libraries, but it does with Java libraries. When there are multiple argument overloads for different functional SAM types on a given Java method, Kotlin gets lost in its inference and needs help. Until JetBrains resolves this issue, you will need to work around this either by being explicit or by using RxKotlin's helpers.

One of the most notorious examples is the `zip()` operator. Try to run the code as shown in the following example and you will get a compile error due to failed inference (the `ch12_12.kt` example):

```kotlin
import io.reactivex.rxjava3.core.Observable

fun main(args: Array<String>) {
    val strings = Observable.just("Alpha", "Beta", "Gamma", "Delta")
    val numbers = Observable.range(1,4)

    //compile error, can't infer parameters
    val zipped = Observable.zip(strings, numbers) { s,n -> "$s $n" }
    zipped.subscribe(::println)
}
```

One way to resolve this is to explicitly construct the SAM type with a lambda expression. In this case, we need to tell the compiler that we are giving it a `BiFunction<String, Int, String>`, as shown here (the `ch12_13.kt` example):

```kotlin
import io.reactivex.rxjava3.core.Observable
import io.reactivex.rxjava3.functions.BiFunction

fun main(args: Array<String>) {
    val strings = Observable.just("Alpha", "Beta", "Gamma", "Delta")
    val numbers = Observable.range(1,4)
    val zipped = Observable.zip(strings, numbers,
                    BiFunction<String,Int,String> { s,n -> "$s $n" }
```

```
        )
        zipped.subscribe(::println)
    }
```

The output is as follows:

```
Alpha 1
Beta 2
Gamma 3
Delta 4
```

Unfortunately, the preceding code is pretty verbose. Many use RxJava and Kotlin to have less code, not more, so this is not ideal. Thankfully, RxKotlin provides some utilities to work around this issue. You can use the `Observable`, `Flowable`, `Single`, or `Maybe` utility classes to invoke implementations of the factories affected by the SAM problem. Here is an example of using this approach (the `ch12_14.kt` example):

```
import io.reactivex.rxjava3.core.Observable
import io.reactivex.rxkotlin3.Observables

fun main(args: Array<String>) {
    val strings = Observable.just("Alpha", "Beta", "Gamma", "Delta")
    val numbers = Observable.range(1,4)
    val zipped = Observables.zip(strings, numbers) { s, n -> "$s $n" }
    zipped.subscribe(::println)
}
```

There are also extension functions for non-factory operators affected by the SAM issue. The following is our example using a `zipWith()` extension function that successfully performs inference with our Kotlin lambda argument. Note that we have to import this extension function to use it (the `ch12_15.kt` example):

```
import io.reactivex.rxjava3.core.Observable
import io.reactivex.rxkotlin3.zipWith

fun main(args: Array<String>) {
    val strings = Observable.just("Alpha", "Beta", "Gamma", "Delta")
    val numbers = Observable.range(1,4)
    val zipped = strings.zipWith(numbers) { s, n -> "$s $n" }
    zipped.subscribe(::println)
}
```

It should also be pointed out that `subscribe()` on `Single` and `Maybe` is affected by the SAM ambiguity issue as well, so there are `subscribeBy()` extensions to cope with it, as shown in the following code (the `ch12_16.kt` example):

```
import io.reactivex.rxjava3.core.Observable
import io.reactivex.rxkotlin3.subscribeBy

fun main(args: Array<String>) {
    Observable.just("Alpha", "Beta", "Gamma", "Delta", "Epsilon")
            .count()
            .subscribeBy ({ println("There are $it items") })
}
```

Try not to let the issue of SAM ambiguity deter you from trying Kotlin. It is a nuance when interoperating Kotlin lambda expressions with Java SAM types. The issue has been acknowledged by JetBrains and should be resolved pretty soon. Also, there has been a discussion in the Kotlin community to create a ReactiveX implementation in pure Kotlin for other reasons, and we will touch on the future of RxKotlin at the end of this chapter.

Using let() and apply()

In Kotlin, every type has `let()` and `apply()` extension functions. These are two simple, but helpful, tools to make your code more fluent and expressive.

Using let()

The `let()` function simply accepts a lambda expression that maps the invoked object `T` to another object `R`. It is similar to how RxJava offers the `to()` operator, but it applies to any type `T` and not just `Observable/Flowable`. For example, we can call `let()` on a `String` value that has been lowercased and then immediately do any arbitrary transformation on it, such as concatenating its `reversed()` value to it. Take a look at this operation (the `ch12_17.kt` example):

```
fun main(args: Array<String>) {
    val str = "GAMMA"
    val lowerCaseWithReversed = str.toLowerCase().let { it + " " +
    it.reversed() }
    println(lowerCaseWithReversed)
}
```

The output is as follows:

gamma ammag

The `let()` function comes in handy when you do not want to save a value to a variable just so you can refer to it multiple times. In the preceding code, we did not have to save the result of `toLowerCase()` to a variable. Instead, we just immediately called `let()` on it to do what we need.

In an RxJava context, the `let()` function can be helpful in quickly taking an `Observable`, forking it, and then recombining it using a combining operator. In the following code, we multicast an `Observable` of numbers to a `let()` operator, which calculates a sum and a count, and then returns the result of the `zipWith()` operator that uses both values to find the average by dividing the sum value by the count value (the `ch12_18.kt` example):

```kotlin
import io.reactivex.rxjava3.core.Observable
import io.reactivex.rxkotlin3.subscribeBy
import io.reactivex.rxkotlin3.zipWith

fun main(args: Array<String>) {
    val numbers = Observable.just(180.0, 160.0, 140.0, 100.0, 120.0)
    val average = numbers.publish()
        .autoConnect(2)
        .let {
            val sum = it.reduce(0.0) { total, next -> total + next}
            val count = it.count()
            sum.zipWith(count) { s, c -> s / c }
        }
    average.subscribeBy(::println)
}
```

The output is as follows:

140.0

The last line in `let()` is what gets returned and does not require a `return` keyword.

In summary, the `let()` function is a powerful and simple tool to fluently convert one item into another item. Using it to fork an `Observable` or `Flowable` stream and then joining them again is one helpful application for `let()` in RxJava.

Using apply()

The `apply()` function is similar to `let()`, but, instead of turning a T item into an R item, which `let()` does, `apply()` executes a series of actions against the T item instead, before returning the same T item. This is helpful in declaring an item as T but doing tangential operations on it without breaking the declaration/assignment flow.

Here is a non-reactive example. We have a simple class, `MyItem`, which has a `startProcess()` function. We can instantiate `MyItem` but use `apply()` to call this `startProcess()` method before assigning `MyItem` to a variable, as shown in the following code (the `ch12_19.kt` example):

```
fun main(args: Array<String>) {
    val myItem = MyItem().apply {
        startProcess()
    }
}

class MyItem {
    fun startProcess() = println("Starting Process!")
}
```

The output is as follows:

```
Starting Process!
```

In RxJava, `apply()` is helpful in adding an `Observer` or `Subscriber` to the middle of an `Observable`/`Flowable` chain, but not breaking the flow from the primary task at hand. This can be used for emitting status messages to a separate stream.

In the following code, we emit five 1-second intervals and multiply each one. However, we create a `statusObserver` and subscribe to it within `apply()` right before the multiplication. We multicast before `apply()` as well, so the emissions are pushed to both destinations. Here is the code (the `ch12_20.kt` example):

```
import io.reactivex.rxjava3.core.Observable
import io.reactivex.rxjava3.subjects.PublishSubject
import java.util.concurrent.TimeUnit

fun main(args: Array<String>) {

    val statusObserver = PublishSubject.create<Long>()
    statusObserver.subscribe { println("Status Observer: $it") }

    Observable.interval(1, TimeUnit.SECONDS)
            .take(5)
```

```
                .publish()
                .autoConnect(2)
                .apply {
                    subscribe(statusObserver)
                }
                .map { it * 100 }
                .subscribe {
                    println("Main Observer: $it")
                }

        Thread.sleep(7000)
    }
```

The output is as follows:

```
Status Observer: 0
Main Observer: 0
Status Observer: 1
Main Observer: 100
Status Observer: 2
Main Observer: 200
Status Observer: 3
Main Observer: 300
Status Observer: 4
Main Observer: 400
```

So again, `apply()` is helpful in taking a multicasted stream of emissions and pushing them to multiple observers without having any intermediary variables.

Similar to `apply()` is the extension function `run()`, which executes a series of actions but has a void return type (or, in Kotlin-speak, Unit). There is also `with()`, which is identical to `run()` except that it is not an extension function. It accepts the targeted item as an argument.

Tuple and data classes

Kotlin supports tuple to a small degree, but it also offers something even better with data classes. We will look at both of these in an RxJava context.

Kotlin supports the quick creation of a `Pair` containing two items (which can be of differing types). This is a simple two-value, but statically-typed, tuple. You can construct one quickly by putting the `to` keyword between two values. This is helpful in doing `zip()` operations between two streams when you just want to pair the two items together.

In the following code (the `ch12_21.kt` example), we zip a stream of string items with a stream of `Int` items and put each pair into `Pair<String, Int>`:

```
import io.reactivex.rxjava3.core.Observable
import io.reactivex.rxkotlin3.Observables

fun main(args: Array<String>) {
    val strings = Observable.just("Alpha", "Beta", "Gamma", "Delta")
    val numbers = Observable.range(1,4)

    //Emits Pair<String,Int>
    Observables.zip(strings, numbers) { s, n -> s to n }
            .subscribe {
                println(it)
            }
}
```

The output is as follows:

```
(Alpha, 1)
(Beta, 2)
(Gamma, 3)
(Delta, 4)
```

An even better approach is to use a data class. A data class is a powerful Kotlin tool that works just like a class, but it automatically implements `hashcode()`/`equals()` and `toString()`, as well as a nifty `copy()` function that allows you to clone and modify properties onto a new instance of that class.

But for now, we will just use a data class as a cleaner approach than a `Pair` because we actually give each property a name instead of `first` and `second`. In the following code (the `ch12_22.kt` example), we will create a `StringAndNumber` data class and use it to zip each pair of values:

```
import io.reactivex.rxjava3.core.Observable
import io.reactivex.rxkotlin3.Observables

fun main(args: Array<String>) {
    val strings = Observable.just("Alpha", "Beta", "Gamma", "Delta")
    val numbers = Observable.range(1,4)
    data class StringAndNumber(val myString: String, val myNumber: Int)

    Observables.zip(strings, numbers) { s, n -> StringAndNumber(s,n) }
            .subscribe {
                println(it)
            }
}
```

The output is as follows:

```
StringAndNumber(myString=Alpha, myNumber=1)
StringAndNumber(myString=Beta, myNumber=2)
StringAndNumber(myString=Gamma, myNumber=3)
StringAndNumber(myString=Delta, myNumber=4)
```

Data classes (as well as just plain Kotlin classes) are quick and easy to declare, so you can use them tactically for even small tasks. They make your code look cleaner and easier to maintain.

The future of ReactiveX and Kotlin

Kotlin is a powerful and pragmatic language. JetBrains put a lot of effort into not only making it effective but also compatible with existing Java code and libraries. Despite a few rough patches such as SAM lambda inference, they did a phenomenal job making Java and Kotlin work together. However, even with this solid compatibility, many developers were eager to migrate entirely to Kotlin to leverage its functionality. Named parameters, optional parameters, nullable types, extension functions, inline functions, delegates, and other language features make Kotlin attractive for exclusive use.

JetBrains has also successfully made Kotlin compliable with JavaScript and will soon support **Low-Level Virtual Machine** (**LLVM**) native compilation. Libraries built in pure Kotlin can potentially be compiled to all these platforms. To solidify Kotlin's position even further, Google officially established it as the next supported language for Android.

So this begs the question: would there be a benefit in creating a ReactiveX implementation in pure Kotlin without relying on RxJava? After all, the Kotlin language has a powerful set of features that could offer a lot to a ReactiveX implementation and bring it to multiple platforms. It would also create a ReactiveX experience optimized for Kotlin, supporting nullable type emissions, extension operators, and coroutine-based concurrency.

Coroutines – a generalization of subroutines – provide an interesting and useful abstraction to quickly (and more safely) implement concurrency in a Kotlin application. Because coroutines support task suspension, they provide a natural mechanism to support backpressure. In the event that a ReactiveX implementation in Kotlin is pursued, coroutines can play a huge part in making backpressure simple to implement.

 If you want to learn about how Kotlin coroutines can be leveraged to create a ReactiveX implementation in Kotlin, read Roman Elizarov's fascinating article at `https://github.com/Kotlin/kotlinx.coroutines/blob/master/reactive/coroutines-guide-reactive.md`.

So yes, there could be a lot to gain by making a ReactiveX implementation in pure Kotlin. At the time of writing, the idea is gaining more traction in the Kotlin community. Keep an eye on it as people continue to experiment and proofs-of-concept creep toward prototypes and then to official releases.

Summary

In this chapter, we covered how to use RxJava for Kotlin. The Kotlin language is an exciting opportunity to express code on the JVM more pragmatically, and RxJava can leverage many of its useful features. Extension functions, data classes, RxKotlin, and functional operators such as `let()`/`apply()` allow you to express your reactive domain more easily. Although SAM inference can cause you to hit snags, you can leverage RxKotlin's helper utilities to get around this issue until JetBrains creates a fix. Down the road, it will be interesting to see whether a ReactiveX implementation in pure Kotlin appears. Such an implementation would bring in a lot of functionality that Kotlin allows and Java does not.

This is the end! If you have completed this book from cover to cover, congrats! You should have a strong foundation to leverage RxJava in your workplace and projects. Reactive programming is a radically different approach, but it is radically effective, too. Reactive programming will continue to grow in pertinence and shape the future of how we model code. Being on this cutting edge will make you not only more marketable but also a leader for years to come.

Appendix A: Introducing Lambda Expressions

This appendix will walk you through lambda expressions. That is an important part of streams, reactive programming, and functional programming in general. Try to make sure that you have a good understanding of this topic, otherwise, much of this book, especially the examples, will be a mystery to you.

Introducing lambda expressions

Java officially supported lambda expressions since Java 8 was released in 2014. *Lambda expressions* are shorthand implementations for **Single Abstract Method** (**SAM**) classes. In other words, they are quick ways to pass functional arguments instead of anonymous classes.

Implementing Runnable using lambda expression

Prior to Java 8, you might have leveraged anonymous classes to implement interfaces, such as Runnable, on the fly, as shown in the following code snippet:

```
public class A_01 {
    public static void main(String[] args) {
        Runnable runnable = new Runnable() {
            @Override
            public void run() {
                System.out.println("run() was called!");
            }
        };
        runnable.run();
    }
}
```

The output is as follows:

```
run() was called!
```

To implement `Runnable` without declaring an explicit class, you had to implement its `run()` abstract method in a block immediately after the constructor. This created a lot of boilerplate and became a major pain point with Java development, becoming a barrier to using functional programming in Java. Thankfully, Java 8 officially brought lambdas to the Java language. With lambda expressions, you can express the same functionality as in the preceding example in a much more concise way, as follows:

```
public class A_02 {
    public static void main(String[] args) {
        Runnable runnable = () ->
                        System.out.println("run() was called!");
        runnable.run();
    }
}
```

Awesome, right? That is a lot less code and boilerplate noise, and we will now dive into how this works.

Lambda expressions can target any interface or abstract class with one abstract method, which is called a functional interface. In the preceding code, the `Runnable` interface has a single abstract method called `run()`. If you pass a lambda that matches the arguments and return a type for that abstract method, the compiler will use that lambda for the implementation of that method.

Everything to the left of the `->` arrow is an argument. The `run()` method of `Runnable` does not take any arguments, so the lambda provides no arguments with the empty parenthesis, `()`. The right side of the arrow `->` is the action to be executed. In this example, we are calling a single statement and printing a simple message with `System.out.println("run() was called!");`.

Java 8 lambda expressions can support multiple statements in the body. Let's say we have this `Runnable` anonymous inner class with multiple statements in its `run()` implementation, as shown in the following code snippet:

```
public class A_03 {
    public static void main(String[] args) {
        Runnable runnable = new Runnable() {
            @Override
            public void run() {
                System.out.println("Message 1");
                System.out.println("Message 2");
```

```
            }
        };
        runnable.run();
    }
}
```

You can move both `System.out.println()` statements to a lambda expression by wrapping them in a multiline { } block to the right of the -> arrow. Note that you need to use semicolons to terminate each line within the lambda expression, as shown in the following code snippet:

```
public class Launcher {
    public static void main(String[] args) {
        Runnable runnable = () -> {
            System.out.println("Message 1");
            System.out.println("Message 2");
        };
        runnable.run();
    }
}
```

Making a Supplier a lambda

Lambda expressions can also implement methods that return items. For instance, the `Supplier` interface introduced in Java 8 (and originally introduced in Google Guava) has an abstract `get()` method that returns a `T` item for a given `Supplier<T>`. If we have a `Supplier<List<String>>` whose `get()` method returns `List<String>`, we can implement it using an old-fashioned anonymous class as follows:

```
import java.util.ArrayList;
import java.util.List;
import java.util.function.Supplier;

public class A_05 {
    public static void main(String[] args) {
        Supplier<List<String>> listGenerator =
                new Supplier<List<String>>() {
                    @Override
                    public List<String> get() {
                        return new ArrayList<>();
                    }
                };
        List<String> myList = listGenerator.get();
    }
}
```

But we can also use a lambda expression, which can implement `get()` much more succinctly and yield `List<String>` as follows:

```
import java.util.ArrayList;
import java.util.List;
import java.util.function.Supplier;

public class A_06 {
    public static void main(String[] args) {
        Supplier<List<String>> listGenerator = () -> new ArrayList<>();
        List<String> myList = listGenerator.get();     }
}
```

When the lambda is simply invoking a constructor on a type using the `new` keyword, you can use a double colon `::` syntax to invoke the constructor on that class. This way, you can leave out the symbols `()` and `->`, as shown in the following code block:

```
import java.util.ArrayList;
import java.util.List;
import java.util.function.Supplier;

public class A_07 {
    public static void main(String[] args) {
        Supplier<List<String>> listGenerator = ArrayList::new;
        List<String> myList = listGenerator.get();
    }
}
```

Similarly, any method that accepts the single parameter of the same type as the emitted element can be presented with the double colon symbol. This syntax is called a *method reference*. For example, you can replace `s -> System.out.println(s)` with `System.out::println`.

Making a Consumer a lambda

The `Consumer<T>` interface has a single abstract method, `accept()`, that takes a `T` argument and performs an action with it but does not return any value. Using an anonymous class, we can create a `Consumer<String>` that simply prints the string as shown in the following code snippet:

```
import java.util.function.Consumer;

public class A_08 {
    public static void main(String[] args) {
        Consumer<String> printConsumer = new Consumer<String>() {
```

```
            @Override
            public void accept(String s) {
                System.out.println(s);
            }
        };
        printConsumer.accept("Hello World!");
    }
}
```

The output is as follows:

Hello World!

It can be implemented using a lambda expression as follows:

```
import java.util.function.Consumer;

public class A_09 {
    public static void main(String[] args) {
        Consumer<String> printConsumer =
                (String s) -> System.out.println(s);
        printConsumer.accept("Hello World");
    }
}
```

The compiler can actually infer that s is a String type based on the Consumer<String> declaration. Consequently, you can leave that explicit type declaration out, as shown in the following code:

```
import java.util.function.Consumer;

public class A_10 {
    public static void main(String[] args) {
        Consumer<String> printConsumer = s -> System.out.println(s);
        printConsumer.accept("Hello World");
    }
}
```

And, as we have mentioned already, for a single-parameter method invocation, you can actually use a method reference. Declare the type you are targeting on the left-hand side of the double colon and invoke its method on the right-hand side of the double colon as follows:

```
import java.util.function.Consumer;

public class A_11 {
    public static void main(String[] args) {
        Consumer<String> printConsumer = System.out::println;
```

```
            printConsumer.accept("Hello World");
        }
    }
```

Making a function a lambda

Lambda expressions can also implement the `Function` interface, which has a single abstract method that accepts arguments and returns an item. For instance, RxJava 2.0 (as well as Java 8) has a `Function<T, R>` interface that accepts a `T` type and returns an `R` type. This means that you can declare a `Function<String, Integer>`, whose `apply()` method accepts a `String` and returns an `Integer`. For example, we can implement `apply()` by returning the string's length in an anonymous class, as shown here:

```
import java.util.function.Function;

public class A_12 {
    public static void main(String[] args) {
        Function<String,Integer> lengthMapper =
                new Function<String, Integer>() {
                    @Override
                    public Integer apply(String s) {
                        return s.length();
                    }
                };
        Integer length = lengthMapper.apply("Alpha");
        System.out.println(length);
    }
}
```

We can make this even more concise by implementing `Function<String, Integer>` as a lambda expression as follows:

```
import java.util.function.Function;

public class A_13 {
    public static void main(String[] args) {
        Function<String,Integer> lengthMapper = (String s) -> s.length();
        Integer length = lengthMapper.apply("Alpha");
        System.out.println(length);
    }
}
```

As in the previous examples, we can use other syntaxes alternately to implement the
Function<String, Integer> interface. Java 8's compiler is smart enough to see that the
input parameter s is a String based on the Function<String, Integer> type we have
defined. Therefore, we do not need to explicitly declare s as follows:

```
Function<String,Integer> lengthMapper = (s) -> s.length();
```

And we do not need to wrap our input parameter s in parentheses, (s), either, as those are
not needed for a single argument (but are needed for multiple arguments, as we will see
later):

```
Function<String,Integer> lengthMapper = s -> s.length();
```

And, since we are simply calling a one parameter method or property on the incoming
item, we can use the double colon :: syntax (method reference) to call the method on that
type:

```
Function<String,Integer> lengthMapper = String::length;
```

The Function<T,R> interface is heavily used in RxJava by Observable operators to
transform emissions. The most common example is the map() operator, which turns each T
emission into an R emission and derives an Observable<R> from an Observable<T>, as
shown in the following code:

```
import io.reactivex.rxjava3.core.Observable;

public class A_14 {
    public static void main(String[] args) {
        Observable.just("Alpha","Beta","Gamma")
                .map(String::length) //accepts Function<T,R>
                .subscribe(System.out::println); //accepts Consumer<T>
    }
}
```

The output is as follows:

```
5
4
5
```

Note that there are other flavors of `Function`, such as `Predicate` and `BiFunction`, which accept two arguments, not one. The `reduce()` operator accepts a `BiFunction<T,T,T>`, where the first `T` argument is the rolling aggregation, the second `T` argument is the next item to put into the aggregation, and the third `T` argument is the result of merging the two. In this case, we use `reduce()` to add all the items using a rolling total:

```java
import io.reactivex.rxjava3.core.Observable;

public class A_15 {
    public static void main(String[] args) {
        Observable.just("Alpha","Beta","Gamma")
            .map(String::length)
            .reduce((total,next) -> total + next) //BiFunction<T,T,T>
            .subscribe(System.out::println);
    }
}
```

The output is as follows:

14

Appendix B: Functional Types

They are called *functional interfaces* because each of them has only one abstract method—a **Single Abstract Method** (**SAM**). They are also called functional types because they are used as method parameters (by `Observable` operators, for example). You have to be very familiar with them in order to avoid re-inventing the wheel and creating a custom interface while a corresponding interface is already provided with the library.

Functional types

Here are all the functional types available in RxJava 1., 2., and 3.0 at the time of writing. You may recognize many of these functional types as being almost identical to those in Java 8 (in the `java.util.function` package) or Google Guava.

However, they were copied to an extent in RxJava to make them available for use in Java 6, 7, and 8. A subtle difference is that RxJava's implementations throw checked exceptions. This eliminates a pain point from RxJava 1.*, where checked exceptions had to be handled in lambda expressions that yielded them.

In the following table, the RxJava 1.* equivalents are listed as well, but note that the SAM column corresponds to the RxJava 2.* and 3.0 type. Another important point is that RxJava 1* functions implement `call()` and do not support primitives. Also, RxJava 2.* and 3.0 implements a few functional types with primitives to reduce boxing overhead where reasonably possible.

Here are all the RxJava functional types:

RxJava 2.x and RxJava 3.0	RxJava 1.x	SAM	Description
`Action`	`Action0`	`run()`	Executes an action, much like `Runnable`
`Callable<T>`	`Func0<T>`	`get()`	Returns a single item of type T
`Consumer<T>`	`Action1<T>`	`accept()`	Performs an action on a given T item, but returns nothing
`Function<T,R>`	`Func1<T,R>`	`apply()`	Accepts a type T and returns a type R
`Predicate<T>`	`Func1<T,Boolean>`	`test()`	Accepts a T item and returns a primitive `boolean`
`BiConsumer<T1,T2>`	`Action2<T1,T2>`	`accept()`	Performs an action on a T1 and T2 item, but returns nothing
`BiFunction<T1,T2,R>`	`Func2<T1,T2,R>`	`apply()`	Accepts a T1 and T2 and returns a type R
`BiPredicate<T1,T2>`	`Func2<T1,T2,Boolean>`	`test()`	Accepts a T1 and T2 and returns a primitive `boolean`
`Function3<T1,T2,T3,R>`	`Func3<T1,T2,T3,R>`	`apply()`	Accepts three arguments and returns an R type
`BooleanSupplier`	`Func0<Boolean>`	`getAsBoolean()`	Returns a single primitive `boolean` value
`LongConsumer`	`Action1<Long>`	`accept()`	Performs an action on a given Long, but returns nothing
`IntFunction`	`Func1<T>`	`apply()`	Accepts a primitive `int` and returns an item of type T

Not every primitive equivalent for a functional type has been implemented in RxJava 2.0. For example, currently, there is no `IntSupplier` like the one in Java 8's standard library. This is because RxJava 2.0 does not need it in order to implement any of its operators.

In addition, RxJava 3.0 includes the following new functions in the `io.reactivex.rxjava3.functions` package:

- `Function4<T1,T2,T3,T4,R>`: Accepts four arguments of type `T` and returns a `R` type
- `Function5<T1,T2,T3,T4,T5,R>`: Accepts five arguments of type `T` and returns a `R` type
- `Function6<T1,T2,T3,T4,T5,T6,R>`: Accepts six arguments of type `T` and returns a `R` type
- `Function7<T1,T2,T3,T4,T5,T6,T7,R>`: Accepts seven arguments of type `T` and returns a `R` type
- `Function8<T1,T2,T3,T4,T5,T6,T7,T8,R>`: Accepts eight arguments of type `T` and returns a `R` type
- `Function9<T1,T2,T3,T4,T5,T6,T7,T8,T9,R>`: Accepts nine arguments of type `T` and returns a `R` type

Appendix C: Mixing Object-Oriented and Reactive Programming

Mixing object-oriented programming with reactive programming is not only permissible but can even be beneficial. The following discussion presents such cases and demonstrates how such a mix can be done.

Mixing object-oriented and reactive programming

As you start applying your RxJava knowledge to real-world problems, something that may not immediately be clear is how to mix it with object-oriented programming. Leveraging multiple paradigms such as object-oriented and functional programming is becoming increasingly common. Reactive programming and object-oriented programming, especially in a Java environment, can definitely work together for the greater good.

Obviously, you can emit any type `T` from an `Observable` or any of the other reactive types. Emitting objects built off your own classes is one way in which object-oriented and reactive programming work together. We have seen a number of examples in this book. For instance, Java 8's `LocalDate` is a complex object-oriented type, but you can push it through an `Observable<LocalDate>`, as shown in the following code:

```
import io.reactivex.rxjava3.core.Observable;
import java.time.LocalDate;

public class C_01 {
    public static void main(String[] args) {
        Observable<LocalDate> dates = Observable.just(
                LocalDate.of(2020,11,3),
                LocalDate.of(2020,10,4),
                LocalDate.of(2020,7,5),
                LocalDate.of(2020,10,3)
        );
        // get distinct months
        dates.map(LocalDate::getMonth)
```

```
                  .distinct()
                  .subscribe(System.out::println);
           }
       }
```

The output is as follows:

NOVEMBER
OCTOBER
JULY

As we have seen in several examples throughout the book, a number of RxJava operators provide adapters to take a stateful, object-oriented item and turn it into a reactive stream. For instance, there are the `generate()` factories for `Flowable` and `Observable` that build a series of emissions of a mutable object that is updated incrementally. In the following code, we emit an infinite, consecutive sequence of Java 8 `LocalDates`, but take only the first 60 emissions. Since `LocalDate` is immutable, we wrap the seed `LocalDate` of `2020-1-1` in an `AtomicReference` so that it can be mutably replaced with each increment:

```
import io.reactivex.rxjava3.core.Emitter;
import io.reactivex.rxjava3.core.Flowable;
import io.reactivex.rxjava3.functions.BiConsumer;
import io.reactivex.rxjava3.functions.Supplier;

import java.time.LocalDate;
import java.util.concurrent.atomic.AtomicReference;

public class C_02 {
   public static void main(String[] args) {
      Supplier<AtomicReference<LocalDate>> initialState =
              () -> new AtomicReference<>(LocalDate.of(2020,1,1));

      BiConsumer<AtomicReference<LocalDate>,
              Emitter<LocalDate>> generator =
                 (AtomicReference<LocalDate> next,
                     Emitter<LocalDate> emitter) ->
              emitter.onNext(next.getAndUpdate(dt -> dt.plusDays(1)));

      Flowable.generate(initialState, generator)
              .take(60)
              .subscribe(System.out::println);
   }
}
```

The output is as follows:

```
2020-01-01
2020-01-02
2020-01-03
. . .
2020-02-27
2020-02-28
2020-02-29
```

RxJava has many factories and tools to take object-oriented imperative operations and make them reactive. Many of them are covered throughout this book.

But are there cases for a class to return an Observable, Flowable, Single, or Maybe from a property or method? Certainly! When your object has properties or methods whose results are dynamic, change over time, and represent an event(s) or a sizable sequence of data, they are candidates to be returned as a reactive type.

Here is an abstract example: say you have a DroneBot type that represents a flying drone. You could have a property called getLocation() that returns an Observable<Point> instead of Point. This way, you can get a live feed that pushes a new Point emission every time the drone's location changes, as shown in the following code:

```
import io.reactivex.rxjava3.core.Observable;

public class C_03 {
    public static void main(String[] args) {
        DroneBot droneBot = null; //create droneBot
        droneBot.getLocation()
            .subscribe(loc -> System.out.println("Drone moved to " +
                                        loc.x + "," + loc.y));
    }
    interface DroneBot {
        int getId();
        String getModel();
        Observable<Location> getLocation();
    }
    static final class Location {
        private final double x;
        private final double y;
        Location(double x, double y) {
            this.x = x;
            this.y = y;
        }
    }
}
```

This `DroneBot` example shows another way in which you can mix object-oriented and reactive programming effectively. You can easily get a live feed of that drone's movements by returning an `Observable`.

There are many use cases for this pattern: stock feeds, vehicle locations, weather station feeds, social networks, and so on. However, be careful if the properties are infinite. If you wanted to manage the location feeds of 100 drones, flat-mapping all their infinite location feeds together into a single stream is likely not going to produce anything meaningful, apart from a noisy sequence of locations with no context. You will likely subscribe to each one separately, in a UI that populates a `Location` field in a table displaying all the drones, or you will use `Observable.combineLatest()` to emit a snapshot of the latest locations for all drones. The latter can be helpful in displaying points live on a geographic map.

Having reactive class properties is useful when they are finite as well. Say you have a list of warehouses, and you want to count the total inventory across all of them. Each `Warehouse` contains an `Observable<ProductStock>`, which returns a finite sequence of the product stocks currently available. The `getQuantity()` operator of `ProductStock` returns the quantity of that product available. We can use `reduce()` on the `getQuantity()` values to get a sum of all the available inventory, as shown here:

```
import io.reactivex.rxjava3.core.Observable;
import java.util.List;

public class C_04 {
    public static void main(String[] args) {
        List<Warehouse> warehouses = null; // get warehouses
        Observable.fromIterable(warehouses)
                .flatMap(Warehouse::getProducts)
                .map(ProductStock::getQuantity)
                .reduce(0, (total, next) -> total + next)
                .subscribe(i -> System.out.println("There are " +
                                        i + " units in inventory"));
    }
    interface Warehouse {
        Observable<ProductStock> getProducts();
    }
    interface ProductStock {
        int getId();
        String getDescription();
        int getQuantity();
    }
}
```

So, a finite `Observable`, like the ones returned from `getProducts()` on `Warehouse`, can be helpful, too, and is especially helpful for analytical tasks. Note, however, that this particular business case decided that `getProducts()` would return the products available at that moment, not an infinite feed that broadcasts the inventory every time it changes. This was a design decision, and sometimes, representing snapshot data in a cold manner is better than a hot infinite feed.

An infinite feed would have required `Observable<List<ProductStock>>` (or `Observable<Observable<ProductStock>>`) to be returned, so logical snapshots are emitted.

You can always add a separate `Observable` that emits notifications of changes and then uses `flatMap()` on your `getProducts()` method to create a hot feed of inventory changes. This way, you create basic building blocks in your code model and then compose them together reactively to accomplish more complex tasks.

Note that you can have methods that return reactive types and accept arguments. This is a powerful way to create an `Observable` or `Flowable` catered to a specific task. For instance, we could add a `getProductsOnDate()` method to our `warehouse` that returns an `Observable` emitting product stock from a given date, as shown in the following code:

```
interface Warehouse {
    Observable<ProductStock> getProducts();
    Observable<ProductStock> getProductsOnDate(LocalDate date);
}
```

In summary, mixing reactive and object-oriented programming is not only beneficial, but also necessary. When you design your domain classes, think carefully about what properties and methods should be made reactive and whether they should be cold, hot, and/or infinite. Imagine how you will be using your class and whether your candidate design will be easy or difficult to work with. Be sure to not make every property and method reactive for the sake of being reactive either. Only make it reactive when there is a usability or performance benefit. For example, you should not make a `getId()` property for your domain type reactive. An ID of the class instance is unlikely to change, and it is just a single value, not a sequence of values.

Appendix D: Materializing and Dematerializing

Two interesting operators we have not yet covered are `materialize()` and `dematerialize()`. We did not cover them in Chapter 3, *Basic Operators*, with all the other operators because it might have been confusing at that point in your learning curve. But hopefully, the point at which you are reading this means that you understand the `onNext()`, `onComplete()`, and `onError()` events well enough to use an operator that abstractly packages them in a different way.

Materializing and dematerializing

The `materialize()` operator takes the three events `onNext()`, `onComplete()`, and `onError()`, and turns all of them into emissions wrapped in `Notification<T>`. So if your source emits five emissions, you will get six emissions where the last one will be `onComplete()` or `onError()`. In the following code, we materialize `Observable` emitting five strings, which are turned into six `Notification` emissions:

```
import io.reactivex.rxjava3.core.Observable;

public class D_01 {
    public static void main(String[] args) {
        Observable<String> source = Observable.just("Alpha", "Beta",
                                    "Gamma", "Delta", "Epsilon");
        source.materialize().subscribe(System.out::println);
    }
}
```

The output is as follows:

```
OnNextNotification[Alpha]
OnNextNotification[Beta]
OnNextNotification[Gamma]
OnNextNotification[Delta]
OnNextNotification[Epsilon]
OnCompleteNotification
```

Each `Notification` has three methods – `isOnNext()`, `isOnComplete()`, and `isOnError()`, to determine what type of `Notification` event it is. There is also `getValue()`, which returns the emission value for `onNext()`, but returns null for `onComplete()` or `onError()`. We leverage these methods on `Notification`, as shown in the following code, to filter out the three events to three separate `Observer` subscriptions:

```
import io.reactivex.rxjava3.core.Notification;
import io.reactivex.rxjava3.core.Observable;

public class D_02 {
    public static void main(String[] args) {
        Observable<Notification<String>> source =
                Observable.just("Alpha", "Beta", "Gamma",
                                         "Delta", "Epsilon")
                    .materialize()
                    .publish()
                    .autoConnect(3);

        source.filter(Notification::isOnNext)
                .subscribe(n -> System.out.println("onNext=" +
                        n.getValue()));

        source.filter(Notification::isOnComplete)
                .subscribe(n -> System.out.println("onComplete"));

        source.filter(Notification::isOnError)
                .subscribe(n -> System.out.println("onError"));
    }
}
```

The output is as follows:

```
onNext=Alpha
onNext=Beta
onNext=Gamma
onNext=Delta
onNext=Epsilon
onComplete
```

You can also use `dematerialize()` to turn `Observable` or `Flowable` emitting notifications back into normal `Observable` or `Flowable`. It produces an error if any emission is not `Notification`. Unfortunately, at compile time, Java cannot enforce operators being applied to `Observable` or `Flowable` emitting specific types as Kotlin does, so the corresponding Java code may look as follows:

```
import io.reactivex.rxjava3.core.Observable;

public class D_03 {
    public static void main(String[] args) {
        Observable.just("Alpha", "Beta", "Gamma", "Delta", "Epsilon")
                .materialize()
                .doOnNext(System.out::println)
                //.dematerialize()                    //RxJava 2.*
                .dematerialize(v -> v)
                .subscribe(System.out::println);
    }
}
```

The output is as follows:

```
OnNextNotification[Alpha]
Alpha
OnNextNotification[Beta]
Beta
OnNextNotification[Gamma]
Gamma
OnNextNotification[Delta]
Delta
OnNextNotification[Epsilon]
Epsilon
OnCompleteNotification
```

So what exactly would you use `materialize()` and `dematerialize()` for? You may not use them that often, which is another reason why they are covered here in the Appendix, but they can be handy in composing more complex operators with transformers and stretching transformers to do more without creating low-level operators from scratch.

For instance, RxJava2 Extras uses `materialize()` for a number of its operators, including `collectWhile()`. By treating `onComplete()` as an emission itself, `collectWhile()` can map it to push the collection buffer downstream and start the next buffer.

Otherwise, you will likely not use `materialize()` and `dematerialize()` often, but it is good to be aware that such a possibility exists if you need it to build more complex transformers.

Appendix E: Understanding Schedulers

You will likely not use schedulers in isolation, as we are about to do in this section. You are more likely to use them with `observeOn()` and `subscribeOn()`. However, we would like to demonstrate how they work in isolation outside of an Rx context so that you can understand their functionality better.

Understanding Schedulers

A `Scheduler` is RxJava's abstraction for pooling threads and scheduling tasks to be executed by them. These tasks may be executed immediately, delayed, or repeated periodically depending on which of its execution methods are called. These execution methods are `scheduleDirect()` and `schedulePeriodicallyDirect()`, which have a few overloads. For example, we can use the `Scheduler` computation to execute an immediate task, a delayed task, and a repeated task, as shown here:

```
import io.reactivex.rxjava3.core.Scheduler;
import io.reactivex.rxjava3.schedulers.Schedulers;
import java.util.concurrent.TimeUnit;

public class E_01 {
    public static void main(String[] args) {
        Scheduler scheduler = Schedulers.computation();

        //run task now
        scheduler.scheduleDirect(() -> System.out.println("Now!"));

        //delay task by 1 second
        scheduler.scheduleDirect(() ->
                System.out.println("Delayed!"), 1, TimeUnit.SECONDS);

        //repeat task every second
        scheduler.schedulePeriodicallyDirect(() ->
                System.out.println("Repeat!"), 0, 1, TimeUnit.SECONDS);

        //keep alive for 5 seconds
        sleep(5000);
    }
```

```
        public static void sleep(long millis) {
            try {
                Thread.sleep(millis);
            } catch (InterruptedException e) {
                e.printStackTrace();
            }
        }
    }
}
```

The output will likely be the following:

```
Now!
Repeat!
Delayed!
Repeat!
Repeat!
Repeat!
Repeat!
Repeat!
```

The scheduleDirect() method executes a one-time task only and has an overloaded version that accepts a time delay. The schedulePeriodicallyDirect() method repeats infinitely. Interestingly, both of these methods return a Disposable to allow cancelation of the task it is executing or waiting to execute.

These methods automatically pass tasks to a Worker, which is an abstraction that wraps around a single thread that sequentially does work assigned to it. You can actually call the createWorker() method on a Scheduler to explicitly get a worker and delegate tasks to it directly. Its schedule() and schedulePeriodically() methods operate just like scheduleDirect() and schedulePeriodicallyDirect() (of a Scheduler), respectively, and return Disposable too, but they are executed by the specified worker.

When you are done with a worker, you should dispose of it so it can be discarded or returned to the Scheduler. Here is an equivalent of our earlier example using a Worker:

```
import io.reactivex.rxjava3.core.Scheduler;
import io.reactivex.rxjava3.schedulers.Schedulers;
import java.util.concurrent.TimeUnit;

public class E_02 {
    public static void main(String[] args) {
        Scheduler scheduler = Schedulers.computation();
        Scheduler.Worker worker = scheduler.createWorker();

        //run task now
```

```
        worker.schedule(() -> System.out.println("Now!"));

        //delay task by 1 second
        worker.schedule(() -> System.out.println("Delayed!"), 1,
                TimeUnit.SECONDS);

        //repeat task every second
        worker.schedulePeriodically(() ->
                System.out.println("Repeat!"), 0, 1, TimeUnit.SECONDS);

        //keep alive for 5 seconds, then dispose Worker
        sleep(5000);
        worker.dispose();
    }

    public static void sleep(long millis) {
        try {
            Thread.sleep(millis);
        } catch (InterruptedException e) {
            e.printStackTrace();
        }
    }
}
```

The output will likely be the following:

```
Now!
Repeat!
Repeat!
Delayed!
Repeat!
Repeat!
Repeat!
Repeat!
```

Of course, every Scheduler is implemented differently. A Scheduler may use one thread or several threads. It may cache and reuse threads, or not reuse them at all. It may use an Android thread or a JavaFX thread (as we have seen with RxAndroid and RxJavaFX in this book). But that is essentially how schedulers work, and you can perhaps see why they are useful in implementing RxJava operators.

Other Books You May Enjoy

If you enjoyed this book, you may be interested in these other books by Packt:

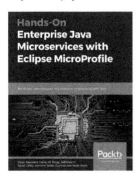

Hands-On Enterprise Java Microservices with Eclipse MicroProfile
Cesar Saavedra, Heiko W. Rupp, Et al

ISBN: 978-1-83864-310-2

- Understand why microservices are important in the digital economy
- Analyze how MicroProfile addresses the need for enterprise Java microservices
- Test and secure your applications with Eclipse MicroProfile
- Get to grips with various MicroProfile capabilities such as OpenAPI and Typesafe REST Client
- Explore reactive programming with MicroProfile Stream and Messaging candidate APIs
- Discover and implement coding best practices using MicroProfile

Hands-On Cloud-Native Applications with Java and Quarkus
Francesco Marchioni

ISBN: 978-1-83882-147-0

- Build a native application using Quarkus and GraalVM
- Secure your applications using Elytron and the MicroProfile JWT extension
- Manage data persistence with Quarkus using PostgreSQL
- Use a non-blocking programming model with Quarkus
- Learn how to get Camel and Infinispan working in native mode
- Deploy an application in a Kubernetes-native environment using Minishift
- Discover Reactive Programming with Vert.x

Leave a review - let other readers know what you think

Please share your thoughts on this book with others by leaving a review on the site that you bought it from. If you purchased the book from Amazon, please leave us an honest review on this book's Amazon page. This is vital so that other potential readers can see and use your unbiased opinion to make purchasing decisions, we can understand what our customers think about our products, and our authors can see your feedback on the title that they have worked with Packt to create. It will only take a few minutes of your time, but is valuable to other potential customers, our authors, and Packt. Thank you!

Index